Contents

Jocasta
INNES
PAINT
magic

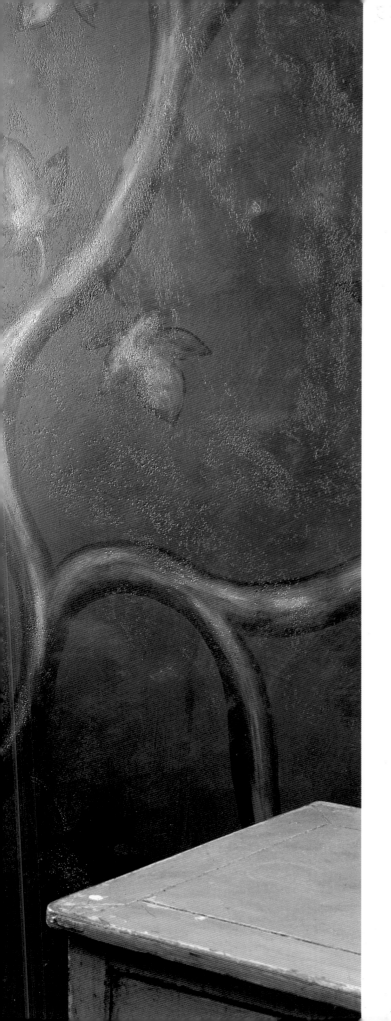

Jocasta
INNES
PAINT
magic

FRANCES LINCOLN

FRANCES LINCOLN LIMITED

4 Torriano Mews, Torriano Avenue, London NW5 2RZ

www.franceslincoln.com

Paint Magic

Copyright © Frances Lincoln Limited 1981, 1987, 1992

Text copyright © Jocasta Innes 1981, 1987, 1992, 2000

First published in hardback under the title *Paint Magic* 1981

Reprinted 1982, 1985 (twice)

First published in paperback 1983

Reprinted 1984, 1985 (twice)

Second edition published 1987

Reprinted 1987, 1989, 1990

Third edition published 1992 under the title *The New Paint Magic*

Fourth edition published 2000 under the title *Paint Magic*

Reprinted in paperback 2003

This edition was designed and edited by Walton and Pringle for Frances Lincoln

www.waltonandpringle.com

Picture Research

Sue Gladstone

British Library Cataloguing-in-Publication data

A catalogue record for this book is available from the British Library

ISBN 0 7112 2272 X

Printed and bound in China

Introduction

It is quite a challenge to re-write the introduction to a book I first published 20 years ago. In that time, there have been radical changes on the decorative painting front, particularly in paint technology, resulting in a new range of colours, products, tools and equipment. Fashions and preferences have also changed considerably, and there is an entirely new generation of readers to consider.

Neither my publishers nor I anticipated that there would be quite such an uptake of the paint effects and possibilities that I showed in my original book, which contrary to all expectations established itself as the 'bible' for anyone interested in new decorative painting techniques. Strange as it now seems, before my book appeared, special effects (known in the USA as 'faux finishes') were both current and well tested by smart interior decorators, but their use was to a considerable extent a trade secret reserved exclusively for wealthy clients. This gave the techniques mystique, and yielded a healthy profit to the decorators concerned.

Although the book was controversial in professional circles, I think it is fair to say that it gave the secretive world of decorative painting skills an astonishing new lease of life, providing steady work for those same professionals, as well as giving others who were artistically inclined a creative opportunity. It also launched a minor revolution in DIY. When the book was first published, trade shops would complain about 'daft women queuing up to ask silly questions'. Today, the shop windows are packed with enticing samples, and their shelves hold the latest DIY materials, from specialist brushes to convenience-orientated products. Smart, informed amateur decorators have provided a whole new market, profitable enough to shift old prejudices and inspire a more helpful and commercially inventive approach.

New technology

In tandem with a new market-led response to a recent but demanding market, paint technology in its widest sense has been speeding ahead. Surveys carried out in Germany and Scandinavia have established that solvents in oil-based media could be toxic enough to cause brain damage and allergies among tradespeople, notably decorative painters, working with them over many years in confined spaces. This led, in many countries, to new legislation, and the banning or phasing out of traditional oil-based media such as paints, tube colours, varnishes and glazes. Many painters have been understandably concerned to transfer their skills and practice to the water-based acrylic media that are superseding the oil-based ones. Acrylics are improving all the time under consumer demand, but to date

A glowing wash, wavering between rose and terracotta, makes a delectable cocoon of colour for a frosty pavilion of a bed draped in muslin and spread with embroidered linen. By way of contrast, everything else – floor, furniture – is dark, plain and shiny.

cannot compete in all respects, lacking flexibility, drying almost too fast for comfort, and being less 'juicy' in use, though flow enhancers, gels and other additives can improve performance. But acrylic paints have an aesthetic appeal of their own, a chalky matt texture applied in thin washes that looks as fragile as watercolour but dries immovably, making them an ideal medium for stencilling, or for mural work in a fresco style. Their 'lean' quality, together with their toughness, is reminiscent of a more ancient medium, egg tempera.

Some decorative painters work almost exclusively in the new acrylics, while others work in both acrylics and oils, depending on the nature of the job. DIY painters, generally short of time, are grateful for the new, faster-drying acrylic systems, starting with the acrylic primer, through emulsions [latex] and colour-washes, to finishing scumbles. A paint system that allows furniture to be trans-formed in a day from start to finish, and floors in two days, is understandably appealing. New finishes or treatments have been developed that lend colour depth, tonal variety or surface interest to the rather blank effect and hard colour of these convenience paints, notably colourwashing with a water-based glaze over emulsion [latex] walls, and distressing over furniture. Both of these have been universally popular, as they are easy enough for amateurs to use and enjoy.

While neutral colours still bulk large in paint sales, there are signs that people are becoming more adventurous in their use of colour, encouraged by a spate of TV home shows and home interest magazines. Retro chic – 1950s, 1960s and 1970s – has led to a revival of the one strong, solid colour wall as a dramatic focus to a room, or its even more popular variant, one vivid square of colour (see page 21).

Texture   Probably the chief innovation in home decorating over the past decade has been the growing popularity of textured walls. As well as a need to warm and soften stark spaces, there is a divergent interest in ancient paints such as limewash and soft distemper, both of which are richly textured and beloved of conservationists for their 'breathing' properties. Neither of these is a convenience paint by contemporary standards – distemper covers beautifully but is not washable, and though limewash (see page 42) is unsurpassed in the right situation, due to the lapse of traditional skills and know-how in the West, it is still at a somewhat experimental stage. Both are steadily gaining converts as people re-discover their homespun texture and glorious colour possibilities. Easier convenience routes to texture range from painted texture (via colourwash or tinted glazes) to tactile texture achieved with paints, such as impasto or a new combing paste, which deliver a diversity of surface interest, soft as blotting paper, rough like Mediterranean plaster work, or ridged as corduroy. Suede paint, with a matt bloom, belongs to the same family, and is as easy to apply as emulsion [latex].

Simple painted squares are
an effective cover-up for softwood boards,
patched and re-laid over the years. One coat
of acrylic primer was followed by two coats of
white emulsion and alternate squares were
filled in with black emulsion. Water-based
lacquer then sealed the floor.

Plaster coatings may seem anomalous in a book about paint, but paint skills enter into their application. They represent the ultimate in textured wall finishes, and their popularity is growing thoughout Europe and the US – they are now available in a DIY ready-to-go formulation from specialist paint outlets. To date, two versions (marmorino and stucco lustro) are available; used singly or together, they can come up with textured surfaces as different as ancient, weathered stone, or glassy-smooth, polished marble. The surprising fact about them, compared to their historic ancestors, is that they can be applied on virtually any surface (except glossy finishes or wallpaper) and look impressively solid, though no single application should be much thicker than icing on a cake. Roman stucco, as seen in the crumbling walls of Pompeii, was applied in as many as twelve layers, from rough to lime-smooth, and could be up to 3 cm (1¼ in) thick.

Watery blue, flat cream and tarnished gold make a splendidly effective colour scheme with a strong Scandinavian neoclassical flavour. The blue grows softer as it goes upwards, becoming more nebulous on the ceiling. The dado has been stencilled, and the floorboards painted white and waxed.

Quick cover-up

Home decorators frequently inherit a previous owner's taste, in the form of un-attractive fitted units, hideously tiled bathrooms or woodchip paper, which they lack the finances to do more than disguise in the short term. Though we always stress that paint can only provide a temporary solution over tiles or melamine, the calls for help have been so urgent and numerous it seemed only sensible to devise a special primer, or bonding agent, that would permit a standard water-based emulsion [latex], or acrylic, paint to cover up these inherently paint-resistant surfaces. When properly applied, these new primers – basically powerful adhesives – allow a total cover-up which can last, with reasonable care and proper varnishing, until you are ready to save up for a more permanent solution. Stark-white melamine fittings can be distressed to look gently aged, or alternatively, as dashingly glossy as a newly sprayed car. Woodchip wallpaper can be transformed with a colour-wash applied over a base coat of emulsion [latex]. This reduces the bumpy effect and gives a softly coloured finish. The same trick works well over those prickly surfaces left by old-style textured paints.

Past, present and future

As someone who has been passionately interested in and professionally involved with paint effects, old and new, primitive and high-tech, arty and naive, for the past 20 years, I am often asked about future trends. Whatever these might be, my paint 'philosophy' is not so different from what it was 20 years ago, when I was writing the first edition of *Paint Magic*, and recognized, with generous help from serious practitioners like Graham Carr (out of the John Fowler stable), just what a hitherto unexplored potential for DIY-decorators was locked up in the highly exclusive decorative painting scene. These were skills, tricks and notions I instantly longed to try for myself. I was sufficiently excited by the results, crude as they then were, to be confident that they deserved to be more widespread, because they offered people so much more scope when it came to creating a very personal space, even when on a limited budget or with no hands-on experience. I was – and still am – an ardent experimenter, prepared to take risks and paint them out if they failed to deliver the effect I was looking for. I persevered with this fascinating new area of decorative paint effects, learning as I went, meeting the experts and reading up the relevant, if scanty, literature. The learning curve was thrilling – I remember Graham Carr demonstrating a tortoiseshell finish, deftly brushing a series of unrelated brushstrokes in assorted colours onto a board, then subtly softening and blending them with a soft, clean brush into 'tortoiseshell' under my eyes. For me, this was pure 'paint magic', hence the title of the subsequent book and my various Paint Magic outlets in Europe, the Far East and the US, where we sell a range of products for the DIY market. The magic is still there, for me at least, many years and decorating fashions later.

opposite Squares of copper transfer leaf, laid in a regular grid, create a rich glow of metallic colour. Walls must be smoothly plastered for metal leaf. The squares were laid, slightly overlapping, on a coat of water-based metal size, and the completed surface given two coats of bleached shellac to stop tarnishing.

below One square of marmorino (see pages 30–32) distressed for texture, tinted and colour-washed in grey and green, and waxed to a marble sheen, offers the only decoration in this simple bedroom, with limewashed walls.

While there are many attractive wallpapers on the market, paint still remains the easiest, fastest and least expensive way to transform a soulless place into your personal haven – somewhere that tells the world who you are, how you see your space and what colours turn you on. We all have a very ancient deep and powerful response to colour. The main point to bear in mind is to take risks with colour, and never be afraid to make mistakes (they inevitably happen, and you will always learn from them). Remember, any paint scheme that goes wrong can be done over again; a re-paint costs less than a pair of shoes, or a good meal at a restaurant. So take a few chances – a room, a wall, or even a mere square, will offer you an exciting and liberating colour experience. Paint is magic that we can all afford.

Walls

Walls not only define and shape the given space that is a room, they also make up the largest surface area, so that what you add to them in the way of colour, pattern or texture is bound to have a considerable effect. Many people make the mistake of thinking that treating walls to the most lavish finish they can afford – handprinted wallpaper, adhesive-backed felt, pine cladding or panelling – will make the room come together and look good, regardless of shabby furniture and ill-assorted carpet and curtains. What happens in fact is that the room appears unbalanced and uneasy, with the favoured walls making themselves oppressively felt. Furthermore, should the lavish finish turn out to be an expensive mistake, which can happen even to old hands at the game, you are stuck with it. A wall finish should be inexpensive enough to let you approach decisions about colour and texture in a relaxed frame of mind, which is the state most likely to produce the right decisions. And it should be flexible, so that if the colour does turn out to be wrong for the room, or just difficult to live with, you can retrieve your mistake without creating too much labour for yourself. What is more, you should be able to change it all quite easily every few years – walls are subject to a lot of wear and tear and one's tastes alter.

Effecting transformations

The short answer, as you may have guessed, is to stick with the traditional solution to all these problems that has been time-tested: paint. Paint is the most practical, the most flexible and, I am increasingly convinced, the most interesting and beautiful and, in some mysterious way, the most appropriate way in which to cover a wall. 'There is no limit to what you can do with paint', a master-decorator friend is fond of saying. I don't think the claim is exaggerated. By paint, you must understand, he does not mean simply the standard three coats of emulsion [latex] paint with which most of us are familiar. Emulsion [latex] paints are useful of course, but sticking with them exclusively certainly limits the range of decorative possibilities. Paint that is imaginatively and knowledgeably used, however, as it is by a professional decorator (in the manner of an artist rather than a do-it-yourself expert), can be made to produce a quite breathtaking range of effects – subtle, extraordinary colours, textures and patterns.

One advantage of not being an expert (that is, someone who trained as a decorative painter) is that one can approach the subject unhampered by tradition and come up with some unorthodox ideas. In the various dry and technical treatises I have read I have rarely seen it mentioned that most of the finishes I shall be describing go on more rapidly than a conventional paint job, that they give an elegant effect for a ridiculously small outlay, or that doing them is engrossing, even exhilarating. Nor is it mentioned that you don't have to use specialized equipment – improvised tools and materials can produce equally good results, though perhaps

previous page Stencilled designs are often most effective on walls with a distressed finish. Here, two thin, slightly different orange washes were slapped loosely over one another on a white emulsion [latex] base, for a brushy effect. The stencilling is a modern version of an eighteenth-century wallpaper design.

An elegant reminder of just how a full-blown dragged finish in subtle tones can enrich fine eighteenth-century joinery. The same glaze, progressively lightened with white, has been used throughout, the darkest tone establishing a firm framework, a mid-tone filling the panels, and a light shade picking out mouldings.

at some sacrifice of slickness and speed. And none of the books emphasize what to me was the most surprising discovery about these finishes – that they are not all that difficult to do. Exceptions are the higher flights of trompe l'oeil and mural painting, although even there you can bring off unexpected successes if you are not over-ambitious, and aim for naive realism or light-hearted abstraction.

In addition, learning to use these techniques has other advantages. The more you know about decorating, the more powerful (in the sense of being able to control your environment) and independent you become. Take choosing a colour, for instance: knowing what to use to make up your own colours opens up exciting possibilities. You can mix colour to match or complement a favourite picture or rug,

Several paint finishes add definition to a Regency hallway. Buff colourwashed walls give way to a granite-spattered dado, with a simply painted rail, and a typically Regency black skirting [baseboard] topped by dull red. The old pine doors have been mahogany grained, for richness. The black detailing adds visual muscle.

play about with different glazes to create a totally new and personal colour effect, blend woodwork colour to match walls, or add just a squeeze of this and that to transform a commercial paint that turned out to be five shades brighter than you expected. It's a very satisfying feeling to know that with a tin of suitable white paint – or a pot of glaze – and a battery of universal stainers [tinting colours] you can achieve just about any colour scheme you fancy.

As you go along you pick up all sorts of useful decorators' tricks. You will find that some finishes make a room appear larger, or sunnier, while others give the meanest little box of a place a sumptuous air. Try a sponged-marble effect in a bathroom, or colourwashed stripes in a cramped hall. If too many cupboards and doors are the problem, 'lose' them by glazing them to match the walls. Emphasize good proportions by stencilling an elegant border in a contrasting colour at ceiling level, above the skirting [baseboard], or round doors and windows. Or, conversely, if achingly empty expanses of wall are the problem, break them up visually with stencilled borders at chair-rail height, or borders and motifs painted to suggest panelling. A collection of old prints or photographs – any pictures for that matter – gain enormously in significance when hung on walls dragged to suggest coarsely woven fabric. Distressed colour finishes are certainly considerably more flattering than solid colour when used as a background to polished wood or gilt, or rich colours and textures.

Versatility is the keynote to all of these special paint finishes. If you are going for a country-cottage freshness and simplicity, the finishes can be as artless and understated as you like. Colourwashing – applying transparent coloured washes blurrily over a white base coat – is one of the prettiest and airiest effects I know; dragging or stippling gentle pastel colours on a white ground looks appealing too. Alternatively, by applying layers of different coloured glazes on top of a textured paint, you can achieve a luscious finish which would not look at all out of place in a Venetian palazzo.

Mastering glaze work

Many of the paint effects described here are based on glaze work and have been used by fine artists, as well as marblers, grainers and other decorative painters, for hundreds of years. However, they were something of a trade secret, and I stumbled on the subject quite by accident.

Staying with friends at a country house over 20 years ago I came across a couple of decorators running busily up and down ladders and doing something to the wall with brushes that I had never seen before. They told me it was called 'dragging'. I coveted the effect it created immediately. One thing led to another and the upshot was this book, now entering into its fourth edition just in time for the (millennium) year 2,000.

MAKING GOOD & PREPARATION

There is no denying the fact that conscientious preparation pays off, ensuring a long-lasting, professional-looking paint surface. Top decorating firms allow considerably longer for 'prepping' than for the final paint treatment. Thorough preparation means that repainting later will be much less onerous. Amateurs are perfectly capable of matching professional standards if they can spare the time and don't begrudge the physical effort or domestic disruption, but if you just want a rapid colour change, or a quick upgrading of your surroundings, you may prefer to settle for less than perfect underpinnings.

A decent minimum

Washing down painted surfaces and filling any irregularities in the wall surface are the two basic minimum requirements of a respectable redecorating job. Washing down ensures that surfaces are cleared of grease, dust and dirt, all of which would interfere with the bonding of new paint, while filling cracks, holes, chips and other blemishes gives a sound, streamlined foundation for your work. Rooms with walls that are in reasonable condition will need little more preparation than this. Tougher measures may be indicated, however, if the plasterwork is crumbly or the paint on woodwork or mouldings is layers thick and really unsightly. A heat stripper [heat gun] gets rid of old paint with less mess than blow torches or chemical solvents and the hard work involved using a heat stripper [heat gun] is rewarded by newly smooth surfaces and crisp detailing.

Old whitewash or distemper, usually on ceilings, can be dealt with in two ways. It can be repainted, using the same kind of paint – see page 210 for information here. Or, where you wish to switch to an emulsion [latex] paint, it should be scrubbed off with a scrubbing brush and warm water, and sealed with a stabilizing sealer. Emulsion [latex] paint will not adhere properly to old powdery paint surfaces.

Washing down

Where possible, clear the room completely of furniture, curtains, pictures and picture hooks, mirrors and so forth. If taking up the carpet is too difficult, try to roll it back from the skirtings [baseboards] and cover it with plastic dust sheets. Begin cleaning by sucking up as much dust as possible using the appropriate vacuum cleaner attachment, paying special attention to picture rails, cornices, the top of cupboards, and door and window architraves. Use a broom to clear any cobwebs. Make up a bucketful of hot water plus a little ammonia, soda crystals or standard cleaning fluid to cut grease, and use a large sponge to swab down all the paintwork on walls and woodwork, starting at the top and working downwards, and changing the water frequently. Rinse with clean water if the surfaces are really dirty. Remember to clean the ceiling as well. Open the windows, leave some sort of heating on where possible and allow the room to dry thoroughly overnight. The surfaces will now be ready for filling.

Papered walls   Wallpaper makes a satisfactory base for paint as long as it is well stuck down and sound. Simply brush down to clean, paste back any loose edges, and level holes or gaps with filler [spackle] – see below.

Patching plaster   Seriously defective plaster is best left to a professional, but odd holes – even big ones – can be patched up with an all-purpose filler [spackle]. Lining paper rescues plaster that is beginning to go, providing a taut clean surface for decoration. Fill any holes, sand them flat, then hang paper with butt joins. Brush a thin coat of decorators' glue size or diluted PVA over the paper to seal it.

Rubbing down paintwork   Gloss [enamel] painted surfaces need rubbing down with abrasive paper and special primer before repainting, especially if a water-based paint is being applied. This roughens the surface and gives the paint something to grip onto. Use aluminium oxide paper or wet-or-dry sandpaper used with water. Rub down gloss [enamel] paintwork even if you are repainting with oil-based paint. Tile primer allows water-based media to bond with gloss finishes (see page 214).

Filling   Use an interior grade of all-purpose filler [spackle] to fill cracks, chips and holes. Brush out loose material to ensure the filler [spackle] bonds. Mix powder with water to a stiffish consistency, and fill with a metal spatula, overfilling to counteract the shrinkage as it dries. Sand level with the walls when dry, and spot seal with emulsion [latex] or undercoat. Filling the gaps between walls and skirtings [baseboards] or door and window frames takes time but is worthwhile. Professional decorators are adept at gauging the consistency of filler [spackle] for this (a little sloppier than you might think) and at smoothing the filler [spackle] with a damp rag after it has begun to harden but before it is too dry – test by running your finger along first. You can also use a caulking gun, which operates like a cake-icing nozzle and bag.

Applying undercoat and primer   When using emulsion [latex] paints on previously emulsioned walls, there is no need for a special undercoat, unless a radical colour change is involved. Two coats of the new colour will usually be enough; three coats may be needed when applying a pale over a dark colour. Use an oil-based undercoat under oil-based paints, acrylic primer under emulsion [latex]. For speed, apply by roller (see page 228), using a brush to cut in at the top and bottom of the walls.

Before painting with emulsion [latex], prime new plaster with an acrylic primer or with a proprietary primer sealer, or simply with thinned decorators' size to reduce absorption and make the paint go further. Emulsions [latex] or distempers are the only paints suitable for new plaster; for any other paints the plaster must be six months old or the residual moisture will cause flaking and other problems.

PAINTING

Oil-based eggshell, or the newer water-based eggshell, remains the preferred and most efficient ground for glaze work, because it is less absorbent and thus allows the glaze to stay 'open' and malleable for longer. Emulsion [latex] paint is porous, giving less 'open' time before the glaze hardens. A coat of acrylic varnish before glazing helps counteract this, and a vinyl silk emulsion [latex] is a satisfactory compromise. The highest quality work is still achieved using a brush, but rollers undoubtedly save time and muscle power. These are, however, better suited to emulsion [latex] than to oil-based paints.

Equipment

You will need: an appropriate roller and tray (see page 228) or decorators' brush (wide enough to speed application, but not so large and heavy it tires you to handle it); small brush for cutting in; light aluminium stepladder; plastic paint kettle; rag for wiping up spills; plastic or cotton dust sheets; dusting brush.

A whole room decked out in scarlet might be hard to live with, but one painted panel in this rousing colour sparks a sober scheme to life, and acts as a focus point for the whole interior. All this needs is a paint can, masking tape and a dash of assertiveness. And don't overlook the matching cushion.

Method Decant paint into the plastic kettle or roller tray rather than working from the tin; not only is this lighter to hold, but less paint is exposed to the air this way. Spread dust sheets over the floor. Make sure that the stepladder is stable. Start painting from the top corner of a window wall. Don't overload the brush or roller; two thinner coats are still preferable to one thick one. When using a brush, hold it by the handle for emulsion [latex] paints, and by the stock for the thicker, more resistant oil paints.

Cover the wall area a block at a time, moving down and then across. As one patch of wall is painted move on down to the next, brushing it into the first. Painting should always be done methodically, but speedily, to keep the 'wet edge' going so that one patch doesn't begin to dry before you can get around to blending the edges in with the next. If you have to break off before finishing a room, try to stop in a corner, so that there is no obvious join when you start painting again. A first coat can be quite sketchy because the second will even things out. Try for a smooth texture, however, softening pronounced brushmarks with a nearly dry brush (wipe it on a rag) or rollering in all directions to spread paint evenly.

Walls are painted after ceilings but before woodwork. Touch out colour that has strayed onto a ceiling with the ceiling paint afterwards. Always allow one coat to dry thoroughly before applying the next. When using oil-based paints, rub the surfaces down lightly when dry with a fine grade abrasive paper to remove 'nibs' or flecks of dust trapped in the paint. This is particularly important when you want to create a superfine finish or 'faux lacquer' effect.

VARNISHING

To varnish or not to varnish is a question that frequently concerns people. There are no hard and fast rules, other than those suggested by common-sense considerations. Decoratively painted woodwork is commonly varnished on the assumption that it will need wiping down often and get rougher treatment. The more fragile wall finishes, either glazed or colourwashed, do last longer if protected by a varnish. One or two coats of matt or mid-sheen clear polyurethane varnish is the usual choice over oil glaze work. Over the popular 'washy' water-based effects, a coat of clear matt oil-based varnish or a matt emulsion [latex] glaze, gives some protection without spoiling the airy, chalky look that is their special charm. Alternatively, you may decide to settle for repainting more often. Polyurethane varnish provides the toughest protection of all but gradually yellows and darkens, which matters over pale colours or wherever you might need to shift pictures around frequently. Hallways, kitchens and bathrooms always take a bit of a beating one way or another, and are probably better off given one or two coats of a tougher polyurethane varnish. Carriage varnish is used for lacquer effects. (See pages 214–215 for more information on varnishes.)

High shine walls are undoubtedly dramatic, catching the light and harbouring reflections. They have always attracted those with a liking for the theatrical, from Japanned boudoirs to the lustrous stucco favoured by Italian Carlo Scarpa. Shine gives a staircase wall presence, and the look is easy to create with varnish.

Whatever varnish you choose, there are some rules to follow for successful application. Use a clean, soft varnish brush or 'glider', which should be kept for this purpose alone. Thin the first varnish coat with the appropriate solvent (white spirit [mineral spirit] or water) in roughly 3:1 proportions. Make sure that the room is as dust-free as you can make it, cleaned and vacuumed first. Then, when you have finished, shut off the room until the varnish is dry. Try not to leave 'skips' (unvarnished areas) and check the walls in a good light. Varnish, even matt varnish, looks wet and shiny on first application so skips should be easy to spot. Any varnishing will look better for being lightly smoothed over with fine abrasive paper when it is hard dry; this removes the inevitable grit, dust and hairs that become trapped in the surface while it is still wet. Then re-coat.

Special Paint Finishes

FRESCO

An interesting development in interior decoration in the past few years is the enhanced prestige of wall finishes based on polished, tinted plaster. Until relatively recently these 'stucco' finishes were both exclusive and expensive, and usually executed by teams of Italian craftsmen. With the advent of DIY stuccos, ready-to-use pastes that are applied paper-thin with special floats or trowels, all this has changed. Trained plasterers do it quicker and better, but handy amateurs can also acquire the knack with practice. These state-of-the-art formulations can be applied over all but high gloss surfaces.

However, I think it is useful to know something of the history and evolution of these coatings. As with fresco painting, lime, sand and marble dust are the staple ingredients, yielding fine-textured surfaces that can be coloured in different ways and/or given a final waxing to give depth and complexity. Depth of colour with subtle texture points the way decoration is moving today.

Buon fresco

There exists considerable confusion over the precise meaning of the term 'fresco', which in Italian simply means 'moist' or 'fresh', in this context referring to the dampness of the freshly applied lime plaster on which the pigments were applied. From ancient times onwards, the technique has been widely used in mural decoration for its beauty, simplicity and permanence, so that in time the word 'fresco' has become almost interchangeable with painted mural decoration, at least certainly among laymen.

Buon or true fresco describes one technique only, where lime-compatible pigment in powder form is mixed with water and painted onto freshly applied and finely textured lime plaster. On wet plaster the watered pigment glides off the brush, such is the absorbency of the base. A base coat of coarse lime plaster, known as the *arriccio* was applied first; the late medieval and early Renaissance masters of fresco, Giotto, Masaccio and others, roughed out their mural schemes in charcoal and red pigment on this surface. Then the second layer of plaster, using finer sand and more lime putty and known as the *intonaco* was trowelled over the base coat. Only a relatively small area of *intonaco* was applied daily; this area was known as the *giornata*, and might be a metre square or more, depending on the delicacy of execution needed. A madonna's head, with its gold-leafed aureole, might require a whole day, whereas a much larger area of straightforward drapery or background could be completed in the same time, often with the help of apprentices.

A richly baroque *mélange* of painted foliage with geometric ceiling decoration, trompe l'oeil columns and cornice, brings a lordly swagger back into contemporary decoration in this early eighteenth-century house. Though the skills shown here are beyond your average amateur decorator, there are rich ideas to ponder or plunder.

To modern eyes, the revelation of the fresco technique in its simplest form is the astonishing beauty of colour that results. It is so clean and pure as to be almost incandescent, but is relieved from inhuman perfection by the minute variations that are to be found in the *intonaco* surface. The brilliance of the colour has to do with several factors – the purity of the powder pigment itself; the fact that the lime surface on which it is applied dries naturally to a dazzling whiteness, so creating a reflective base without equal; and the manner in which the wet pigment is sucked into and bonds with the drying plaster.

A fresco finish can last all of 2,000 years, although this hardly recommends it to the modern interior decorator, given the speed with which many clients weary of any scheme that is devised for them. If, as a devotee of pure colour, you do nevertheless feel moved to try fresco work, first you will need to find an adventurous

An easy way to evoke a sense of ancient fresco work is to paint large-scale patterns and borders with bits missing, as in this Italian villa. It is a case of knowing what to leave out as much as what to put in.

plasterer, and an old and dilapidated shell of a room to start with, the walls of which have been hacked back to brick or stone masonry, or stripped down to lime plaster on laths. From here, you could create a lime-plastered room onto which pigments can be brushed quite plainly, with perhaps a simple contrasting border at the top and bottom. If you have artistic skills, you might be tempted to try a more elaborate scheme, maybe one that is inspired by the fresco painting that survives today, for example from Roman Pompeii, where marble dadoes, trompe l'oeil niches, swags and draperies and other visual conceits were used to expand and elaborate on the architectural spaces. Marbling on lime plaster works remarkably well, as the Romans discovered; while the plaster is still moist, the crude veining can be trowelled further, to produce adventitiously softened and blended effects, which nonetheless dry with a pure brilliance that lends them extraordinary presence and dignity. Plastic sheets can be used to delay drying time on hot days.

Mezzo fresco and fresco secco

In cool, damp northern climates a freshly plastered room's surface can be kept suitably moist for up to two weeks, according to fresco painters working in these conditions today, but in the Mediterranean it often happened that the *giornata* surface quickly dried to a point where it no longer absorbed colour cleanly and evenly. In these situations fresco painters resorted to other expedients. The first was *mezzo fresco* where the same pigments were used, but were diluted in 'lime water', the clear liquid that settles on a body of slaked lime, best used while the plaster was still on the moist side. Although less integrated than *buon fresco* colours, these applications were still to some extent absorbed into and bonded with the surface. A contemporary use of tinted 'lime water' deserves a mention here, used as a final coat over limewashed walls in order to strengthen the limewash colour itself. The whiteness of lime invariably gives chalky shades. Tinted 'lime water', which is clear, brushed over these in the manner of a glaze, boosts the colour without affecting the lime bond.

Fresco secco is the term used for any work that is done on dried lime plaster surfaces, for which the usual medium used historically was egg tempera, where egg yolk was mixed with dry pigment. *Fresco secco* was used to apply the blue pigments lapis lazuli and ultramarine, because these were adversely affected when used on wet lime plaster, the colour darkening and becoming discoloured. It was also used for details, highlights and other additions that were applied once the work could be seen and evaluated as a whole. Sadly, the blues, such an essential note in medieval fresco work, being *secco* and therefore more fragile, have suffered most from time and wear, leaving so many Madonna and Child subjects, for example, bereft of their original colouring. Not all pigments are lime compatible. In general, earth or mineral pigments are the most reliable, unaffected by time.

FAUX FRESCO

It seems a pity that we should not be able to enjoy something of the quality of true fresco without going to the lengths of a complete replastering job. This is a challenge that has exercised many decorative painters, myself included, and we have come up with effects of varying degrees of complexity, which convey something of the subtle flow of colour which is luminous, yet matt and a touch chalky, of the ancient *buon fresco* method. The techniques are borrowed chiefly from the *fresco secco* method. They are all done with water-based paints, for although it is also possible to imitate the fresco look with oil-based media, the colour is not as pure and tends to alter over time.

APPLYING A SKIM COAT

One faux fresco effect decorators experiment with, and which gives something of the requisite chalky colour and texture without going to the lengths of replastering, consists of applying a 'skim' coat of various plaster-type substances to create a 'thirsty' surface that takes up watercolour like blotting paper.

An inexpensive 'skim' compound for amateurs to work with is a standard filler [spackle], mixed up with water to a creamy consistency and skimmed over the existing wall plaster with a trowel and metal scraper. Alternatively, textured paint like impasto can be used.

Preparation

Walls should be well washed to remove grease and grime; paint may need sanding to create a 'bite' for the skim, but fillers [spackles] are obligingly adhesive and will spread out thinly and smoothly (although some people prefer a slightly rough texture) without further assistance in the way of sizing, primer or undercoat.

Materials

Standard filler [spackle] or impasto; plasterer's trowel or float; paint kettle or other container for skim mixture; abrasive paper; face mask; powder pigments or gouache or acrylic colours; artists' brushes for the decorative painting; stepladder.

Method

A disadvantage of filler [spackle] in this context is its drying speed; don't mix too much, or it will set solid before you have covered one wall. Make up enough to fill a small paint kettle to start with, scoop it onto the wall surface with a plasterer's trowel and use this with the float to spread it out thinly as far as it will go. 'Thinly' means 2–3 mm [½–⅛in], just thick enough to obliterate the previous surface and give a fine new one. With practice, you will find the skim goes on as fast as paint.

If you want a roughened effect, like old plaster, simply ease up on the trowelling and scraping, leaving slight bumps and 'cracks' for instant age. Conversely, if you want an extra-smooth coat, abrade it with a sanding block (abrasive paper wrapped round a small chunk of wood) in the same way as when you fill cracks. There will be a considerable amount of dust, so always wear a mask and overalls.

True, or buon fresco, has an ineffable purity of colour. It is a demandingly skilled process, and mostly today we tend to fake it.

When the skim coat is dry, you are ready to apply colour and/or decoration. The simplest, most authentic form of colour is pigments in dry, powder form, which are obtainable from good artists' suppliers (see page 234). These pigments are dissolved in water, and applied with soft brushes of varying sizes, depending on whether you want to cover the whole area with colour or build up some applied decoration with fine brushwork. The colour will dry several shades lighter. Once it is dry, further watercolour can be brushed on top to create deeper tones or patterns. As with all new paint effects that you have not attempted before, it is a good idea to practise first on a skim-coated board, or in a corner of the room that will be hidden by furniture.

Gouache and acrylic colours, both of which can be diluted in water, may be used instead of dry pigments.

OTHER TYPES OF SKIM COATING

A young American painter (Suzanne Bellehumeure) has evolved her own faux fresco method based on a ready-mixed substance known in the US as 'jointing compound'. This is trowelled and spread on walls in just the same way, but has the advantage that it will not set hard as rapidly as filler [spackle] and needs no mixing. She photocopies her design onto a clear acetate sheet and projects it with an overhead projector onto the wall before lightly drawing out the design with coloured chalk. She has used this approach successfully to create mural designs based on wall paintings at Pompeii, Italy that were originally executed in fresco. She uses dry pigment in water for authenticity, and deliberately creates a slightly distressed roughness on the skim coat.

The UK equivalent to jointing compound is one of the proprietary textured finishes available at specialist paint shops such as impasto, available either in powder form or ready mixed. These are normally associated with systematically textured surfaces obtained by combing or stippling the material while still wet, but they can also be applied smoothly using the trowel method (see above). It offers a hard, compacted surface, much harder than filler [spackle], not unlike traditional stucco (the plaster or cement used to coat the outer walls of a house). Its chief disadvantage is the difficulty of removing it from the surface.

COLOURED SKIM FINISHES

An interesting alternative to the effects described above is to mix the skim compound itself with pigment. In the sense that the colour becomes part of the skim coat, this in some respects bears a close resemblance to true buon fresco, though the colour achieved will not have the same luminosity. People who like the honesty of unpainted plaster are likely to find this approach appealing. There is something 'real' about built-in rather than brushed-on colour. The main difficulty is controlling the colour: wet tinted plaster is many shades darker than it is dry.

Method Dry colour can be added in spoonfuls to the powder before combining it with water to make your skim. Acrylic colour should be added to the mixing water. In either case, mix well to distribute the colour evenly. Remember how quickly it hardens, and only mix up a bowlful at a time, making a careful note of the proportions of colour to filler [spackle]. Then apply with a trowel and scraper as above.

This approach need not be limited to skim made up of filler [spackle], but can be extended to ordinary plaster; use decorators' white plaster, rather than 'pink thistle' for the finishing coat. If you are employing a professional, you can arrive at an integrated colour by mixing pigment into the finishing coat before application. You will need a plasterer tolerant of unfamiliar procedures, and time spent experimenting with colour. Try various mixes and leave them to dry before deciding. Earth colours, ochres, siennas and umbers are authentic and pleasing as tints.

The mixed-up colour will seem almost to vanish as the plaster dries, but it will reappear when you apply a thin coat of soft white wax and burnish it lightly with a soft cloth. This final waxing can also be used with the skim coat of standard filler [spackle] to equally dramatic effect. In both cases, the waxing will create a soft sheen, not unlike the texture of what Italians call *stucco lustro*, or polished stucco.

DECORATIVE PLASTERS

Stand-alone plastered finishes go back to classical times. Surviving remnants – as at Pompeii – reveal just how lengthy and skilful the process was. As many as twelve coatings, from gravelly to porcelain-fine, were not unusual. What survives testifies to Roman mastery of this laborious but refined and versatile coating material.

Happily for anyone seduced by these intrinsically handsome, long-lived and low-maintenance surfaces, experts have produced ready-to-go contemporary versions of the Roman prototypes. These can look as good as their classical ancestors, will bond with most substrates (not shiny), require only two applications no more than 1 mm [1/16 in] thick, and can be tackled by DIY-beginners. Marmorino and stucco lustro are the versions currently available, offering a range of effects, from aged, weathered limestone and marble (marmorino) to polished, poreless smoothness (stucco lustro). Both can be tinted, colourwashed for extra depth of tone, and waxed. Though more expensive and trickier to apply than paint, these coatings represent state-of-the-art advances that open up new possibilities for decorators.

MARMORINO A skilled plasterer can work this up to a smooth finish, but the most popular DIY version is distressed for surface interest. Colourwashing directly onto dry marmorino rapidly mimics old stone or marble, and colourwashing tinted marmorino allows depth and subtlety of colour. Waxing protects the surface and adds a complexity of colour.

This intriguingly roughed-up plaster surface, colourwashed to mimic the weathered, bleached tonality of old limestone and marble, lends a certain nobility to any wall. The finish represents a new take on textured, plastered, painted surfaces. At Paint Magic, we call it 'distressed marmorino', and it comes in a tub.

Materials Acrylic primer; marmorino (coverage approx 10.5 m² per 8kg/13 sq yds per 16lb); steel plasterer's float; hawk or board; colourwash; coloured waxes; universal stainers [tinting colours]; sponge or decorators' paintbrush.

Method The walls should be sound, dry and filled. Prime the walls if they are coloured, with an acrylic primer. Open the windows and turn off the heating to delay it from drying too quickly. Stir the marmorino until smooth. With a steel float, scoop up a dollop onto a hawk, or clean board. Pick up a bit on the float and spread, with overarm action, firmly over the wall, working with the float to create a layer thick enough to cover, but papery-thin as possible; overly thick layers can lead to surface 'crackling'. Let it dry hard: about four to six hours. The first coat will dry gritty, like coarse sandpaper. Coat two is applied in the same way, but holding the float at a slight angle, spreading the marmorino with enough force to smooth it out, and leaving irregular 'skips' here and there where the first coat shows through. Don't overdo this. Leave for 20–30 minutes, and smooth again. Leave another 20 minutes and repeat. If dark bruises appear, let it dry for longer and then repeat. Wipe the float often: bruises come from the steel being abraded by the gritty coating. Colourwash with a brush, or sponge, coaxing colour into the gritty bits. Finally, wax when dry if a low-sheen finish is desired.

STUCCO LUSTRO First, apply a base coat of marmorino. Before the marmorino base is fully dry, take up a pat of stucco onto the float or trowel and work with an underarm action across the wall, aiming at a very thin 1 mm [1⁄16 in] layer, and working the trowel marks out. After 2–3 m² [2½–3½ sq yds] clean off the trowel, and re-work the stucco finish until it is smooth and polished. Two people are ideal: one applying the stucco, the other following behind smoothing and polishing. Areas that look dark are still too wet – leave these for 10–15 minutes and re-work (a hair dryer will hasten drying). Apply wax, for protection and shine, after 3–7 days. Rub wax on with a soft cloth, leave to harden, then buff with a lamb's wool pad on a mechanical buffer.

RUBBED FINISHES

Colour can be rubbed onto, or off, walls to give further variants on the fresco look. Rubbed on colour can be layered, colour on colour, to give greater richness of tone, and more options as to the final result. Suddenly tiring of my own pink rubbed walls, I rubbed over the pink with a brownish red oil glaze [glazing liquid], to give a pleasing terracotta shade, matt and cloudy in texture. Rubbing off is both more arduous and less predictable – you need to make a sample board or patch of wall – but because the colour that remains is driven right into the plaster, it creates an interestingly grainy surface and mysterious bloom of colour.

RUBBED ON COLOUR This goes faster, and gives greater control, done over a slippery base paint. A professional would use an eggshell base, but I have used vinyl silk emulsion [latex], which is easier and quicker to apply for DIY painters, with complete success. Any colours are suitable; those in the fresco range (see page 29) are particularly good.

Materials Vinyl silk emulsion [latex] or eggshell paint as a base colour for walls; oil glaze [glazing liquid]; a little white undercoat; small container for holding the glaze; artists' oil colours, universal stainers [tinting colours] or dry colour which should be dissolved in white spirit [mineral spirit]; soft cotton rags; matt varnish; stepladder.

Method For the rubbed colour mixture, the trick is to mix up a colour much darker than the final shade you are after, using a basic glaze recipe (see page 224) and adding some white undercoat for a chalkier matt look. Tint with artists' oils or universal

This passionately coloured bedroom was achieved by rubbing paint on, a technique that is remarkably simple yet effective. Be daring, and experiment with colours – unusual colour combinations can often yield unexpectedly stunning results.

stainers [tinting colours] and, optionally, some dry colour. I find dry colour helps the required powdery look, but it needs to be finely ground, and steeped in white spirit [mineral spirit] first. Wear a mask when handling it, as with all powdery substances.

Have some cards prepared with your basic vinyl silk emulsion [latex] or eggshell wall colour to use as a reference while mixing and testing the rubbed on colour. Use a soft lint-free rag (old sheets are ideal) to apply the colour, dabbing it on and immediately spreading it out finely to cover the base with a transparent film. When the depth of colour is satisfactory, ensure you have enough glaze. Very little is needed, not more than ½–1 litre [1–2 US pints] for a decent-sized room. Start on a window wall, in the top corner, working down and across. Try to avoid patchy build-ups of colour and 'skips', or bald patches, standing back to check from time to time. Build-ups can be softened by teasing the colour out further while it is still malleable. 'Skips' can be evened out later by stippling glaze very finely over the bare spots with a brush. A second rubbed coat, especially if it is a deeper shade like my terracotta, evens out most irregularities. Note that colour applied this way will tend to show up cracks, bumps and other imperfections.

If your first rubbed colour looks too thin, leave it to harden for several days before rubbing a second coat of the same or a different colour over the first. If the first coat threatens to 'lift' while you are applying the next, seal it with an isolating coat of extra pale matt oil-based varnish, then apply coat two of rubbed colour.

Seal the rubbed colour with matt oil-based varnish. This allows another chance to modify the rubbed colour, by slightly tinting the varnish with artists' oils, dissolved in solvent.

RUBBED OFF COLOUR This discovery came about by accident. A painter friend rollered a terracotta emulsion [latex] onto walls in a passage in my house. It dried to a dark, stifling shade, and the only alternative to painting it out (two or three coats over that particular colour) was to rub it off again, which we did with silicone carbide paper. It was hard work, but after clearing a large patch we looked at it with new eyes, and saw that it looked superb just as it was. We used it as the background to a mural of dancing Greek figures. It may seem perverse to put paint on only to rub it off again, but it remains a greatly admired surface. Perhaps one to try over a small space?

My terracotta emulsion [latex] went straight over new 'pink thistle' plaster, which being new would absorb more colour. Choose a colour many shades darker than the one you require, roller it on, then sand off with sanding blocks. On walls previously painted with many layers of colour, rubbing down produces surprising effects. To make sure these are acceptable, sand a patch before you embark on further repainting and rubbing back. The walls come up very smooth, excellent for applying further decoration on. I don't think there is any need to varnish this effect as it is more or less integrated with the plaster. If you must, use clear polyurethane.

COLOURWASHING

Generically, the term colourwash denotes any soft, dappled wash of transparent colour applied over appropriate substrates to add depth, complexity and texture. Three versions are described below: soft distemper (a traditional finish), oil media (a semi-traditional finish), and pre-tinted, ready-to-go formulations, which are state-of-the-art and the DIY favourite.

SOFT DISTEMPER COLOURWASHING Historically the inspiration for all colourwash effects, this was invented by the late John Fowler, doyen of imaginative paint finishes for the British 'upper crust'. It is inexpensive if you make your own distemper and beautifully soft-looking – distemper is a 'blotting-paper' paint – but non-washable, so of limited use.

Old-fashioned distemper (used to be dubbed 'whitewash') does not have the chemistry of limewash, nor is it washable. However, it 'breathes', dries to a velvet bloom and covers any existing surface well, including wallpaper or emulsion [latex].

overleaf An attic kitchen in Spitalfields, London, seems a little closer to heaven thanks to the ethereal blue that has been washed over the walls and ceiling. Bands of deeper blue colourwash define windows and a former fireplace alcove.

HOMEMADE DISTEMPER You will need whiting, available from builders' merchants, trade outlets or artists' suppliers, sold in 3kg [7lb] bags, which is enough for a small room. Also needed are rabbit skin glue granules – make these up according to the package instructions – usually 500g [1lb] size to 9 litres [9 US quarts] water. Stand the glue container in a pan of hot water, or *bain-marie*, and heat slowly, until warm and runny. You will also need a large plastic bowl, powder pigments for tinting, large spoons, card for colour testing, and a large metal heatproof container.

To make distemper, half-fill the plastic bowl with cold water, then tip in the whiting until it forms a peak a few inches above water level. Leave to fatten overnight. Stir with a wooden spoon, or the propeller attachment of an electric drill, to make a smooth, thick gruel or paste. Dissolve the powder pigments in hot water.

Vivid yellow colourwash is wiped over white emulsion [latex] to give an instantly sunny effect.

Blue colourwash has been wiped thinly over a mid-blue matt emulsion [latex] to give a vivid colour that almost matches the intensity of lapis lazuli.

These 'ancient' walls are a few hours' work, using complementary shades of proprietary colourwash, lettuce green and terracotta, brushed over a stone coloured basecoat of emulsion [latex]. The colours neutralize each other and when dry create a mellow dappled effect like weathered stone or old parchment.

The crossways brush movement used for colourwashing counteracts the liquid colour's natural tendency to run straight down the wall.

Add, little by little, to the whiting mix, stirring until evenly coloured. Now gradually add the warmed glue size mixture. Your distemper should be the consistency of mayonnaise. If it stiffens unmanageably, stand it in hot water until it becomes runny. Test the mix for colour on card, using a hair dryer for speed. Wet distemper is many shades deeper than when dry, because of the whiting (chalk) content.

Do not make up more distemper than you can use at a time – it will not keep longer than a day or two. New distemper formulations, based on casein, that keep for longer are now available (see page 212–213) but are more expensive. Use the distemper as it is for the ground coat. For a colourwash to go on top, thin it considerably with water to the consistency of milk.

Method

To colourwash with distemper, especially to achieve stronger shades, first apply a solid covering of distemper base. Allow it to dry. Mix a much-diluted distemper wash, milk-thin, with desired pigments to make a highly pigmented wash. Test several samples to check the colour. When you are happy with the shade, brush loosely over the distemper base with a large brush, cross hatching, leaving some base coat showing. Allow to dry, and repeat, brushing over any bare patches, as well as over some previous washing. Although it looks intense when wet, it dries to the softest finish imaginable.

Many people use much-thinned emulsion [latex] paints as a short-cut to colour-washed effects over emulsion [latex] base coats. I find these counter-productive, because all standard emulsions contain a high proportion of filler [spackle], for opacity, which works against the ideal transparency of a colourwash. However, many professionals who are trained on oil media still prefer to fake a colourwash, using oil or acrylic glazes (see below). The advantage of these is that they have a slower drying and longer 'open' time, allowing the most delicate and uniform effect. The disadvantage is the potential health risk of using evaporating solvents.

OIL GLAZE COLOURWASHING

PAINTS AND COLOURS A colourwash oil glaze is thinned considerably more than those used for other finishes in the book – about nine parts solvent, to one part paint. 500ml [1 US pint] of paint should be ample for at least two coats of colourwashing in a small room. See pages 210–213 for types of paint, and pages 220–226 for instructions on mixing, thinning and tinting washes and glazes. Oil paints are thinned with white spirit [mineral spirit] and tinted with universal stainers [tinting colours] or artists' oil colours; emulsion [latex] paints are thinned with water and tinted with universal stainers [tinting colours] or artists' gouache or acrylic colours.

OTHER EQUIPMENT Paint kettle, preferably lidded, for the colourwash glaze; wide soft brushes, 100 or 125 mm [4 or 5 in]; stepladder; clean rags.

Method The application is the same whatever type of paint you use. Dip your brush into the wash, then slap the colour on loosely and irregularly in all directions, trying to avoid heavy brushmarks and hard edges. Leave a good bit of ground colour uncovered. When dry repeat the process, brushing over most of the bare patches and also over some of the first coat of colour. This gives nicely varying intensities of colour, and a dappled effect.

Thinned paint of any kind will dry very quickly, but it is probably best to leave each wash overnight to settle before applying the next, or you may find you are taking the colour off rather than putting it on. If this happens, the bare patches can be rescued by patting on colour with a sponge. Don't be alarmed if a very watery wash runs off copiously to begin with. It may need to be gone over assiduously with a soft brush to persuade it to stick. Put lots of waterproof protection on the floor and expect the first coat to look a mess. The next coat makes a miraculous difference – the colour suddenly comes alive, and the walls knit together with the inimitable radiance that watercolour alone can give.

VARNISH A matt, slightly aged and non 'finished' look is the aim with colourwashing, but if you think you will need to wash the walls, varnish them for protection with a clear, matt acrylic varnish, or matt emulsion [latex] glaze.

READY-TO-GO COLOURWASHES Water-based, pre-tinted and ready-to-go, branded colourwashes are now widely available. These are all clones of the Paint Magic Colourwash I pioneered in the late 1980s, looking for a convenience finish that would add texture, surface interest, colour depth and complexity to plastic-looking standard emulsion [latex] paints, both matt and silk. It was designed to be, and remains, a DIY product, and has been hugely popular. It softens woodchip papers, artex finishes and other inherited nasties successfully, while rapidly delivering a painterly texture and colour intensity over emulsion [latex] base colours, which can look hard and blank when undoctored. It is a finish that requires understanding to apply well. It is not a paint to be applied thickly, but a transparent wash that is best worked by two painters working together, one sponging or brushing on, the other following behind, softening and smoothing out, for a delicate layer of modifying colour. The final colour depends very much on the base shade. I would recommend light emulsion [latex] shades under the lighter colourwash shades, but a mid-tone of the same colour for stronger colourwash shades. This makes for a richer, less splodgy final result. Colourwashes are excellent at achieving the brushy textures that are coming up as updates on the 1980s' perfect, expert glaze work. Paint Magic's non-absorbent emulsion [latex] paint range makes the ideal base for all colourwashing, giving more 'open' time, and manageable effects.

Preparation   Walls should be clean, dry and previously washed down to remove grease or stains. Filler [spackle] needs to be rubbed back and 'stopped out' with a lick of the basic paint, to make absorbency uniform. Turn off central heating appliances for the interim. On internal party walls, which are warmer and thus more absorbent, a light misting with a water-filled plant spray can adjust temperature differences prior to colourwashing. Colourwash seems to dry rapidly, but needs at least 48 hours to cure, or harden. It looks exaggerated until it dries matt, but settles down visibly in a few days. If varnishing, which is recommended over such a watery finish, use a matt acrylic varnish or emulsion [latex] glaze, applied after several days curing time.

Method   Most colourwashes are sold in plastic kegs or jerrycans. A 500ml [1 US pint] keg will cover up to 50 m² [60 sq yds] of wall if properly applied and brushed out. Apply

Colourwashing works as well with crisp, contemporary interiors as old, beamed cottages. Buff, the shade used here, has been the consistent bestseller, an undemanding neutral rescued from being flat and dull by its attractive tonal variations.

with a decorator's cellulose sponge, every which way, then follow behind with a softening brush, to smooth out concentrations of colour. Work fast – the drying time varies, but is shorter than with oil glazes. Only stop at a corner, never halfway across a wall (this rule applies to most paint finishes).

If you want a brushy texture, leave the colourwash to settle for a minute or two, then brush firmly, for the look required, up-and-down or cross-hatched as in the newest wallpaper paint effects.

LIMEWASH

Limewash is still used in third world countries and peasant communities, despite the boom in convenience paints; this is because of its utter simplicity in both ingredients and manufacture. There is, however, a fascination about lime (limewash in particular), which may explain the growing numbers of lime devotees in the developed world; these people organize hands-on demonstrations and conferences and debate the pros and cons of lime in specialist journals like *Lime News*.

So what is it about lime that accounts for its renaissance? Why is it that sophisticated architects, conservationists, and a growing body of home owners are seduced by a product whose origins are lost in pre-history, which can be made in limestone areas by anyone who can assemble a rudimentary kiln?

Building lime, for use in mortars and renders as well as limewash, is made by firing quarried limestone at a high temperature in a lime kiln for several days. The resulting product is unslaked lime, a coarse powdery material resembling lumpy washing powder, but so active chemically that the addition of water sends the temperature of the mix rocketing to boiling point. This process, known as slaking, is dramatic to see: the mixture seethes and steams furiously for a few minutes, before suddenly going quiet and inert, and subsiding into a thick, dazzlingly white pasty substance that looks remarkably like yoghurt. This is slaked lime putty, which is still mildly caustic, but safe to handle with care (wear gloves, and avoid contact with sensitive body parts). If mixed with water, in an approximate 2:3 ratio, the slaked lime will produce limewash, the most ancient and structurally simple of paints (if mixed with aggregates, it will yield building mortar and render).

Limewash in no way resembles the twentieth-century convenience paints that we are all familiar with. It is as fluid as skimmed milk and there is no appreciable build-up after regular applications; in fact, each new coat not only enriches the colour but re-activates and strengthens previous coats. Limewash is whiter than white, hence the incredibly dazzling brilliance of Greek villages under the sun. It makes vivid colours mixed with pigments, preferably mineral or earth colours, with a radiance (lime is crystalline, thus refractive) that stands out from a row of buildings painted with masonry paints.

Left-over limewash can be kept indefinitely in a lidded plastic container, but it will need thorough stirring before re-use. However, limewash tinted with non-compatible pigments (blues chiefly) will alter in colour over time, so it is best to use these up on the job. A cerulean blue left to stand, for example, will develop a violet tint.

Another peculiarity of limewashing is that each new coat 'transparentizes' previous ones, which is heartstopping until you realize that the paint becomes opaque as it dries. Several coats, depending on the substrate, are needed to give total cover and colour intensity. But since the paint is so fluid it can be slopped on with a mop or a long-handled broom, this is less arduous than it sounds.

Carbonation For carbonation to occur, whereby your sloppy wash hardens through exposure to the air to an opaque, stony, tough film, the substrate must be porous (lime render is best, also brick, stone, old cement render, even breeze blocks). Also, drying needs to be slowed down as much as possible. Work in cool conditions, 'mist' surfaces with sprayed water, tape up plastic sheeting to ward off direct sunlight, and allow two to three days before re-coating.

If fully carbonated, limewashing delivers a stony-hard finish, which looks soft owing to its dappled colour. This will not rub or wash off, although the colours do

On the proper substrate – porous, free of anything plastic in the paint line, PVA, and dampproofing sealants – there is nothing to touch simple, ancient limewash. It dries stony hard, has texture, makes radiant colours that can last centuries, and you can slop it on with a mop or a hearthbrush.

Dragging in parchment colour on white makes a soothing foil for the pretty green mouldings painted in trompe l'oeil, which do so much to improve the proportions of a turn-of-the-century drawing room. Note the ingenious windowseat in the bay window. A cut-out grille painted in with the walls conceals the radiator.

tend to gradually and pleasingly mellow with time and fade in bright sunlight over the years. Don't expect solid, opaque colour: slight colour variation provides much of the beauty of limewash.

Limewash is the conservationist's first choice because it clings like a leech and 'breathes', allowing moisture to pass through the building fabric and evaporate instead of penetrating gradually with a destructive effect. Where a limewash is appropriate (on a porous substrate or in a historical context) it is undoubtedly the best choice.

Final tips Mist surfaces to be limewashed with a plant spray first to prevent the wash being sucked back into the porous surface; a coat of white limewash acts as a luminous primer to further coloured washes. Conservationists sometimes prime with Snowcem, a branded product, for speed. A spoonful of PVA added to a tub of limewash helps it 'stick' to non-porous finishes, like emulsion [latex], but it can never carbonate and will remain soft, powdery and rub off, though it still looks attractive. Adding a dollop of skimmed milk powder, or oil, gives exterior limewash extra weather resistance.

DRAGGING

A dragged finish consists of controlled brushmarks, usually arranged vertically on walls, while on woodwork and other surfaces they echo the grain of the wood beneath. When a firm brush is 'dragged' through a tinted glaze it creates a finely striped surface with a subtle, slightly 'shot silk' appearance. Dragging looks most at home in well proportioned period rooms, with decent-sized skirtings [base-boards] and cornices. It is generally considered the most difficult wall finish because of the difficulty of keeping brushstrokes straight down a length of wall and of preventing a build-up of glaze at the start and finish of each stroke. Beginners find a rougher rustic dragging easier, and this can look very decorative too. Other variations on the theme include dragging first vertically, then horizontally, to give an attractive handwoven texture.

Some suggest that the technique was developed in colour by the late John Fowler, as an extension of a basic graining procedure. It has also been claimed that dragging imitates the finely ridged surface obtained when brushing on lead paint. On walls it makes a dignified background to paintings and antiques, but latterly dragging seems to have been used chiefly on woodwork, in neutral colours, to make discreet colour contrasts and give a 'finished' appearance.

Colours Pastel glazes dragged on white, or deeper colours dragged over a pastel base, always look effective. Blue on blue, green on green are popular wall colours, but

This detail of the glaze work on the previous page homes in on the charm worked by a transparent glaze finish in slender mouldings, which creates 'panels' in this nineteenth-century London house. These are applied mouldings, defining wall proportions attractively, but the trompe l'oeil trick on page 89 would give much the same effect.

dragging one colour over another – blue on green or lilac on grey – accentuates the 'shot silk' effect. Unusual colour combinations can also work well – grey-blue over orange, warm brown over light blue; I am fond of dragged red walls, using a darkish tone of red over a warm buff or coral pink.

Preparation

For the best work, dragging is done in a tinted transparent oil glaze [glazing liquid] over a non-permeable eggshell base, and finished with a colourless oil-based matt varnish for protection. It is possible to drag other types of paint but the traditional formula still gives the most elegant effect. Walls do need to be in good shape for dragging, as it shows up bumps and cracks in an unappealing way. They can either be well filled and sanded before base coating, or lined, sized and base coated.

Materials

Professionals all have their favourite glaze formulae, but one based on a proprietary transparent oil glaze [glazing liquid] tinted with artists' oil colours or universal stainers [tinting colours], thinned copiously with white spirit [mineral spirit] and 'softened' with the addition of a varying amount of standard white undercoat, is widely used. See page 224 for recipes and page 220 for colour mixing instructions. Try out dragged colour schemes on card or paper before you start, letting them dry before going ahead on the wall, since wet glaze colour calms down a lot as it dries

The quantity of oil glaze needed will vary with the absorbency of the base paints.

Hold the dragging brush in a firm but relaxed grip, and steadily draw it down through the wet glaze or wash.

1 litre [2 US pints] of glaze [glazing liquid] will be enough for an average-sized room painted with a non-porous eggshell paint. Over vinyl silk and matt emulsion [latex] you should allow for greater absorption – 1½–2 litres [3–4 US pints]. Acrylic scumble is not recommended for this most testing of glaze finishes.

BRUSHES The brush shown below is a long-bristled 'flogger', much used in graining. It creates pronounced stripes, but most people find the longer bristles hard to control down the length of a wall, as they offer no real resistance. A 'glider' or varnishing brush is a good alternative. A standard decorating brush, 100 mm [4 in] wide, gives enough bristle to press against the glaze and produces fine, clear stripes. For more rustic, irregularly striped effects, a wide paperhanging brush is useful; beginners often feel more comfortable with this, since it has shorter, thinner bristles. These are the ones to snip into for pyjama stripes. Being so much wider they make the dragging go faster too.

OTHER EQUIPMENT A vital piece of equipment is a sturdy, light aluminium stepladder. To contain the glaze you also need a paint kettle with a wire handle, or a roller tray for the paperhanging type of brush. Rags, newspaper or kitchen roll are essential for wiping excess glaze off the brush now and then.

Method Experts can drag-paint solo, but two people usually do a more efficient job. Painter A brushes on the glaze down one strip of wall at a time, usually about 45 cm [18 in] wide, and painter B follows behind, firmly dragging the brush through the wet glaze to produce the characteristic pin stripes. Meanwhile, painter A applies glaze onto the adjacent strip, overlapping the first strip by about 1 cm [½ in] to keep the 'wet edge' going. If the glaze edge dries it cannot be dragged, and the result is an unattractive thick stripe of colour. If this occurs, wipe off the glaze edge with solvent on a rag and repaint it.

Make sure you get the glaze consistency right before starting. If it is too over-thinned and runny the stripes will tend to blur and merge again. Correct this by adding a little more oil glaze. For distinct stripes, let the glaze 'set up' for up to a minute before dragging; for softer stripes, increase the quantity of white undercoat. Too much glaze gives a jammy look, which is not attractive, though a slightly jammy glaze is good for two-way dragging, since it gives a slight three-dimensional texture, like cloth weave.

Dragged walls should be almost matt when dry, with the base well covered, but if you end up with a sheen you dislike, flatten it out with a matt, colourless varnish, which also gives protection.

The most difficult part of dragging is avoiding a build-up of denser colour at the top and bottom of each stroke, always recognizably the mark of a beginner. The trick is to use the lightest pressure on the brush at the start and finish of each stroke, without fumbling or smudging. This knack comes with practice. One neat way round the problem is to make a positive feature of this colour build-up by painting it as a solid colour band afterwards.

Colour that strays onto the ceiling or cornice is best touched out afterwards. On the woodwork it can be wiped off with a clean rag by either of the painters involved. To avoid obvious breaks, always stop at a corner, never half way across a wall, where it will be noticeable. Wipe the dragging brush frequently on a rag to remove any excess glaze. It is helpful to begin dragging where a vertical already exists, at a door frame or in a corner, for example.

Rather than two people alternately using the stepladder, two ladders are simpler and safer, or use a lightweight stool. It is difficult to drag vertical lines without wobble on tall walls, though dragging from cornice to dado is quite manageable. A painted dado is a solution where there is no real one. In time, the glaze becomes tough enough to wash down carefully, but professional decorators usually complete dragged walls with a coat of clear matt varnish.

STIPPLING

Stippled walls make a flattering, uninsistent background to any sort of soft furnishings. The art of stippling has been practised by generations of decorators to soften colours and eliminate brushmarks from painted walls or woodwork. Using a large, fine stippling brush, the painter went over newly applied glazes closely and quickly to distribute it as evenly as possible, in order to create a matt, just perceptibly grainy, texture.

A decorative stippled finish can be achieved by pressing firmly against an area of thinly applied wet glaze with a stippling brush or soft wad of cloth or a roller, so that the glaze is drawn up into tiny pinpricks of colour, and the ground allowed to 'grin' through. Depending on the tools used, the effect varies from a fine freckle of colour to a soft mottling.

Brush stippling gives the most delicate, even finish, like the bloom of colour on a peach. It is slow and tiring to do, however, and best reserved, I think, for small areas of wall, woodwork or furniture. The brushes, too, are expensive as brushes go, though an ordinary painter's dusting brush makes a cheap substitute.

Stippling with wads of soft cloth (pad stippling) gives an effect halfway to rag-rolling (see pages 53–56) but is tighter and more uniform.

A mohair roller can be used over wet glaze to create a broken, coarsely stippled effect very quickly.

opposite Vellum and parchment were buzz words in 1930s decoration, and this interesting pastiche of a 1930s interior makes use of stippling in shades of cream to give walls the air of having been papered with squares of vellum. Aluminium leaf has been laid on the cornice and door frame.

The specially commissioned cabinet, shown here close up, from the 1930s-style room featured on the previous page, has been stippled to match the walls, in handkerchief-sized squares.

Colours Stippling is usually done in transparent colours over a white or light-coloured base coat. Just enough of the base colour shows through to soften and lighten the glaze, so that raspberry red over white will appear as deep pink, coffee brown over cream as *café au lait*, and so on. Pastel colours are attractive and make a good background for stencils.

An interesting variant of the technique, popular in the 1930s, was to stipple an opaque coat (usually white or cream) over a bright and shiny base colour, such as scarlet, emerald green or cobalt blue. An opaque coat used in this way is usually called a 'scumble' (not to be confused with the transparent oil glaze sometimes sold as scumble glaze). The effect of tiny flecks of shiny colour surfacing through a matt, opaque scumble is an appealing one, but it must be done with a brush and so is probably best kept for furniture – though it is a feasible way of softening a shiny wall finish you have grown tired of. Another 1930s trick was to use stippling to blend and shade bands of different wall colour into each other, creating the softly graded effects that were so popular in Art Deco hotel powder rooms, cinemas and cocktail bars. Overall stippling allows one colour to merge into another gradually and almost imperceptibly, with no demarcation line.

Preparation   Wall surfaces should be sound and reasonably smooth, though bumps and cracks won't be so obvious as with a directional finish such as dragging. It is important, however, that the ground coat be a non-porous paint for the stippling to register effectively and evenly. One coat of oil-based paint with a mid-sheen finish over one of undercoat gives the right kind of base. Roller stippling, being coarser and bolder, can be done over a ground of emulsion [latex] paint, but the results will be patchier unless the base coat is varnished (matt acrylic) to seal it.

Materials   GLAZE Transparent oil glaze [glazing liquid], or a glaze of thinned oil-based flat paint, undercoat or mid-sheen finish (see pages 210–213) can all be used for the stippling coat, depending on whether you want a shiny or matt finish. Exact quantities are difficult to give, but 1½ litres [3 US pints] is enough for a small to average room. Left-over glaze should be stored in a sealed jar for touching up later. For stippling ordinary emulsion [latex] paint, use a sponge. As the paint is brushed on, the sponge is used to break up the surface, which dries to a soft mottled finish. A marine sponge gives the most pleasing, random effect.

Use universal stainers [tinting colours] or artists' oil colours to tint the glaze yourself. See pages 222–25 for instructions on thinning and tinting. Note, glazes made of diluted paint tinted with universal stainers [tinting colours] give a slightly different effect from tinted transparent oil glaze [glazing liquid]. They look softer, muzzier and less glowing, because of the white pigment on which most paints are based.

TOOLS What you need will depend on which type of stippling you have decided upon. Stippling brushes come in various sizes, the largest being the most time-saving for wall treatments. A roller should be the textured variety, lambswool, mohair (or synthetic equivalent) or coarse polystyrene, not the smooth foam sort. These are so inexpensive that you may think it worth buying a couple of detachable roller heads to save time cleaning off the build-up of glaze. Stippling with a cloth wad offers plenty of scope for experimentation. Using rags of different textures gives different effects – a soft finish with muslin, net curtains, glass curtains, or old sheeting; a crisper look with hessian, burlap, or sacking. Whichever you start with, make sure you have a plentiful supply, because the cloth pads will become hard with paint and have to be jettisoned fairly often, and changing the type of cloth halfway will give a marked change of texture to the walls. Some painters use crumpled soft paper. Experiment with various effects before you decide which method to use.

OTHER EQUIPMENT White spirit [mineral spirit] or water for thinning; paint kettle, bucket or wide flat tin to hold the glaze; stepladder; plenty of clean rags.

Method   **BRUSH OR PAD STIPPLING** For this sort of stippling, two people definitely get on better than one. When you have mixed up your glaze, one member of the team brushes it evenly and finely, no thicker than a film, over a vertical strip of wall while the other follows behind stippling the surface while it is still wet and malleable. Keep the pressure on the stippling brush steady and even. Efficient teamwork is important in brush stippling because this takes quite a time, and it helps if you can be stippling the top half of a wall while your partner is brushing glaze onto the bottom. Keeping a wet edge is important for a professional-looking wall finish. If a glaze seems to be drying too fast to keep a wet edge going, add a little raw linseed oil, which acts as a retardant. Stippling with cloth pads is less tiring than brush stippling but needs the same quick, decisive touch.

Remove surplus glaze from the brush periodically, by brushing out on waste paper or rags, to prevent it from overloading to the point where it puts on more glaze than it takes off. Change cloth pads occasionally for the same reason. Unevennesses can be touched out, if necessary, after you have finished a strip. Stand back for an overall impression. Darken light patches by picking up a trace of glaze on pad or bristle tips and touching the colour in lightly. But go easy, colour builds up faster than you expect, and take care to clean the brush before re-using it. Build-ups of glaze, where you have gone over one place twice with a loaded brush, can be toned down either by re-stippling with a clean brush or rag or, if very stubborn, by a brush or rags moistened with a little white spirit [mineral spirit] to soften the drying glaze.

ROLLER STIPPLING This is a different animal. It takes longer to brush the glaze on than to roller stipple it off again, since a roller flashes up a vertical surface in no time. Roll the roller up and down over the wet glaze, using quite firm pressure, until the colour is evenly textured. Take care not to let the roller skid over the glaze, because this wipes off streaks of colour, which then have to be patched up and re-stippled. Clean the roller head frequently by rolling vigorously on waste paper to mop up surplus colour. It is more difficult to cut in neatly at the top and bottom of a wall with a roller, and glaze may accumulate here or smudge on to the woodwork or ceiling. Keep clean rags handy for wiping off smudges, and even out built-up colour by stippling over the area with a soft rag moistened with white spirit [mineral spirit]. Clean the roller at the end of the session by rolling on paper, then in white spirit [mineral spirit] – which has to be squeezed out by hand – then on clean paper.

VARNISH If the walls are likely to need frequent washing down, varnish with a clear matt or mid-sheen varnish (if you have used a wash this is certainly necessary). Matt varnish dries almost invisibly, giving a tough finish that can be wiped clean.

RAGGING & RAG-ROLLING

Ragging leaves an elegant flow of softly variegated texture over wall surfaces. Rag-rolling is a striking variant of the same finish.

For a ragged finish, a bunched-up rag or chamois leather is pressed onto wet glaze. By varying the pressure on the rag, rolling it this way and that and re-arranging it from time to time, subtly varied impressions are left that create a pleasantly uninsistent but lively flow of textured colour.

For a rag-rolled finish, rags or leathers are rolled up into a small bolster shape. This is then rolled up (or down) the wet glaze to give a directional pattern of broad blurry stripes, reminiscent of watered silk. The rolling movement needs to be carefully controlled as the stripes must be more or less vertical, parallel and equidistant. Professionals often pencil or chalk in guidelines with a spirit level or plumbline.

Twisting rags into a loose rope, which is then knotted into a figure of eight and rolled up the wet glaze, gives a highly dramatic patterning similar to the bold 'graining' on eighteenth-century American country furniture.

Colours   Because of the relative obtrusiveness of a ragged finish, it is best confined to softer colours. The more 'interesting' pastels – blue-green, brownish-pink, greyish-mauve – all look attractive ragged over a slightly 'dirty' white ground – that is, a white base

right Ragging off by dabbing the bunched-up cloth onto the wet glaze.

far right Here the glaze or wash is being ragged onto the wall using a rag-rolling movement. Since it goes so quickly, ragging on is a particularly suitable method for applying a fast-drying wash.

opposite The owner of this room, tired of her chilly white walls, rag-rolled them on the spur of the moment with sky-blue emulsion [latex] paint. No setting could be more delicately atmospheric, or could more perfectly complement the blue green colour of the painted wicker chair.

tinted with a little raw umber for a cool greeny-grey cast, or a little ochre and raw sienna for a warmer cream. Colour on colour looks fetching if the colours are of similar intensity or tone. One of the most attractive ragged finishes I have seen was a warm duck egg blue – a greeny blue – ragged over a transparent faded-brick colour tinted with burnt sienna. In complete contrast a parchment-tinted glaze – a little white plus raw or burnt umber – ragged over plain white gives an ultra-refined, 'laid-back' finish.

Preparation

Ragging can be done with both oil and acrylic scumbles tinted with appropriate tinting media. See Fundamentals, page 216. As with all glaze work, a nonabsorbent base paint gives best results, as it leaves more 'open' working time. Oil-based eggshell was the traditional choice and is still used in quality jobs, but many people substitute silk vinyl emulsion [latex], or a standard emulsion [latex] given a coat of acrylic varnish to make it less absorbent.

Materials

Oil scumble glaze should be coloured with artists' oils, or universal stainers [tinting colours]. Oil glaze is thinned before use with solvent such as white spirit [mineral spirit], and a little white oil-based paint is often added to the glaze to give softer markings and prevent a sticky jam effect.

Acrylic scumble can be tinted with liquid tinters or universal stainers [tinting colours]. Some people use emulsions [latex] for tinting, thinned first with a little water and thoroughly stirred into the scumble. Acrylic scumble looks milky white when wet, turning transparent as it dries.

For mixing and tinting instructions, see pages 222–225. A 500ml [1 US pint] keg of oil glaze [glazing liquid] is enough for a small to average-sized room. Allow approximately twice this amount for acrylic scumble.

RAGS AND BRUSHES You need a wide, soft brush to apply the glaze or wash and a good supply of rags or a piece of chamois leather to distress it. Rags can be of varying texture (old sheet, gauze, or even hessian or burlap), but they must be well washed and lint free, and the same type must of course be used throughout. Rags and leather can be used dry or – with a glaze – wrung out in white spirit [mineral spirit] for a softer effect.

Method

Apply the glaze over a fairly large section of wall with a large soft brush. Transparent oil glaze needs to be worked over quite a lot to even out brushstrokes. The oil glaze made from the recipe on page 224 is easier to brush out than a proprietary glaze, though much slower drying.

There are two ways of using the rag to make a pattern. Either bunch it up in one

hand and dab and push it about on the glaze with a 'loose wrist', or wrap it into a loose but compact bundle and, using both hands, roll this about over the wet glaze in various directions like a rolling pin. The idea is to make an irregular pattern, but one that looks fairly uniform overall. From time to time you will have to change your rag, as it will become stiffened with glaze or paint. With oil glaze [glazing liquid] or oil paint, chamois leather should be used wrung out in white spirit [mineral spirit], as this allows you to clean it now and then.

If the wet edge dries while ragging with oil-based paint, try softening it with a clean rag soaked in white spirit [mineral spirit]. A wash of acrylic scumble dries fast so if possible have two people on the job at the same time. Paint a small strip of wall at a time and fade out the wash toward the edge of the strip so that the overlap is not too thick. If the wash starts to dry before it has been ragged, dabble it with a wet sponge to make it more workable. Misting with a plant spray should also soften a hard edge.

VARNISH A ragged finish can be protected with a coat of clear matt or mid-sheen acrylic varnish.

SPONGING

Sponging is a really jolly decorative finish, quick and easy to do, and capable of infinitely varied effects according to the type of sponge, the way you wield it and the number of colours used.

SPONGING ON OR OFF The most commonly used sponging technique differs from most of the decorative finishes described here in that the sponge is used to dab the tinted glaze or wash on, taking up the colour from a large flat surface, such as a plate or tray. However, you can brush on a glaze in the usual way and then use a clean sponge to distress the wet surface – a sponge wrung out in solvent gives a very regular, prettily granulated appearance, like a close-textured stone, or knobbly knitting.

SPONGING ON WITH TWO COLOURS The sponging-on method, carried out with two different coloured glazes or washes over a light ground, is a speedy way of obtaining a marbled effect that can look extremely opulent in a small room. To obtain the most emphatic patterning, the wall surface should be painted first with a light-coloured, mid-sheen or flat paint. An emulsion [latex] paint ground coat makes the most suitable base for sponged-on water-based colours. The sponged-on colours should be thinned to transparency with the appropriate dilutent. Test the effects on paper first.

Materials   GLAZES AND WASHES A tinted transparent glaze (oil or acrylic scumble) gives the most translucent 'marble' effect, plus the longest working or 'open' time. Thinned paints, either oil- or water-based, can be substituted but tend to dry fast, giving less scope for second thoughts and any subsequent retouching. Experiment on boards first to help you decide which medium works best for you. For a small room, 1 litre [2 US pints] of any of the above should be ample for either sponging on or off. See pages 223–224 for instructions on thinning and tinting glazes and washes.

Use universal stainers [tinting colours], artists' oils, gouache or acrylic colours as appropriate for tinting. Thin transparent oil glaze [glazing liquid] with white spirit [mineral spirit] and acrylic scumbles with water.

EQUIPMENT A marine sponge is essential for sponging-on tinted transparent glaze; it doesn't have to be brand new. If this is too expensive, the best substitute is a pad of soft crumpled muslin or cheesecloth fabric, held bunched up in the hand. (Change this for a new piece of fabric especially when it gets hard with paint.) Cellulose sponge makes hard-edged identical prints that don't flow together attractively. However, it can be used for the sponging-off method, where it will produce a regular stippled effect.

right Sponge on the glaze or wash using a light 'pecky' movement, to produce a soft, cloudy impression.

far right For two-colour sponging, wait until the first colour is quite dry, then apply your second colour in the same way, for a gently marbled effect.

You will also need a bucket or paint kettle for mixing up the glaze; a clean, flat container to use as a palette; a stepladder; and plenty of spare rags or waste paper for wiping up as you sponge the wall surface.

Method **SPONGING OFF** For a simple, uniform, one-colour sponging, brush the thinned glaze out over a strip of wall in the usual way, then press the sponge – wrung out in white spirit [mineral spirit] – evenly over the wet glaze. This finish needs to be regular, so spend a little time working over thicker patches of colour to get the whole thing evenly distressed. You may need to wash out the sponge from time to time in white spirit [mineral spirit] if it becomes loaded with glaze.

SPONGING ON For two-colour sponging to produce a marbled effect, soft, transparent glazes [glazing liquids] and a light touch with the sponge help give the impression that the colour was floated on. Keep the glaze in a flat container large enough to dab the sponge into, and have waste paper handy to test the colour on before dabbing it on the wall. Thick wet prints mean the sponge is overloaded. Go on dabbing the paper until you get a soft cloudy impression; then dab over the wall surface with a light, 'pecky' hand movement, keeping the sponged prints fairly spaced out. A good bit of ground colour should show through the first sponged colour, say two-fifths of the total area. When the first glaze colour is quite dry, sponge on the second colour. Concentrate on the blank areas, but overlap with the previous prints too, to give a dappled effect that must not be allowed to become too regular and predictable. Change the position of the sponge regularly, and wipe it clean now and then on clean rags, or rinse out in solvent – but take care to squeeze it out well, or this will make the next lot of paint very diluted.

previous page Sponging is the easiest and fastest of the special finishes to apply and can look particularly stylish when three related colours are sponged in separate 'continents', as in this room, then softened and blended slightly at the edges. The handsome wall painting is a crib from a museum postcard.

VARNISH Apply varnish after 24 hours, or when the glaze is hard, using a clear matt or mid-sheen acrylic varnish (thinned three parts varnish to one part water).

IMPASTO

This was originally a fine art term used to describe a thick, textured paint application. Rembrandt's famous 'highlights' – on armour, fabric or faces – when seen close up, break down into thick swipes of paint, probably applied with a palette knife. Stand back, and they coalesce magically, as dramatic flashes of intense light.

This technique of using a thick layer of paint inspired the manufacture of impasto, a wall paint designed to add surface interest, or texture. Effects range from a well-brushed-out, soft 'blotting paper' finish (excellent for ceilings) to a roughed-up surface resembling walls you may have seen in the Mediterranean. Unlike most textured finishes, impasto can look soft despite its toughness. For the

The delight of impasto is that you can do with it what you will: brush it on for a matt 'blotting paper' surface or heap it on and trowel it for a rough tough plastery look. Alternatively, you could apply it over a suitable stencil for a low relief effect, as here, painted over in white or cream and reminiscent of embroidery or lace.

rough plastered effect, it should be brushed on generously, then worked over with a trowel or spatula. It can be tinted, using media suited to water-based paints, or can be colourwashed on completion for a softer, dappled look, which most people prefer. Because of its absorbency, colourwashing on top needs to be applied quickly, with rapid 'softening' to disperse the colourwash fairly evenly, so colour does not collect in cracks and hollows. One bonus – impasto is an excellent finish for walls that are not in particularly good condition, since it is thick and tough enough to 'fill' and smooth out cracks and unevenness in the wall surface, unless of course you want to emphasize these.

Compared with most textured finishes, the impasto made by Paint Magic is easy to apply, with a brush and/or spatula. It dries to a pleasant creamy white, untinted matt finish, while many other commercial versions have a repellent sheen. One disadvantage, however, is that the paint is not fully opaque, which means that it should be applied over a white priming coat, like acrylic primer, especially where the existing finish is strongly coloured, or patterned.

Experienced painters have no problem applying colourwash directly to impasto-treated walls. Nervous beginners, however, may feel more comfortable applying a nonabsorbent emulsion [latex] base first, then following with the colourwash, as this system allows a longer 'open' time. As with all unfamiliar paint products, test its performance on a board before you start. The 5 litre [10 US pints] tub size will cover approximately 15–20 m^2 [18–24 sq yds], depending on whether it is brushed out, in a similar way to paint, or trowelled in a thick layer.

Materials   Standard brushes; plasterer's trowel and/or float or artist's spatula (for rough surfaces); water-based liquid tinters or dry pigments, previously soaked in water; emulsion [latex] base or colourwash, as required. Varnish (matt acrylic) is needed over a colourwashed finish, which is inherently fragile – it can be wiped over lightly with a damp sponge, but would not withstand serious scrubbing.

Method   Impasto, like paint, can be brushed on and laid off with a standard brush. As a textured finish, it is brushed on thickly, then worked over with a trowel or float to the roughness and texture desired. Let it dry thoroughly before colourwashing or base coating, about 24 hours. To colourwash directly, dilute the colourwash with water, apply it with a sponge to cover the largest area, then soften with a brush.

GESSO

Gesso is a fluid plastery substance that offers a pristinely white and thirsty surface for paint. If properly applied and sanded between coats, it provides a surface as fine and smooth as porcelain, making it a superlative primer for furniture destined for a lavish painted finish. In addition, gesso has a variety of other uses. It makes an excellent surface for applying gold leaf, and also lends itself to creating low-relief decoration, achieved by 'dribbling' it from a brush to build up the layers, as done by those who practised the art of japanning (European imitation of oriental lacquer work) in the seventeenth and eighteenth centuries. Another use of traditional gesso that has surfaced recently among experimental decorators is to use it as a refined coating for walls, as a plaster and/or paint. Some people like to stress the brush-marks, like finest pin tucks, and its natural dazzling whiteness; others sand it back, using increasingly fine grades of abrasive paper to achieve porcelain smoothness, either to leave bare, displaying its lovely subtle sheen, or to decorate with washes of watery colour in an abstract or figurative design.

Today, you can buy an acrylic, ready-to-go gesso (Liquitex, available from artists' supply shops). However, it is a lot more costly than the traditional gesso (see below), and the final surface lacks porcelain smoothness.

Materials   Rabbit skin glue granules; artist's whiting; *bain marie*; measuring jug; spoon; sieve; assorted brushes; silicone or wet-or-dry abrasive paper; sharp tools for carving.

Method   Tip a cupful of rabbit skin glue granules into a bowl with cold water to just cover. Leave to 'fatten' overnight until the granules have soaked up the water. Turn the mixture into the top part of a *bain marie* and heat over simmering water, stirring until melted and liquid. This is the gesso 'stock', which must not boil or the gesso loses strength. Dilute the stock with a little water, and brush a thin coat over the

Gesso takes on a contemporary look. Here it has been used both as a base for silver leaf, and to form raised lettering, a new take on its sculptural uses. Chopped cooked egg whites laid on top of the silver leaf gave the dusky patina. Silver leaf was also used to back a sheet of glass to make a hazy but reflective mirror.

furniture or wall; leave to dry. Add the whiting gradually to the rest of the stock, stirring to break up lumps, until the whiting begins to settle on the bottom of the pan. Push the mix through a sieve into a bowl, then return it to the pan to keep warm.

Three parts water to two parts gesso makes thick gesso (*gesso grosso*), used as a primer. Follow this with six coats of thin gesso (*gesso sotile*), made by diluting with a further two parts water. Brush vertically, then horizontally, to form a crisscross pattern. In between coats, once the gesso has dried and hardened, rub the gesso back with silicone or wet-or-dry, fine-grade paper.

LACQUER FINISH

A rich surface gloss and depth of colour are the *lac-de-chine* characteristics that decorators are after when they suggest a 'lacquer' wall finish to their clients. I don't mean by this the sort of effect you get by simply painting everything with gloss or enamel paint. That is certainly shiny, but it looks thick and lifeless compared to more complex effects built up with matt colour and glaze or varnish. Lacquer-look finishes are a demanding background, unkind to shabby furnishings and oddly shaped rooms. Shiny colour needs a high degree of finish everywhere else as well – sound plasterwork, handsomely moulded cornice, well-painted woodwork, elegant furniture – in short, an expensive effect. An exception to the rule might be a room where something nearer to worn old lacquer has been contrived, using dark base colours – crimson, vermilion, olive-green, deep blue, chestnut – brightened with a little discreet gold stencilling and given a semi-gloss varnish for sheen rather than shine.

Creating a lacquer-type finish

There are three ways to get a lacquer-type finish. The first, if you simply want shine, is to apply one or two coats of clear varnish (carriage varnish for rapid shine, semi-gloss for sheen) over walls painted in your chosen colour. The second method, though similar, gives richness of colour as well: you apply the varnish in the same way, but tint it to tone with the paint beneath. In the third method, the base coat is covered with a toning glaze, and then varnished. If you apply a number of coats of glaze and varnish, all tinted differently, you can achieve a wonderful depth of colour.

Preparation

A lacquer finish requires perfectly prepared walls. Choose a base paint colour that will look good through clear varnish, or to tone with subsequent coats of glaze or tinted varnish. When it is dry, lightly sand it to remove dust, but don't grind away so hard that you cut through the paint. Dust the walls down, then wipe them over finally with a damp cloth. As for any varnishing job, the room itself should be immaculate before you begin, to prevent dust from settling on the sticky wet surface. Remove curtains or draperies and rugs, cover furniture with dust sheets, and vacuum and dust everything. Keep doors and windows closed.

Materials

For a lacquer-type finish with one coat of varnish (thinned three parts varnish to one part white spirit [mineral spirit]) for a small room – 3 x 4 m [10 x 12 ft] – you need 1 litre [2 US pints] of clear gloss polyurethane varnish or carriage varnish (see pages 214–215).

To glaze the same room you need 500 ml [1 US pint] of mid-sheen oil-based paint or transparent oil glaze [glazing liquid]. Or, for speed, use fast-drying acrylic scumble glaze tinted with acrylic colours or universal stainers [tinting colours]. See pages 210–213 for information on paints and pages 222–225 for tinting glazes.

OTHER EQUIPMENT Brushes should be fairly wide, 75 or 100 mm [3 or 4 in], and of extra-good quality. Varnish brushes should be kept for varnishing only (see page 232), as you don't want bits and pieces of old paint marring your smooth finish. Other equipment includes white spirit [mineral spirit]; fine sandpaper; stepladder; pan, paint kettle or bucket for the thinned glaze; plenty of clean rags.

An old-fashioned tack cloth is a useful accessory in a high-quality job. Basically a soft cloth impregnated with varnish, and kept 'sticky', this cleans off any grit or nibs. Today they can be bought ready-to-go from specialist trade shops. The tack rag picks up surface dust and grit quickly and easily without disturbing the finish.

Deeply glossy painted walls can be chic and alluring. Dining rooms are an ideal venue for such theatrics, reflecting back candle-light. Strong colours, as here, look vivid and dramatic seen through the glassy surface created by the layers of varnish. Tinting the varnish gives extra depth.

Method **TINTED VARNISH** To tint oil-based varnish, dilute a blob of universal stainer [tinting colour] or artist's oil colour in a little white spirit [mineral spirit], then add a cupful of varnish. Stir well, then add the rest of the varnish, thinning as above. Varnish should be applied with a full brush and brushed out fast, lightly and evenly to avoid brushmarks. Applied too liberally, varnish will curtain or sag. Thick coats of varnish tend to wrinkle so two thin coats are always better than one thick one. Likewise, try to avoid going over the same spot twice, as this can leave sticky deposits that dry darker. Although the varnish won't take long to dry, allow longer than stated on the can if the room is not heated – ideally, varnish should be applied in a mildly warm room, to help flow and drying. One coat may be enough, but two will give greater depth of colour and shine. Let the first coat dry really hard before putting on the second – it may take several days. Read the manufacturer's instructions carefully.

GLAZING Apply glaze [glazing liquid] with a large soft brush over the entire wall surface, keeping it even and as fine as possible. Brush out well to avoid brushmarks – stippling over an oil-based glaze will eliminate them. Leave for 24 hours until it is perfectly dry, then varnish over, thinning gloss or semi-gloss varnish as suggested and using a clean brush.

ANTIQUE LACQUER For an antique lacquer effect, the colours should be softened to the patina of antique lacquer, not used hot and strong. This can be done by painting the walls with an antique glaze (see page 168) before or after stencilling, or by adding a little of the same antiquing colours to the final varnish. Try the effect of raw and burnt umber on a patch that won't show – raw umber is particularly flattering to greens and blues, while burnt umber is richer over reds. A speck of black can be added too, to age the whole surface even more. One coat of varnish is enough, but two – both thinned – are better. I think semi-gloss varnish gives a softer, prettier texture than gloss, but takes longer to build up.

STENCILS Designs stencilled in metal powder can look splendid on a lacquer finish. The stencilled motif might be a simple fleur-de-lys or Tudor rose, which always look good spaced out on a diagonal grid. Or adapt the quaint chinoiserie figures that decorated eighteenth-century japanned pieces: a flower-spray motif or a man fishing from a sampan, for example. Remember that the stencils can be used back to front for a slight change of emphasis. Alternatively, of course, you could limit yourself to a simple gilt border stencil. Use Indian ink with a fine sable brush for detail and antiquing glazes to 'dirty' and age the work. Carriage varnish, as used for royal coaches, gives an ideally hard, fine, shiny finish for a high-class job.

TEXTURED PAINTS

Texture may be tactile, such as the effects created by marmorino and stucco lustro (see pages 30–32), combing, or suede paints; alternatively, it can be introduced visually by glaze work, giving the impression of texture.

BRUSHY EFFECT

The finish shown below is the new spin on the dragged finish that was popular in the early 1980s. The brushmarks are conspicuous, adding visual texture. The walls here were finished with an acrylic scumble glaze, tinted a few shades deeper than the light red emulsion [latex] base. The glaze was laid on in narrow strips, from top to bottom, then left for a few minutes, before brushing down firmly with a wide wall-paper brush. Acrylic scumbles dry with a distinct sheen, so a coat of emulsion [latex] glaze (see pages 214–215) was used to knock back the shine and protect.

COMBING

At first glance, combing could be mistaken for the classic dragged finish, but a closer look shows that the stripes are raised, like corduroy, lending a subtle richness of texture. The striping is also looser, occasionally with deliberate curves.

A dragged finish makes a come-back with this vivid brushy effect, which has a painterly looseness people like today. Walls here were painted first with a soft pinky red, then glazed and brushed out with an acrylic scumble glaze tinted to a deeper, warmer red. The resulting look is textured.

Combing paste is semi-transparent and needs tinting with white and raw umber to an opaque off-white shade. The most popular finishes use off-white paste over a coloured emulsion [latex] base. The base colour needs to be deeper than the overall shade you want. For example, off-white over a warm pink gives a rosy shell-pink, over *café au lait* a warm cream, and over aquamarine a sky blue. For a funkier effect, tint the paste to give stronger shades, such as charcoal over gold.

Materials

Combing paste (allow 1 x 2.5 litre [5 US pints] tub for approximately 16 m² [19 sq yds] of wall surface, remembering to subtract doors, windows, etc); rubber comb; emulsion [latex] base shade, two coats; standard decorating brushes, as close to the comb width as possible; acrylic varnish (matt or eggshell), optional; stepladder.

Method

Prepare the wall for painting. Fill the cracks and hollows, sand until smooth, then apply a layer of primer, followed by two coats of emulsion base. When dry, brush

Combed walls are the latest in textured finishes, with a ridgy three-dimensional surface like corduroy. Colour contrast between the combed stripes and emulsion [latex] base adds further depth of texture. Off-white combing over mid-tone shades of emulsion [latex] plays up the chalky, ceramic look.

The first emulsion [latex] paint with built-in texture, suede paint dries to a matt, 'blotting paper' surface that looks rich and inviting. It should be applied with a wide brush in cross-hatch strokes, not laid off in the usual way.

on the combing paste from top to bottom, a narrow strip at a time (20 cm/ 8 in is ideal), applying it thickly and laying off with the brush tips for a smooth icing effect. Then, starting in one corner, comb the paste from top to bottom, using less pressure at the start and finish of the 'drop', but keeping up firm and even pressure all the way. You are, in effect, scraping off the paste to reveal the base colour as you go. The lesson here is to tackle one wall at a time, without stopping. Don't worry if your stripes are a bit wobbly. Dashing spontaneity in the execution is part of the appeal – liveliness, not neatness, is the aim.

Ideally, this is a job for two decorators, one brushing on the combing paste, the other combing it off. The important thing is to avoid letting the leading edge of the paste harden before brushing on the next strip (the paste stays 'open' for between eight and ten minutes). If this happens, wetting with a plant spray may help. Alternatively, you may need to scrape off 2.5–5 cm [1–2.5 in] of paste and re-brush. Comb into a corner, but leave a space before applying the next strip on the adjoining wall, or you risk messing up the previous combed strip. Go back and complete the area once the combing paste has dried hard, about 24 hours later, switching to a smaller brush if necessary.

Varnishing is optional. A coat of matt acrylic varnish will give protection without altering the 'chalky' look. A semi or full gloss varnish is preferred in the US, being both tougher and bringing up the base colour more emphatically. However, this is a tough finish, and varnishing is not essential.

SUEDE PAINT Suede leather has staged a come-back lately, in upholstery and soft furnishings, so it was only a matter of time before a wall paint was developed with something of the deeply matt, sensuous appeal of the real hide. Suede paint shares the soft look of old-fashioned distemper (see pages 34–39), but it is essentially an emulsion [latex] paint with additives, making its application comfortably familiar. But there are points to bear in mind. Suede paint is less opaque than standard emulsions [latex], so works best applied over a base colour close to the final suede shade. The first coat may be rollered, but the second should be brushed on, using a brush as wide as you can handle easily, brushing colour on in all directions rather than laying off smoothly. This emphasizes its 'suede' texture. It should not be varnished; marks can be wiped off with a damp sponge. The usual objection to emulsion [latex] paints is that they look 'plastic'. Suede paint eliminates that problem decisively, with its blotting paper mattness and friendly texture.

Suede paint makes a warm finish for large loft spaces, and looks good with spiky metal furniture; in a different context, it flatters polished antiques and old gilt. Remember, always aim for contrast when working with texture. Colours in the suede paint range (see pages 210–211) include off-white, cream and duck egg blue.

Decorative Painting

STENCILLING

Stencils are an essentially simple but versatile decorative tool, a way of painting repeat patterns which has been known for thousands of years. They were popular among the rulers of medieval Europe for 'powdering' painted walls by disposing a motif over a regular grid. (Henry III of England had green walls powdered with gold stars stencilled in this way.) A great revival of stencilling took place in the latter part of the nineteenth century when elaborate polychrome schemes were used to decorate churches, public buildings and the newer royal residences like Osborne House. Medievalists such as William Morris and William Burges made frequent use of stencils in their interior designs, with multiple overlays.

Stencilling has also flourished as a poor man's approximation of fashionable printed wallpaper as a means of imitating overall repeat motifs. One tends to find examples of this use in the remoter country districts, from New England and Scandinavia to Sicily. Stencilling is undeniably laborious, but the result can be delicious and it need not have the homespun simplicity of these rural examples.

left Stencilling like this was done in imitation of wallpaper at a time when labour was cheap and wallpaper was imported and expensive. Note how the bands of motifs keep to a wallpaper spacing regardless of cracks in the boarded walls. Stencil patterns may be one of the best records of forgotten early designs.

right This lively diamond design was stencilled by Vanessa Bell and Duncan Grant in their home, Charleston Manor. The overall pattern has a slight jazz-age feel to it and provides a vivid background to gentler treatments on furniture and ornaments. A similar effect can be reproduced using two rubber stamps.

Modern designers such as John Stefanidis and Renzo Mongiardino make use of highly sophisticated versions of the stencil-as-wallpaper idea, using many 'faded' colours, and much variation of tone to suggest antique embroideries or tapestry. Such ambitious schemes, sadly, demand the specialized expertise of these designers but stencilling with 'powdered' motifs is an easy and dramatic way to give impact to almost any decorating scheme, and it is perhaps surprising that few people experiment with these techniques. Strong self-contained motifs such as stars, fleur-de-lys, scallop shells, oriental seals and heraldic emblems are all suitable. One of the prettiest schemes of this sort, in Sweden, shows a sprig of coral a few inches high, stencilled in pale red on a pale grey ground, not closely, but at intervals at least 1 m [3 ft] apart. After many years of timid floral borders, there are signs that bolder use of stencilled pattern is becoming popular, with ethnic and abstract designs appealing to younger people. There is a great range of pre-cut stencil designs to be found in art shops as well as specialist shops but if you have a pet design or want to devise one based perhaps on a chintz or rug design, it is easy to make your own. The process has been made vastly easier by photocopying machines, with their capacity for enlarging small motifs and vice versa.

Uses of stencilling

Use stencils not just to decorate walls but to improve a room's proportions, draw attention to attractive or quirky features, or to add bold blocks of pattern. Deep borders top and bottom cut a room's height, and can substitute for a cornice. False dadoes were often stencilled at dado height, with different wall colours above and below, another device for shrinking height. For a neoclassical look, stencil 'pilasters' at intervals between dado and ceiling, and marble the dado below. And don't overlook the possibility of stencilling on fabrics (see left), floors, furniture, and even sisal matting. One tiny motif stencilled on a grid is a simple, if painstaking, way to add charm and interest to anything from a papier mâché box to a three-panel screen.

Materials

Oiled stencil card or acetate is used for cutting out stencils. Oiled stencil card, which is opaque, is much easier to cut with a scalpel or craft knife than transparent acetate, which tends to split very easily. Use carbon paper and a sharp pencil to transfer motifs onto stencil card, and a rapidograph drawing pen for drawing on acetate. A 'hot pen' makes cutting acetate much easier. I use layers of newspaper for cutting on, which I find less tiring than plate glass and cheaper than cutting boards. A light craft knife or scalpel is easier to wield than a heavy-duty craft knife. The knife must be sharp; blades need to be changed often.

BRUSHES AND SPONGES Stencillers today rarely use the straight-cut hog bristle brush commonly sold as a 'stencilling brush'. This is tiring to use, with its 'pouncing' or

Stencilling has moved beyond pretty florals and dainty borders: today's use of stencils is bold and punchy. Here, designs adapted from Nigerian wood-blocks do wonders for simple curtains made from cheap calico, an idea that can be transposed just as successfully to walls or lining paper.

above The simplest rosette stencilled in distemper on a regular grid imitates wallpaper in a Swedish farmhouse, and makes a sympathetic background to a wonderful medley of paint effects: primitive marbling and graining plus a burst of folk exuberance on the decorated wall cupboard.

right Stencils today are moving away from floral and pastel designs. This close-up of a farmhouse kitchen wall, distempered a rich Venetian red, demonstrates this trend with a Paisley motif above and a foliage design below – making a handsome backdrop to a colourful collection of pottery.

stamping on of colour. A softer, rounded mop-like brush used in a looser, round-and-round action, gets along faster and gives a fine, dry image that can be as misty as the one achieved by spray paints.

Sponges, marine and synthetic, are used to stencil textured images, and are easy to handle. A felt painting pad is used by some people. Spray paints are less and less popular, because of ecological concerns, though water-based spray paints are now available.

Spray adhesive is excellent for attaching stencils to any surface, especially useful in the case of fragile, lacy stencils, which need to be kept as flat as possible to prevent blurring or tearing the stencil. A light pass with the spraycan over the stencil is all that is needed, and it can be peeled off again easily without damage to the wall paint beneath.

PAINTS Most stencillers use emulsion [latex] for rapid cover and acrylic primer with artists' acrylic tube colours, which also dry fast and immovably to add colour and shading. Mixing acrylic colours into a proprietary medium (see pages 216–217), gives extra transparency, extends the paints and delays hardening. For faded fabric effects I often use colourwashes (see pages 34–42) over a primer or emulsion [latex] base. Professionals rarely use so-called stencil paints, or crayons, owing to their high cost.

OTHER EQUIPMENT Rags; a plate or two for a palette; masking tape; portable stepladder; plumbline; straight edge or long ruler.

Cutting stencils When using acetate, trace designs onto the acetate with a rapidograph; the material is transparent so simply lay it on top of the design. Use transfer paper or carbon paper to transfer designs onto card, then cut it with a 'hot pen'. Card is easier to cut smoothly. An expert, with a strong grip, can easily cut a fine, bevelled edge round each shape. Keep cuts as smooth, clean and lively as possible; with sharp blades you are almost drawing with the knife. One advantage of acetate is that when in use it can bend round corners, and is almost indestructible. Card gradually softens and wears out, so make spares, stencilling your design onto extra card.

Registration Positioning stencils accurately is chiefly a problem when superimposing different 'cuts' for polychrome effects. For such schemes, cut all stencils the same size with notches in the top corners which you mark lightly on the wall with chalk. Borders are simplified by overlapping the beginning and end of the stencil. Grids are best marked out lightly in chalk, or with a chalked 'snap line', which can be purchased from builders' merchants.

The inspiration for this starry sky stencil over a colourwash came from a painted Scandinavian armoire, or *fatehbur*. It is worth noting that the simplest stencil forms, star shapes as here, gain impact from a change of scale, and a random sprinkling looks much more appealing than a tight grid.

Painting Put dabs of colour round the rim of your plate, with a splodge of white acrylic colour in the middle. Experiment with colours, mixing them up on the plate; you need very little colour. The cardinal rule of stencilling is to use an almost dry brush. Pick up colour, then work it up into the bristles on a piece of newspaper. When the colour emerges soft, slightly transparent, without visible moisture, you are ready to start. Fix the stencil in place with spray adhesive or tabs of masking tape, or hold it with one hand. Use a round scrubbing motion to apply the colour, like putting rouge on one's cheeks. Paint as fine as this is easy to shade with a quick further rub of another colour. Designs featuring two predominant colours (from two stencils) say, red apples with green leaves, work well when each colour is shaded with the other: red on the green leaves, green on the apples. This simple trick, you will

find, prevents stencils looking 'jumpy' on the wall. Applied decoration must always 'lie down'. If you are superimposing colours within your stencil design, make sure that the first layer of paint is fully dry before applying the next colour.

Varnishing

On walls, most stencil schemes will not need varnishing. But a coat of clear matt varnish will certainly prolong the life of an ambitious and intricate project. Stencilled floors and furniture can be varnished with matt acrylic or polyurethane for extra strength, though the latter should not be used over pale colours.

RUBBER STAMPING

Not everyone realizes that the invaluable rubber stamp used for countless routine and mundane purposes also has immense decorative potential. Rubber stamp manufacturers, given scale drawings of suitable designs, will convert them into decorative stamps for a modest fee. Using quick-drying paints or inks, you can then stamp designs effectively and speedily on to walls or furniture in any arrangement you favour.

The idea comes from the traditional method of hand printing fabrics with carved wooden blocks. Small floral motifs stamped in a regular grid look like hand-printed Indian cotton, especially if the same design is massed together to make a patterned border surround. A geometric motif, such as a simple diamond, can build up to quite a different effect – Art Deco-like, or 1930s Bloomsbury style in the manner of Duncan Grant and Vanessa Bell. The scope for patterns is immense, but do remember that it is the size and complexity which will determine the cost of making the stamp.

The naive quality of small repeat floral motifs is perfectly suited to small cottage-style rooms. Here, instead of measuring up painstakingly and pencilling in guide-lines, you can – if you feel confident enough – trust your eyes when it comes to positioning the patterns. Smaller designs interspersed with larger motifs for variety will emphasize the hand-printed effect.

In larger rooms, pencilled or chalked guidelines are necessary as small errors have a way of becoming magnified over a large area.

The freshness and charm of this rubber-stamped country bathroom come from the simplicity of its design. The alternation of large prints with small results in a pleasantly uninsistent pattern over the walls. The somewhat random positioning of the motifs adds to the pretty hand-painted effect.

Materials

Rubber stamps; a small sheet of glass with taped edges; artists' acrylic colours plus acrylic medium; a small lino cutters' roller [brayer]; sponge; chalk; plumbline; ruler and straight-edge; waste paper.

Preparation

Walls should be reasonably smooth and freshly painted in matt or mid-sheen paint. For a regular grid pattern, measure and mark out the wall area, using a plumbline to secure verticals and a T-square or spirit level to get horizontals lined up, with 90°

This charmingly random mosaic effect was achieved using acrylic colours and our old friend the potato, carved here like a little waffle iron and used to print colour straight onto the walls of a small bathroom.

angles at intersections. A chalked line (see page 140) is an effective way of marking lines of any length and can be rubbed off again later when no longer needed. If you are using two stamps of different sizes, you will find they look best staggered – a small one equidistant from two larger ones, for example, so that a triangular pattern is formed.

Method Prepare colour in a saucer before transferring it onto the glass sheet. Mix 1 to 1½ tablespoons of acrylic colour with ½ tablespoon of water and ½ tablespoon of acrylic medium. Making a larger quantity of acrylic colour is usually counter-productive, as it tends to harden off within an hour even if retardant is added. Special wet palettes can be obtained that keep acrylic colour soft and usable for days, but these are quite expensive. It is simpler and far cheaper to make a note of what colours were used, in which proportions, and to make up the colour and re-mix as and when necessary.

Once you are satisfied with the colour, transfer a spoonful or two to the glass sheet and roll it out smoothly with the roller. Roll colour onto the stamp and try it out on a sheet of paper. If the print looks clear and crisp, you have got the right amount of colour on the stamp. Stamp the design on the wall surface in the usual way, replenishing the colour when necessary. You will almost certainly find some prints come out cleaner and brighter than others. Extremely blurry or splodgy prints can be wiped off again carefully, using a sponge moistened in water for acrylics, or solvent for printing inks. On the whole, a certain variation in tone and clarity is a bonus, adding to the hand-printed look.

To neaten up the overall effect, the edges of wall surfaces can be outlined with a painted ribbon or stripe, an inch or so wide, in the same colour as the motifs. This can be painted on by hand using a fine brush for the edges and a thicker one to fill in. Alternatively, masking tape can be used to delineate the painted stripe, and then peeled off later.

Another idea, especially attractive in an attic room with interesting sloping ceilings, is to mass the stamp motifs together closely and regularly to make an outside border of solid patterns. This will need setting off from the rest of the wall with a narrower painted stripe. You can also make a feature of cupboard doors by stamping them closely so that they stand out as a dense patch of colour in a more loosely patterned room.

It is worth giving stamped walls a coat or two of varnish or emulsion [latex] glaze to seal them and allow for wiping down from time to time.

NOTE Don't think of decorative rubber stamps as a one-off investment. You can print off matching curtains or blinds, use the motif singly on lampshades or for heading your own writing paper.

WALL PAINTING

Wall paintings have an imaginative freedom that even the most beautiful stencilling cannot match. But it must be some lingering inhibition associated with scribbling on nice clean walls, plus a genuine diffidence about tackling a creative job without training, that accounts for the rarity of this form of decorative work. And yet, really, it is not so difficult. All sorts of untrained people quite unselfconsciously produce vigorous and charming murals. While I admire the sophisticated vistas and colonnaded loggias that artists have conjured up for their rich patrons, I often find these less memorable and pleasing than technically more modest efforts done with greater conviction and involvement.

Those who cannot manage freehand copying will find that the most faithful scaled-up representations can be achieved quite mechanically by using a grid. Once you have chalked the outlines on the walls, all that remains is to reproduce the original colours. The advice given in this book on mixing colours and producing decorative effects, such as stippling or sponging, should be of help here, or use an overhead projector to make it easier.

Designs

Be realistic in your choice of design – flat, two-dimensional treatments that rely on shape and colour rather than modelling and perspective for their effect are easiest to bring off. You need not choose to paint anything strictly representative – think also in terms of pattern. Look at the classical murals, Egyptian, Cretan, Etruscan and Pompeiian, at tapestries, at the paintings of Uccello, Matisse, Le Douanier Rousseau, at Moghul painting and Japanese prints, lacquer screens, Delft, Jacobean crewel work, at samplers and at decorative borders in children's books – these often prove a mine of ideas. Most helpful of all perhaps is folk art in its many manifestations – embroidery, carving, ceramics, painted furniture and, of course, murals. Folk art is living proof of how a feeling for colour and a strong decorative impulse can transcend technical limitations. Some of my favourite wall paintings are those done by the journeyman stencillers and housepainters in eighteenth- and nineteenth-century New England homes. These charming rural scenes, with little hills, winding streams and clumps of sponged-in trees, have a charm and directness that have little to do with technique, only a certain sensitivity to colour and design, and true feeling for the landscape.

Preparation and paints

Use whatever materials are to hand. Odds and ends of paints left over from jobs around the house and felt-tip pens and crayons can all be pressed into use, provided the surface you are painting on is sound and smooth. Flaky, cracked plaster, overpainted lining or wallpaper that has started to peel, old emulsion [latex] finish, will all reduce the life of your work. If you are planning a fairly elaborate mural, it would be worthwhile providing yourself with a durable, nonabsorbent base coat such as the standard mid-sheen oil-based paint advocated for most of the decorative finishes. Use the same paint, tinted with universal stainers [tinting colours] or artists' oils for the decorative painting. Or, if you object to a slight sheen, use flat emulsion [latex] paint or standard undercoat (which dries perfectly flat) for both ground and painting, tinted as before with universal stainers [tinting colours] or liquid tinters (see pages 216–217). On a new, sound emulsion [latex] base you could paint with emulsion paint [latex] tinted with stainers, artists' gouache, or artists' acrylic colours. Used neat, but extended with acrylic medium or water, they give glowing, fast-drying colours, useful for detail but expensive over large areas.

opposite This is a freehand painting, using metallic powders and coloured glazes to dramatize a strong design loosely based on old wallpapers and Jacobean embroidery. Note the emphasis on texture, which is a far cry from the neat finish of a printed wallpaper.

BRUSHES AND OTHER MATERIALS You will need brushes in various sizes: small artists' sable brushes for details and ordinary 12 or 25 mm [½ or 1 in] decorators' brushes (or artists' oil brushes) for brushing in larger areas. A wider, 75 or 100 mm [3 or 4 in] brush might be helpful for filling in sweeps of background colour such as blue sky or green hills. Equipment for stippling, sponging or stencilling may be required. Chalk or charcoal for drawing in rough outlines; white spirit [mineral spirit]; jars with screwtop lids to hold surplus mixed paint colours; saucers to use as palettes, one for each colour; a paint kettle or bucket for larger amounts; stepladder; plumbline; rags and newspapers.

Method A simple project, such as painting orange trees on either side of a door, will give an idea of different ways of using materials and techniques for varying effects. In this example it is decorative shape and colour we are after, not botanical realism. So the trees should be stylized like those in a sampler – mop heads, pyramids or espalier shapes, studded with bright fruit (a stencil might be used to do these) standing in decoratively shaped and textured containers, such as baskets or Versailles tubs. Sketch various shapes and arrangements first, on squared paper in coloured pens, until you find one you like. Copy this on one side of the door with chalk, scaling it up, keeping to the proportions of your sketch. Use the first tree to measure up the second.

COLOUR AND RELIEF Now for colour – decide whether you want the colour simple and flat, which emphasizes shape and colour contrast, or enriched by glaze and surface treatments. If you can't immediately decide, play safe by painting different parts in flat, pale colour – grey trunk, sap-green leaves, pale orange fruit, yellow basket. Surface interest can then be added, if required, using darker tinted glazes – thinned versions of the paint you are using – brown for the trunk, bright green sponged on for foliage, vermilion stippled on the fruit, burnt umber dragged criss-cross over the yellow to suggest basketwork. Glazes – see page 223 for how to thin and tint paint to make them – give depth of colour, and in this case a suggestion of relief or modelling. Stipple highlights on the fruit, by dabbing the bristle tips in off-white glaze, or paler areas of foliage, using yellow-green. Likewise, the basketwork can be given more prominence by shading and highlighting the wicker strands. But it is always as well to pause before elaborating a mural treatment and ask yourself whether you want your tree or whatever to stand out in greater relief. For while the eye happily accepts incongruities, like trees in tubs floating above the skirting board [baseboard] when the treatment is flat and purely decorative, greater realism in the handling might make this sort of thing disturbingly surreal. Trompe l'oeil (see page 88) which is a sort of visual joke, exploits such incongruities. Otherwise, it is

Stencilling, plus freehand overpainting, contributed to this contemporary spin on baroque style – swirling but stylized motifs in subdued monochromatic shades. The tradition of trompe l'oeil imitations of elaborate hand-run plasterwork found in Swedish interiors was a possible influence.

a convention that flat two-dimensional shapes work best unless the mural is actually intended to open up walls by suggesting landscapes seen in depth, framed by columns or fantastic topiary, or a vine-festooned pergola. Even here, though, keep the effects stylized, merely pinching a few tricks for suggesting distance, such as shading the sky from sky blue at the top to the merest wash of blue on the horizon, and using grey-mauve or grey-blue for distant hills.

VARNISH Any mural that you are pleased with should be varnished with clear matt acrylic varnish, because walls are inevitably subject to wear and knocks and may need occasional wiping down. It would be sad to watch your masterpiece fading like Leonardo da Vinci's *Last Supper*.

3-D WALL EFFECTS

While full-blown trompe l'oeil decorating schemes have declined in popularity over the past decade, for a variety of reasons – changing fashion, a shortage of highly skilled painters and expense – there are some decorative wall treatments, such as stone blocking, that are still much in demand. Both stone blocking and trompe l'oeil are, to a greater or lesser extent, intended to fool the eye, and suggest with paint tricks a material other than flat plaster.

STONE BLOCKING

Shown on the left is a minimalist version of stone blocking, in my own London hallway, stopping well short of an attempt to reproduce a stony finish with one of the textured paints or stuccos on the market. It merely alludes to ashlar stonework, with its bevelled edges highlighted on two aspects and shadowed on the other two. There was an historical justification for using it in my house since the scraps of original wallpaper (c.1810), which I unearthed under later papers and paint, were almost identical. Though stone block wallpapers are available, to keep costs down I chose to reproduce the effect in paint myself, with the help of an assistant.

Once the scale of the blocks was established (we used a card template, spirit level and plumbline to pencil accurate guidelines), and the basic wall finish (a buff-colour wash over an off-white non-porous emulsion [latex]) was in place, I was able to leave my assistant to press on with the faux detailing, which consisted of two white lines at right angles, meeting up with two dark (raw umber) lines at right angles, a reference to ashlar coursing seen in a strong light. Blockwork is usually done over a pale stone colour – grey, creamy or variegated, with darker shades interspersed.

I looked into possible short-cuts. Coloured felt pens, in white and sepia, seemed a feasible solution, drawn along a straight edge for speed, but the pen marks were too watery and insubstantial to register visually. Decorative painters like to use tinted oil media for blocking, thinned with scumble and varnish, but these are prone to smudging. We finally settled for acrylic colours with a little liquid flow-enhancer added to help the paint slide easily from one end of the block to the other. Too much starting and stopping makes work look hesitant and amateur. We used the narrowest straight-cut fitch for the lining, with small sable brushes to cut into the corners. Dark and light lines need to meet at a sharp 45° angle to look convincing. The whole area was varnished with a matt varnish for protection.

If 3-D is your aim, a much more textured blocking effect can be executed by masking off painted walls with narrow masking tape, and applying a textured paint, such as impasto (see page 60), over the blocks to create a stony texture. When the tape is peeled off, the blocks stand proud of the painted background, and are then colourwashed in grey, buff or cream tones. The interstices can then be coloured in, as above, or left unfinished, since the minimal raised effect imitates dressed stone and creates its own highlights and shading.

This close-up of paint effects in my hall – stone-blocking on the walls, granite spatter below the dado and graining on the doors – shows how the faux elements come together. Though not strictly period, it works without departing from the convention that halls should be neutrally coloured.

TROMPE L'OEIL Trompe l'oeil means 'to deceive the eye'. In terms of decorative painting this involves using the traditional resources of a skilled artist to suggest three dimensions where there are only two, so that for just a fraction of a moment one believes a painted object to be real. Trompe l'oeil is used as a witty solution to an architectural, or perhaps decorative, problem. For example, a room is unbalanced by having a prettily domed alcove on one side of the mantelpiece, but not on the other. Rather than knocking back walls and commissioning expensive carpentry, a trompe l'oeil artist paints in a matching alcove, achieving symmetry and a talking point all at once. The charm of trompe l'oeil, of course, is that through it you can conjure up just about anything your imagination can create, and your technical skills can cope with.

Apart from its usefulness in disguising architectural defects, I like the jokiness, the element of surprise that never fails to get 'oohs' and 'aahs' as the deception is unmasked. One trompe l'oeil painting I found particularly appealing was a recessed alcove with shelves on a blank bathroom wall, holding a collection of the sort of thing one might not normally associate with bathrooms – pretty old books with gilt tooled bindings, a vase of sweet williams, some china ornaments. As well as filling up the blank wall nicely it gave this most utilitarian room a civilized air.

There is no use pretending trompe l'oeil is easy, like stencilling or even simple mural painting. On the other hand, I think it is worth mentioning in a book for amateur painters and decorators because it is not beyond the reach of anyone clever and patient enough to copy exactly. In other words it is imitative rather than creative. And there are relatively simple, lighthearted trompe l'oeil effects which make for intriguing experiments. You could paint a trompe l'oeil carpet down the middle of a bare wooden staircase, cover a wall with mock Delft tiles, or liven up a room by painting mock panels on the walls, similar to the technique for doors described on pages 104–105.

Architectural trompe l'oeil effects are done in a technique reminiscent of 'grisaille', a decorative development of the old art student's exercise in monochrome painting, or suggesting solid form, perspective and so on, with different shades of one colour only – lightened with white or darkened with black.

Trompe l'oeil painting makes great use of shading to suggest three-dimensional realism. An amateur's best approach to realistic trompe l'oeil is undoubtedly to paint from a model – vase of flowers, blue-and-white china, a pile of old leatherbound volumes, or whatever you like – or from a good colour print. It is unlikely that an inexperienced artist would be able to achieve anything near the juicy realism of an old Dutch still life, but if you choose subjects that are decorative in shape and colour, the result can still be very attractive and a slight stiffness in execution can look quaintly 'naive'.

SOME USEFUL TIPS Don't be afraid of combining stencils with freehand work where the subject seems to admit it, for formalized forest trees, say, or sheep in a landscape, or bunches of grapes. The effect can be both pretty and witty. Using a stippled finish over any large coloured area can be effective, too, giving a pointillist effect. Sponging, as already stated, is always the quickest way to suggest foliage. Adding personal details is a sure way to enliven any mural – try putting familiar buildings into a landscape, or family portraits into scenes with figures, not detailed close-ups so much as characteristic outlines. Finally, over-brilliant colour effects can be toned down most easily by applying a cream glaze (white paint tinted with a little ochre and raw umber) over the whole work, or by applying an antiquing glaze, or wax.

Trompe l'oeil jumps out of its strait jacket in this astonishingly theatrical impression of a room hung with patterned drapes suddenly blown by a freak wind. This is trompe l'oeil in action, an interesting and imaginative reprise of a decorating convention that in the wrong hands can appear lifeless.

Woodwork

The woodwork in a room – doors, windows, architraves, skirting [baseboard] and dado – has the same relationship to the walls as a frame has to a picture. It acts as a boundary, creating a useful visual break between horizontal and vertical surfaces. Chair and picture rails, as well as serving practical functions (to protect walls from chair backs and as an anchor for pictures), are also architectural devices for breaking up flat planes and improving a room's proportions. In the days when wood and labour were cheap, such details were generously scaled, with handsome mouldings, both solid and structural looking. Doors were panelled, architraves of a dignified width, skirtings [baseboards] of a depth and thickness that balanced the height of the ceiling and cornices. Woodwork like this adds greatly to the appearance of a room and is worth making into a decorative feature. Painting it all shiny white makes it compete with wall surfaces instead of framing them, so you might like to consider other ways of treating it: a contrasting colour, or all-in-one with the wall colour perhaps?

previous page A simple but clever notion – a plain cupboard is brilliantly vitalized by diamond-shaped MDF cut-outs and contrasting paint finishes (a mottled glaze against a plain ground). The effect is further enhanced by the elegant monogram on each panel. Attention to detail and the ability to personalize items is the delight of DIY decoration.

MAKING GOOD & PREPARATION

It pays to take special pains in preparing woodwork for painting. These surfaces get a lot of handling. If the paint is full of craters and cracks it will collect dirt that is hard to wipe off. The degree of making good required depends on the state of the old paintwork. If it is reasonably smooth and level it usually needs no more than washing down with weak sugar soap solution to remove grime, plus a little filling and sanding down to hide any cracks or nail holes.

Stripping down

Badly scarred and chipped woodwork can be salvaged by extensive filling and making good. No-one would needlessly undertake the job of burning off paint. However, if the paintwork is really dilapidated, or if it is the sort of finish that is apt to discolour, or 'bleed' into the paint layers on top, you will certainly save time in the long run by cleaning it off.

Burning off with a blowlamp or hot air gun and shave hook is the quickest method. It is worth getting yourself an industrial-type gas blowlamp or heat stripper [heat gun], which will do the job properly. Start at the bottom of the area you are stripping – heat rises and will soften the paint just ahead of your scraper as you work upwards – and put a dust sheet on the floor to catch the hot, melted fragments. Move the blowlamp or heat stripper to and fro, following it with the scraper. Strip mouldings first, then panels, followed by flat surfaces such as skirtings [baseboards]. Strip with the grain of the wood.

Chemical paint stripper is a slow and messy method of getting back to the wood. Follow the manufacturer's instructions, but make sure that you allow time for the stripper to soak into the paint and soften it before you start to scrape – wear

Three panelled doors tightly juxtaposed on a tiny landing look cool and elegant, thanks to the care expended on their preparation and finish. The simpler the concept, the more you pick up on quality in the detailing, which is why minimalist style tends to work out expensive, unless you do it yourself.

rubber gloves to protect your hands. Use a flat scraper for flat areas and a shave hook for working round windows, doors and mouldings.

After stripping, wipe the wood surface with water and a little vinegar to neutralize the chemical in the stripper. Wetting the wood raises the grain, so smooth the surface with sandpaper when dry.

Cracks & knots   To make a quick, neat job of filling hairline cracks along skirting [baseboard], round door panels, or where built-in units meet the walls or ceiling, mix all-purpose filler [spackle] and water to a creamy consistency, and brush this into the cracks with an ordinary decorators' brush. This fills the cracks, and levels off the filler so that

opposite Beds, like fireplaces, need 'anchoring' in a room. A very plain bed, such as this one, jutting out from an equally plain wall leaves a psychological hole. Here, a chequerboard of painted MDF squares hung just behind the bed is a neat, simple, modern solution – it makes a visual point and softens a bleak conjunction.

little or no sanding is required. If you have extensive filling to do, a caulking gun could save time in the long run. For larger cracks, use all-purpose filler [spackle] mixed to a soft paste, and put a dab of undercoat or primer in the cracks first to encourage the filler to grip, and discourage it from shrinking. Fill with a table knife, or artists' palette knife, and then level off while it is still malleable by wiping with a damp rag firmly over the top. Use special wood filler [wood putty] for window frames; it expands and contracts with the wood, and is applied like other fillers.

Touch in new knots with patent knotting [knot sealer] – use one coat on stripped, seasoned old wood, two or three on new wood. This prevents resin from knots seeping up as a yellow stain through subsequent paint layers.

Primer & undercoat

Give new or stripped woodwork a coat of primer, then an undercoat [American readers will probably use an enamel undercoat only], which you can tint to match the top finish. Rub these down lightly with fine sandpaper when dry and hard to give a superfine base for the top coat. Ideally there should be two coats of undercoat – the first being thinned with white spirit [mineral spirit], the second used straight from the tin.

Previously painted woodwork won't need a primer, but sand down old gloss [enamel] paint after cleaning to provide 'bite' for the undercoat. Always leave paint plenty of time to dry out between coats.

Top coat

The woodwork finishes described here are based on a lean, matt look, achieved with a flat oil-based or acrylic paint. This is the effect most decorators prefer, since it is elegantly unobtrusive. Mid-sheen paint, see page 210, can be used if you prefer a slight sheen on woodwork, but don't use semi-gloss or gloss [enamel] unless you intend to get a lacquer effect. If you want a high shine, and a greater depth of colour, use a tinted glaze followed by gloss varnish, or tinted varnish, as for lacquering walls, see pages 64–65.

The classic painters' order of work for painting woodwork was to begin by painting the door first, then windows, fireplaces, chair rails, and finally skirting [baseboard]. This is because when painting the skirting one's brush may pick up stray dust from the floor area, which will get into the woodwork paint and mar the smooth surface you are trying to achieve.

Materials

Narrow decorators' brushes, 50 or 75 mm [2 or 3 in], plus an even smaller one 12 or 25 mm [½ or 1 in] for fiddly 'cutting in'; paint kettle or tin; white spirit [mineral spirit]; fine- and medium-grade sandpaper; newspaper; clean rags; stepladder. See pages 98–99 for how to paint windows and for the sequence to observe in painting panelled doors.

Simple Treatments

SHADES OF WHITE

Decorators often use a palette of 'dirty' or off-whites to emphasize panels on cupboards and doors, shutters, and other decorative details. This sophisticated treatment discreetly brings out their three-dimensional modelling while retaining a feeling of lightness and airiness. Equal discretion is shown in the choice of paint texture, usually flat or matt, occasionally with a sheen, but never glossy. There is nothing precious or arbitrary about this, it just looks better, especially in old houses where it gives the effect of the old lead paints that changed colour with time.

Usually three shades of off-white are used: darkest for panels, a shade lighter for the mouldings round them, and the lightest of all for the surrounds – which would also include linking woodwork areas such as architrave, skirting [baseboard], chair rail and so forth. Some decorators reverse the sequence, using the palest shade for the panels and the darkest for surrounds. The degree of contrast between the three shades will depend on how elaborate the rest of the room scheme is, and therefore how subtle or interesting you want the woodwork to be.

Sequence of painting

To paint all the woodwork in a small room you will need approximately 1 litre [2 US pints] of paint. Begin with the light areas, the surrounds. This may not be orthodox, but makes sense from the point of view of not wasting paint. Paint them in the lightest shade, just perceptibly off-white. To make it, mix a dollop of raw umber and a dot each of black and yellow ochre artists' colours into a flat or mid-sheen white paint to take the glare off the white.

Next, tint some of the remaining paint a shade darker by adding a little more raw umber (very little, since the quantities are much reduced) and another speck of black and yellow. Try the effect before painting all the mouldings – it should be just perceptibly darker. Finally, repeat the tinting process again to get the darkest shade for the panels themselves. The paint by now will be a warm grey, with a slightly greenish cast, a most attractive colour that looks right with almost any wall colour.

Rustic effects and textured surfaces are currently very popular for interiors. The barebones simplicity of this bedroom – the roughly finished painted plank headboard, echoing the whitewashed walls and old beams – is offset by the cool glamour of a luxurious silky quilt and touches of gilding.

MATCHING COLOURS

Colouring woodwork to match the walls is another approach effectively used in many old American houses. It looks particularly fine when there is a lot of woodwork to begin with – shutters, panelling, dado, as well as the usual doors and skirtings [baseboards]. When all these are painted to match one of the gentle but positive colours of the Colonial period – blueberry, cinnamon, or that especially romantic blue-green that is formed by yellowing varnish over faded blue paint – the

Painting plain doors

For a good even surface, a large flat area, such as a flush door, is best painted in sections. Start at the top and work down, going quickly so that the paint doesn't dry before you have completed the routine of laying on, cross-brushing, smoothing out and laying off.

1 Lay paint on, using vertical strokes

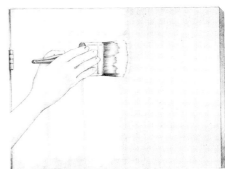

2 Without recharging bristles, cross-brush

3 Lay on and cross-brush a second section

4 Smooth out both sections

5 Lay off, moving away from the wet edge

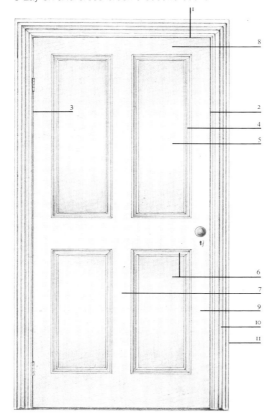

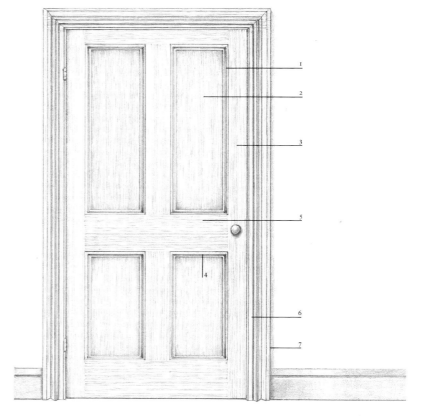

Painting panelled doors

Painting the different parts of a panelled door in a specific order (below, far left) is a proven logical saver of time, mess and effort.

If the door opens towards you, begin by painting (1) the rebates and (2) opening edge. If it opens away, paint the rebates and (3) hinged edge. Paint (4) the mouldings of the top panels next, then (5) the panels themselves – brush the paint well into decorative mouldings, but not so thickly that it spills over into 'runs'. Paint (6) the lower panels in the same way. Next paint (7) the central vertical section, then (8) the horizontal sections, or rails – top middle and bottom in that order – and lastly (9) the outer vertical sections, or stiles. Finally, paint (10) the door frame and (11) architrave. Leave the door wedged firmly ajar until dry.

Direction of dragging

The direction in which you drag the paint on doors and other panelled woodwork (see page 102 for dragging woodwork) usually echoes their construction – that is, the brushwork goes with the grain. Thus (below, left) dragging is vertical on (1) vertical mouldings, (2) panels and (3) stiles, and horizontal on (4) horizontal mouldings and (5) rails. Similarly, on (6) frame and (7) architrave, drag up the sides and across the top. An exception to this rule is a door with three or more crosswise panels – here the grain of the panels usually runs horizontally, and they should therefore be dragged in the same direction.

Painting windows

Like doors, windows should be painted in the correct sequence, which depends upon their construction. Use a metal shield or masking tape to keep paint from getting onto the glass.

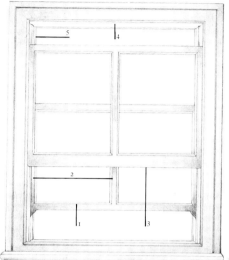

To paint a sash window, raise the lower sash and pull the upper sash down, so you can paint (1) the meeting rail, including its rebate (where the pane meets the wood) and bottom edge. Then paint (2) the bars and stiles on the upper sash, (3) the bottom edge of the lower sash, (4) the soffit, (5) about 50 mm [2 in] down the outside runners.

Close the window almost completely and paint (6) 50 mm [2 in] down the inside runners. Now paint all the (7) rebates, (8) the cross-bars, (9) the remaining cross-rails, (10) the stiles, (11) the window frame and (12) the architrave. Make sure you don't get paint on the sashcords. There is no need to paint the whole length of the runners.

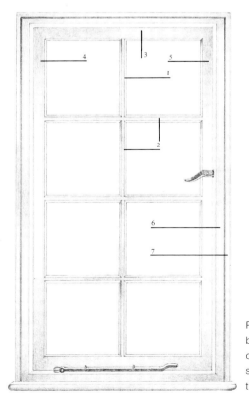

Paint a casement window in similar order beginning with (1) the rebates, then (2) the cross-bars, (3) the cross-rails, (4) the hanging-stile, (5) the meeting stile, and finally (6) and (7) the window frame and architrave.

effect is extraordinarily reposeful, with a rigorous simplicity that gives added value to rich colours in pictures, rugs and furnishings. Again, the paint should be lean-textured, flat and non-reflective. (An all-over gloss [enamel] colour finish can be effective too, but in a quite different way, sleek and sophisticated, not atmospheric.) Both walls and woodwork can be dragged discreetly in a darker tone of the same colour for added texture and to soften and blend everything together.

This one-colour treatment is also useful where skirtings [baseboards] and architraves are meagre and skimpy. In this case it is a mistake to call attention to them. Painting them to match the walls is a good way to fade them out.

CONTRASTING COLOURS

Contrasting colour in woodwork can look rich or architectural. I remember a room with faded red walls and grey-blue woodwork, and another, more eccentric combination of tawny orange walls and pea-green woodwork, which worked well as a background to opulent Moorish pieces and vivid embroideries and rugs. Colours usually look best when they have a similar tonal value – that is, colours that would register identically grey in a black-and-white photograph. Soft reds and blues, or greens, can look very good together. Often these contrasting colour treatments on walls and woodwork are given a dragged finish, in a glaze a tone or two darker, to soften them becomingly. An attractive variant of dragging is to give the tinted glaze a fanciful graining treatment, combing it to suggest some fantasy material between wood and marble. Latterly, the use of dark colours on woodwork (including black) against strongly coloured walls, has become fashionable with younger decorators influenced by the Arts and Crafts movement and Art Deco interiors.

Picking out mouldings

Picking out decorative mouldings, cornices and so on in a contrasting colour is a favourite technique with decorators who want to give a crisply finished look to a room. It is also a good way to break up large expanses of woodwork, such as fitted cupboards. As the surfaces of new cupboards tend to be flat these days, you may need to add mouldings yourself first, mitring them at the corners and glueing them in place. One idea is to paint the prominent parts of the moulding or cornice in a strong colour, filling in between them in a softer tone of the same colour. Choose your colour to reinforce one already in the room scheme – either a straight match or a tone lighter or darker.

Apply the contrasting colour in the form of a watery-thin glaze, made from flat or mid-sheen paint since it should look matt when dry. Try the paint out on a test area first, to check that it is intense enough to register on the decorative mouldings. Use a soft, narrow brush – a 12 mm [½ in] paintbrush or artists' brush – then neaten up the edges with a fine sable brush.

An unexpected mix of colours gives a typically Scandinavian lyricism to this interior of a Swedish house. Scandinavian painters often use the device shown here of a painted dado rail, allowing contrasting colours to be used above and below, so lowering the apparent ceiling height. Note how a plank wall is painted just as if it were plaster, right across the cracks.

DRAGGING

Most of the decorative finishes described for use on wall surfaces – stippling, sponging, ragging – can be adapted to flatter beautiful woodwork or to make the best of the flat, usually meagre, fittings prevalent in so many modern houses. Dragging, particularly, is often employed with painted woodwork, using a thin tinted paint glaze to soften outlines and give a delicate patina of colour.

OFF-WHITE Dragging can be used very attractively in the shades of white treatment described on page 97. To do this, first paint the woodwork surfaces with mid-sheen white oil- or water-based eggshell paint and allow to dry hard. Then mix up a thin glaze, and drag on the three shades of off-white, tinting the glaze as already described with raw umber, black and yellow ochre colours.

COLOUR Woodwork painted to match the walls (see page 97) is sometimes dragged in a darker or lighter tone of the same colour to add texture. If a wall with a distressed finish has woodwork painted in a contrasting colour, it is a useful technique to drag the latter in a darker or lighter tone, since two distressed colours provide a softer contrast than two plain ones. If the contrast between walls and woodwork is very harsh, a glaze tinted with raw umber is an ideal choice as it softens any colour attractively.

Method Follow the instructions for dragging walls (see pages 45–48) using transparent oil glaze [glazing liquid] or thinned oil-based paint (see pages 223–225) tinted with stainers or oil colours, over a flat or mid-sheen base paint. Dragging woodwork presents a directional problem, on panelled doors especially. I have seen these dragged entirely vertically, but the usual method is to drag in the direction of the wood grain beneath. Thus the brushstrokes are vertical on the panels and on both sides of the architrave or door frame, and horizontal on cross timbers and along the top of the frame. The same holds good for window frames and shutters. Skirting boards [baseboards], chair rails and other horizontal pieces of woodwork are dragged horizontally.

VARNISH Apply one or two coats of clear, matt polyurethane or acrylic varnish to protect dragged woodwork. It is especially important to varnish doors, since they get a tremendous amount of wear, handling, slamming and so on.

FROTTAGE

Like so many faux finishes for paintwork or panelling, frottage is probably of French origin. It is of some antiquity, but has recently returned to favour. The technique involves brushing a tinted glaze unevenly over lengths of paper – lining paper, tissue paper, even corrugated paper. The paper is then placed on the prepared wall

A close-up detail of the frottage finish shows the complex 'organic' effect that can be achieved by applying a tinted glaze via sheets of lightly scrumpled tissue paper. Newspaper, lining paper, even clingfilm [saran wrap], can also be used. The underlying metallic paint warms and enriches the final surface.

surface and pressed with both hands on the back in a fairly random way. The paper is then peeled away, leaving a characteristic mottled imprint on the base colour, with considerable variation of tone. The effect has depth, without visible brush-marks or other traces of manipulation of the wet glaze.

Different painters have evolved their own variations on the frottage theme. The tissue sheets can be lightly scrumpled, the glaze can be brushed on the wall instead of the paper, glazes of different shades can be superimposed, and the completed frottage can be coated with carriage varnish for a high shine lacquer finish. Or, for antiqued surface treatment over elaborate decorative patterns a 'dirty' tinted glaze can be applied to the wall as above, but then shifted sideways for a mysteriously distressed effect with 'movement'.

TROMPE L'OEIL PANELLING

Flush doors are a legacy of the 1960s and can look dull. A simple trompe l'oeil device intended to suggest recessed panelling and mouldings is an effective way of breaking up the flat surface. The same trick can also be used to add interest to large, flat expanses of built-in cupboards.

Flush doors tend to be narrow for their height, so a two panel arrangement with the larger panel on top helps to make the door look better proportioned. The convention is to paint trompe l'oeil effects of this kind in monochrome, that is shades of one colour, from near-white to sludgy grey.

Preparation

The ideal way to work is to take the door off its hinges and lay it flat, though of course this is not always possible. Surfaces should be clean, smooth, filled, and well sanded. After undercoating, give the door at least one coat of white mid-sheen oil- or water-based paint.

Materials

White eggshell paint; transparent glaze [glazing liquid]; white spirit [mineral spirit]; artists' colour in raw umber and black; soft bushy brush for stippling; standard 35 mm [1½ in] brush for dragging plus a 25 mm [1 in] brush for dragging the trompe l'oeil mouldings; masking tape; rags; pencil and ruler; bowls or small paint kettles for mixing the glazes.

Method

Pencil in panel shapes lightly to create rectangles enclosed by mouldings. Panel and moulding dimensions may vary depending on the size of the door, and the arrangement of the panels. Looking at existing panelled doors will help you gain a sense of the right proportions. Masking tape makes a useful temporary 'moulding' if you want to experiment with alternative arrangements. The traditional system used for trompe l'oeil panelling was to paint from the lightest element to the darkest, leaving each section to dry in between. This took longer, of course, but made plain sailing of such hazards as smudging new glaze. After the light 'mouldings' were dry, the surround was dragged in a paint a couple of tones darker, then the 'panel' was stippled in tones slightly darker than the surround. Finally the two dark or 'shadowed' mouldings were painted in. The same glaze was used each time, darkened by adding a little more of the tinting colours.

Begin by mixing up a barely tinted glaze, using a little white eggshell, some transparent glaze [glazing liquid] plus a cautious addition of raw umber and a dot of black dissolved in white spirit [mineral spirit] or water. The glaze will register as palest greeny-grey on the white door paint. Use masking tape to mark the mitred corners of one pale section of 'moulding', so that pale and darker glazes do not overlap. Then paint the pale glaze between pencilled lines. Leave the glaze flat, or drag it lightly as shown on page 99. Leave it to dry. Replace the masking tape to mark the mitred corners of the other light moulding adjacent. Paint as before and leave it to dry.

Add a squeeze more of both colours to the glaze, using less black than raw umber. With this glaze paint, then drag, the outside frame to the panels, doing the horizontals first, then the verticals. Any slight excess glaze or ragged edges at each end of the horizontal strips will be tidied into neat right-angled joins as you paint and drag the vertical strips. Another way of cleaning up excess glaze is to wipe it off with a clean lint-free cloth dipped in a little solvent.

While the dragged frames are drying, stipple the recessed panels, using the same glaze again darkened a tone or two with more raw umber and a very little black. To stipple, first brush the glaze over a panel, then with a soft, bushy brush 'pounce' the glaze with bristle tips to create a fine, powdery layer of colour. Repeat on the remaining panels, and let dry overnight.

Finish by painting the shadowed mouldings, which, to look realistic, should be those further from the main source of light in the room. Darken the remaining glaze by adding a little more colour than previously. Using masking tape again to mark the mitred corners, first fill in one side, let dry, then paint the second dark moulding as before. When completely dry give the whole door one or two coats of mid-sheen or matt polyurethane varnish.

This approach to painting trompe l'oeil panelling is slow but foolproof, and is often used by professional painters who are able to slot the steps in between doing other jobs.

These designs can be painted directly onto the glass on the inside of the door frame for a trompe l'oeil version of a period fanlight.

Trompe l'oeil panels can transform plain flush doors into something smarter. Two possible combinations – a four- and a six-panelled door – are shown on the right.

Fantasy Finishes

Grainers and marblers have always been considered the elite of the decorative painting fraternity, working in a tradition reaching back to Classical times (the Romans used both techniques) and beyond. It takes skill, judgment and taste to imitate marble and wood in paint, plus real knowledge of the materials themselves. For sheer technical virtuosity it would be hard to improve on the work of nineteenth-century marblers and grainers like Thomas Kershaw, whose sample boards can be seen at the Victoria and Albert Museum in London. My own personal preference, though, is for the bold exaggerations of the earlier Baroque painters, whose work can be seen at Ham House in Surrey, Belton House in Lincolnshire and Blenheim Palace, Oxfordshire, and whose influence I detect in the spirited style of much early American marbling and graining.

GRAINING

Graining can be pale, as in the 'bois clair' style, warm and ruddy, as seen in mahogany-grained Victorian pubs, or dark like Jacobean oak panelling. One attraction of grained finishes is that they are an ideal disguise for joinery that uses a mix of cheap timber and wood-substitutes like medium-density fibreboard (MDF). A run of new bookcases, for instance, grained to match existing woodwork, immediately gains a long-established air.

Graining can be a highly sophisticated and labour-intensive process, involving skillful play with specialist brushes and tools and many layers of glaze. But it is surprising how easily a warm, woody effect can be arrived at by amateurs using a few brushes and a little tinted glaze [glazing liquid].

Though professionals favour water-based media for graining, (like flat beer, see page 113) I think beginners are better off working with oil-based glazes. These are easier to manipulate and 'soften', and the slower drying time means you can have second thoughts, or even, if need be, rub the whole lot off with a rag dipped in solvent. Simply 'flogging' a wet glaze lightly with the appropriate brush (see page 231) immediately gives a grainy, fibrous texture which is attractive just left as it is.

'Softening', however, is the key process in most of the graining and marbling techniques dealt with in this section. Beginners usually have to force themselves to soften a careful piece of work; at first this feels too much like messing it up. But persevere, and you will soon find that the final subtle flicks with the softener (a small badger softener is a justifiable investment, but any soft brush will do) make all the difference, blurring hard lines and blending colours into each other.

Preparation   A smooth ground of mid-sheen oil-based paint is the usual choice, though water-based eggshell is becoming more popular, and at a pinch vinyl silk emulsion (available in the UK) can be substituted. Eggshell or mid-sheen paint encourages the glaze to stay 'open' or workable for longer. The base colour will obviously vary from wood to wood. A cream or buff base suits most of the paler woods, golden mahogany needs a yellowish base, while red Cuban mahogany is frequently grained over a dull pink or red. The exact shade of the base colour is not critical, however, as it can be modified by altering the graining glaze itself.

Materials   GLAZE Glazes are made up of transparent oil glaze [glazing liquid] (home-made, see page 224 for oil glaze recipe, or proprietary glaze see pages 214–215) thinned with white spirit [mineral spirit] and tinted with artists' tube oil colours (see pages 216–217). Provide yourself with a test card or board painted in your chosen base colour on which to experiment with various graining techniques. A test board will also help you check the glaze colour, and practise particular effects like 'wobbly' brushwork before you apply the graining technique to your chosen surface

Skillful graining, here 'mahogany', provides a handsome and durable finish for old pine panelled doors. Softwood doors, such as pine, deal, or fir, were rarely left bare before stripped pine became fashionable. A grained finish upgraded them and gave protection.

opposite This fine eighteenth-century wainscot has been beautifully walnut-grained, with panels of 'oyster' figuring in black mouldings. The effect is warm, rich and spirited.

right To produce burr walnut graining, mix up a warm mid-brown glaze by adding raw sienna and a little of both raw and burnt umber artists' oil colours to a transparent oil glaze [glazing liquid]. Thin with white spirit [mineral spirit] as appropriate.

Brush this glaze rapidly every which way with a 35–50 mm [1½–2 in] decorating brush onto a base of pale toffee-coloured eggshell (A).

Rag lightly with a soft piece of cotton. Add more burnt umber to the first glaze in a separate dish, and use this darker glaze to add random squiggles and splodges (B).

Fold a soft cotton rag into a squarish pad and use this to roll and swirl the wet glaze, blending the darker patches in with the rest. Use a No. 3 artists' watercolour brush and the darkened glaze to add little dark dots randomly (C).

With a clean glider or varnishing brush, gently soften the graining here and there, or use the bristle tips to stipple areas of glaze (D). Alternatively, you might lightly flog the surface, using the standard decorating brush or, if you have one, a flogger, to create texture. But don't do all these things on the same patch – aim for a variety of flowing texture.

When the surface is completely dry, varnish with one or even two coats of mid-sheen polyurethane varnish.

A

B

C

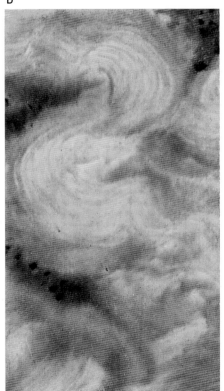

D

A

B

C

D

To produce *bois clair* graining, or blonde wood, paint the surface with an off-white eggshell paint, oil or water-based.

Mix up a tawny but cool-tinted oil glaze with artists' oil colours in raw umber, raw sienna plus a little white to soften the shade. Thin in the usual way with white spirit [mineral spirit]. The glaze should be about the consistency of single cream. Tip some of this into a separate bowl, or paint kettle, and make a slightly darker version using more raw umber.

Paint the lighter glaze loosely every which way over the surface with a standard 35–50 mm [1½–2in] decorating brush (A).

With a glider streak darker colour onto the surface here and there as shown (B).

Wipe the glider on a rag, and then drag it with a wobbly stroke to create continuous grain, aiming to introduce the odd rippling streak of darker colour (C).

Soften lightly with a soft dusting brush (D). Let dry. Rather than polyurethane varnish, finish with one or two coats of eggshell or matt acrylic varnish, which will not yellow or darken – this matters with pale wood-graining.

A

B

above Blonde wood and mahogany graining techniques have been used to create trompe l'oeil panels in this elegant Biedermeier-style bathroom. Fake mouldings have been painted in black to simulate ebony. Several coats of clear matt or mid-sheen varnish should be used in a bathroom to protect the finish from splashes and condensation.

left The first and last stages of mahogany graining are shown here. This technique uses the same basic steps as bois clair (blonde wood) graining (opposite), though of course the colours are different.

To grain mahogany, paint the base a golden shade of either oil-or water-based eggshell for golden mahogany, or a pinky-red for red mahogany. Mix up a rich red-brown glaze using transparent oil glaze [glazing liquid] mixed with artists' oil colours (burnt umber and burnt sienna) and thinned with white spirit [mineral spirit], until it flows easily but is not so thin it trickles and drips. Brush this on quickly and loosely in all directions with a standard 35–40 mm [1½ in] decorating brush (A).

Add more burnt umber to the first glaze in a separate dish, and use this with a glider or flogger to apply darker streaks here and there. Wipe the brush, then draw it through the glaze, wobbling the bristles to create ripples. Flog patches of glaze for texture. Work over the whole area, aiming for a satiny flow of red-brown grain with darker streaks.

Soften the glazed surface to diffuse these darker streaks, and to blur over-pronounced brushmarks (B). Let dry.

Varnish with at least one coat of a mid-sheen polyurethane or acrylic varnish.

To produce oak grain, drag a dry brush over the wet glaze, in a slight ripple (A). Blur the lines very gently with a soft, clean brush (B). Using the sharp edge of a cork, draw heartwood lines into the wet glaze, running roughly parallel (C). Finally, sketch in a knot with the cork edge, then draw in grain lines so they part around it, but do not cross each other (D).

BRUSHES AND TOOLS Professional grainers work with a selection of brushes designed to create certain effects quickly and reliably. These may include overgrainers, swordliners and stipplers as well as a clutch of steel or rubber combs, and rockers to simulate knots and heartwood. There is no point in buying the whole shop to start with, but a 'glider' or varnishing brush, a 'flogger' and a 'rocker' (see section on brushes, pages 230–233) plus one or two fine sable watercolour brushes (Size No. 2 and 3) will give you plenty of scope for experiment. As you become more expert you may decide to invest in a badger softener. A 'knot' tool can be whittled from a cork, or by cutting out the middle of a small stiff stencil brush to make a stamp. A chamois leather is useful for ragging but old rags will do just as well.

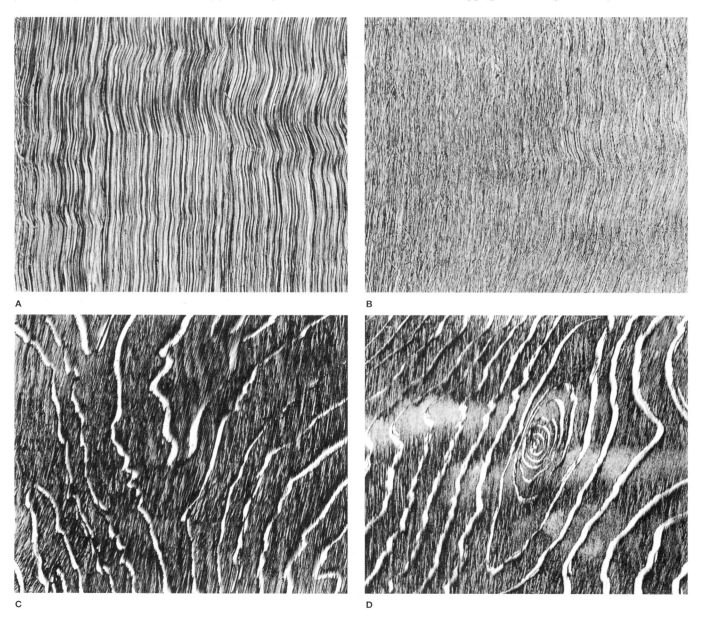

A

B

C

D

Method Study a cleanly figured piece of wood and memorize some of its vagaries – knots, like islands parting the flow of the grain; heartwood, like mountains on contour maps; highlights that ripple like stretch marks across the graining, zigzaggy or wobbly swerves in the basically parallel grain markings. It doesn't matter too much what type of wood you are studying, though the grainier ones – oak, mahogany, walnut, pine – are obviously more stimulating. The point to keep firmly in mind is that nature, most fertile of patternmakers, is never monotonous.

As with all the strongly marked finishes, it makes things easier to treat your painted surface as a series of panels – abstract pictures as it were, in which the decorative elements are differently combined each time. Some conventions should be observed: for instance, the grain should flow the way it would if you were using real wood. Too many knots, unless you want a bird's-eye maple or deal effect, look spotty. A preponderance of smoothly flowing, curving grain, broken here and there by jagged heartwood or knots, is the effect to aim at.

Begin by brushing a thin glaze of colour over your surface. Using the glider, draw the bristle tips over the wet glaze to make fine stripes – like dragged painting – suggesting the general grain flow. Wobble your wrist just a little in mid stroke to give a woody swerve. With the flogger, whip the stripes gently all over to blur them and give a flecked, almost hairy appearance. You now have the basic grain of the wood, a canvas with characteristic woody texture to which you can add highlights, heartwood and knots as desired. See illustration on page 112 (opposite).

When you have blocked in your graining picture – with discretion, don't overdo it – a very gentle softening with the soft brush, bristle tips only, in the direction of the grain usually helps to pull it all together. But do go gently – a big blur is not what you want. If you think part of the surface looks too busy, wipe it out while the glaze is still wet. Try not to smudge the rest of the work. Leave the finished graining to dry hard.

Instructions for graining burr walnut, *bois clair* (blonde woods) and mahogany are given on pages 109, 110 and 111.

BEER OR VINEGAR GLAZES Traditional grainers often worked with water-based glazes using flat beer or vinegar, preferring their special transparency and speedy drying. The vinegar or beer mixture described on page 185 is easier to manipulate than plain watercolour, as its sugar content makes it slightly sticky. Try this if you want a more delicate look.

VARNISH Oil glazes are best varnished for durability. Use clear matt or gloss acrylic varnish, depending on whether you want a quiet or shiny look. Vinegar or ale graining must have a thorough final varnishing to fix and protect it.

MARBLING

Marbling falls into two categories: the highly skilled, closely imitative technique, aiming to deceive the eye into accepting it as real; and a faster, impressionistic, scene-painter technique that merely suggests the rich colours and varied patterning of marble, going for a 'fantasy' effect rather than an identifiable stone. The latter approach is lighter, less demanding, and for our purposes more easily assimilated and successfully executed by amateurs. There is nothing to prevent anyone from getting hold of an example of real marble and experimenting with coloured glazes, brushwork and feathering to get a closer imitation. There are at least nine categories of marble – brecciated, serpentine, travertine, crinoidal, variegated, unicoloured, laminated, statuary, alabaster – so the subject is not one that can be compressed into a few pages. Fantasy marbling, however, is quick and fun and allows a great deal of scope.

A wooden fireplace surround looks impressive given the fantasy marble treatment. A bathroom is a good place to practise one's skills – starting with the bath surround, and extending over woodwork for a coherent effect.

It is a good idea to begin small, but if you are marbling a large surface, 'block' it out into separate rectangles, to be tackled one by one. This gives a more realistic effect, since natural marble tends to be supplied in smallish sheets, and there is less chance of your marble pattern getting too fixed and unvarying. Work quickly and decisively. Don't be afraid of making mistakes; they probably won't show. If they do, wipe them off and start again.

Preparation

The ground coat should be white mid-sheen oil-based paint, quite dry, and lightly rubbed down with fine-grade sandpaper to create a smooth surface.

Materials

White oil- or water-based eggshell paint or undercoat; artists' oil colours in raw umber and black; 50 mm [2 in] decorators' brush; badger softener; small, pointed artists' brush for painting on finer details; marine sponge; white spirit [mineral spirit]; jam jar; saucer; rags.

Method

The steps described here will give you a pale, grey-green marbled finish. Mix up a thin glaze in a jam jar with roughly two parts paint to one part white spirit [mineral spirit]. Add a squeeze of raw umber and a little black, to give a greenish-grey tint strong enough to contrast with the white ground. With the decorators' brush apply the glaze over the area or 'block', then sponge it all over to break up the surface.

VEINING Put a squirt of raw umber and a squirt of black on the saucer. Mix a little black into the umber for a darker shade of grey. With the small brush, pick up some of this colour and put in large veining across the wet glazed surface, using a fidgety

To paint veins, hold the brush loosely and apply them with a fidgety stroke.

114

For pale, greyish marbling, start with a dry ground of white mid-sheen oil-based paint, lightly sanded. Mix up a glaze of two parts flat or mid-sheen white oil-based paint to one part white spirit [mineral spirit], tinted with a squeeze of raw umber artists' oil colour and a dash of black. Brush this over the surface and gently sponge it.

Mix a little black oil colour into some raw umber to produce grey-brown. With a small brush and a fidgety brushstroke apply veins to the wet glazed surface. They should wander across it diagonally, branching off to the left and right, and should have a beginning and an end – genuine marble veining does not start or peter out in the middle of nowhere.

Sponge the veins lightly to remove excess paint. Take a dry paintbrush and gently draw it back and forth across the veining in one diagonal direction (say, bottom left to top right) and then the other, (bottom right to top left) – this softens the harsh lines. Mix up more black with less umber to get a dark grey, and take some up on your little brush. Fidget in some smaller veins, connecting them to the large ones. Like the large ones, they should mostly run diagonally (A).

Use a sponge or paper tissue to soak up the excess paint from the little veins (B). You can then dab this on again in the plain areas, to imitate the variegations of real marble.

Now thoroughly soften the whole surface (C) drawing your dry paintbrush gently back and forth along each diagonal. Go over each diagonal at least three times.

When the surface is quite dry – after a few hours – fidget in extra veins in thinned white paint. Add dabs of the same colour to form pebble shapes (D). After 24 hours, varnish with matt or semi-gloss polyurethane varnish – when this is almost dry, sprinkle it with French chalk or household flour, then polish it with a soft cloth. This will reproduce the sheen of a real marble surface.

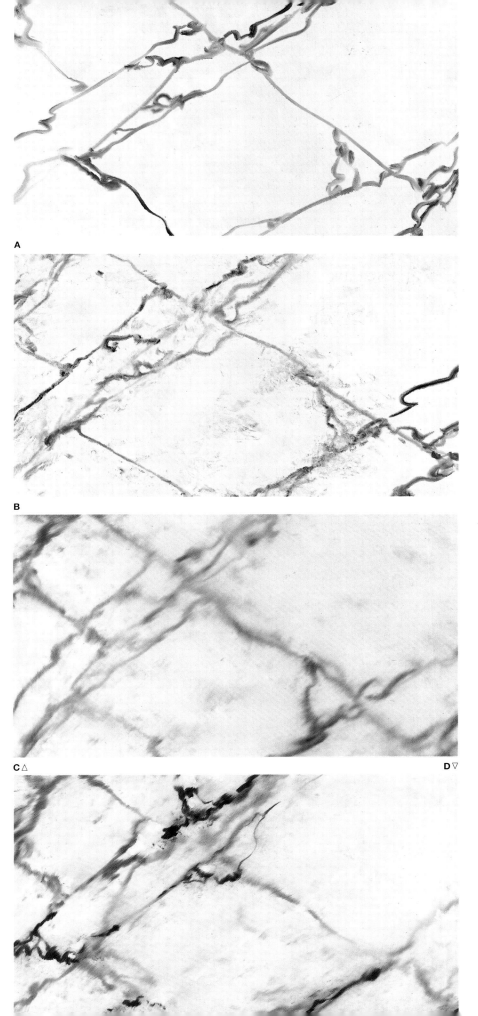

A

B

C △

D ▽

brushstroke. Marble veins tend to meander diagonally, forking off to left and right. But all veining lines should have an end and a beginning, not start in the middle of nothing and fade out again – think of them linking up, like roads on a map. Gently sponge the painted veins to remove excess paint, then brush the veining lightly and diagonally, in one direction and then the other, to soften and blur. Now, with the small brush, take up a darker mix of black and umber, and fidget in smaller veins here and there, linking up the large ones, like secondary roads cutting across between major ones. Sponge lightly again, and soften with the dry brush. The brush softening has a magical effect – suddenly the crude squiggles begin to look like genuine marble.

Stand back and study your handiwork. It may need a bit more veining some-where, or perhaps a space enclosed by veining could be broken up into large and small pebble shapes, lightly drawn in with the small brush. But don't overwork it; half the battle with marbling is knowing when to stop. When the surface is dry (in a few hours), fidget some veins across the surface in plain white, to freshen and 'lift' the marbling. Pebble shapes can be highlighted with a little white too (see photographs on page 115).

VARNISH Leave for 24 hours before varnishing with matt or semi-gloss varnish. When almost dry, sprinkle the varnish with French chalk or household flour and polish it with a soft cloth for a marble-like sheen.

SOME TIPS Study examples of real marble whenever you get a chance, to see the way the surface is broken up. Don't be timid – make your veining bold, thick enough to stand out, and rhythmic. Over a large surface it should change direction fairly often, whereas on a small area it needs to be more balanced.

If you want more colour in your marble or a richer effect, you can repeat the marbling process using a different-coloured glaze – yellow, green, red-brown – on top of the first. The first layer of marbling will show through the second, creating a look of depth, as in the real stone.

FOSSILSTONE MARBLING The marbling technique described on page 118 is particularly effective. It is easy and surprisingly convincing. Fossilstone marbling is suitable for any flat, horizontal surface – a table top or picture frame, for example – but do not try it on a vertical surface, because the colours will run off.

The fossilstone appearance is achieved by spattering wet glaze with solvents. It looks best using low-keyed pebble colours – greeny-grey, dull blue and tawny brown – and is especially impressive on hardboard [particle board or masonite] tiles used as a floor covering or on an MDF tabletop.

For green marbling, start with a dry ground of black oil-based paint. Mix up a glaze of white spirit [mineral spirit] and a little oil glaze tinted with a touch of viridian and a very little Van Dyke brown. Brush this glaze [glazing liquid] over the surface, creating cloudy areas and gently soften it, keeping it subtle. Make up a glaze with a tiny dab of yellow ochre, to create different tones, and repeat the process (A).

Now using more viridian and a touch of emerald green and yellow ochre, with the point of a small artists' brush, apply veins to the wet glazed surface to form 'stones' of different sizes. Do not create stones everywhere, however – keep some areas bare of them. Vary the shades of green here and there, softening as you go, preferably with a badger hair softener (B).

Keep adding more colour and veins, softening as you go; and add more small stones. With a drier brush put in some smaller veins in a lighter colour, and link them with the existing ones (C).

When the surface is dry, add in some white veins and a few white pebble shapes (D). When dry, varnish it with a semi-gloss polyurethane varnish, preferably two coats to give a better finish.

A

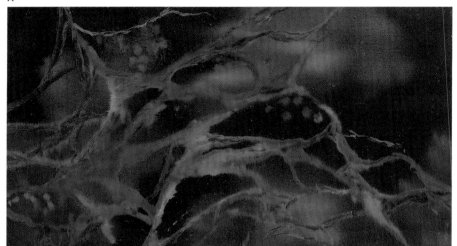

B

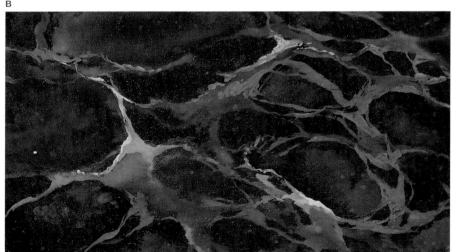

C △

D ▽

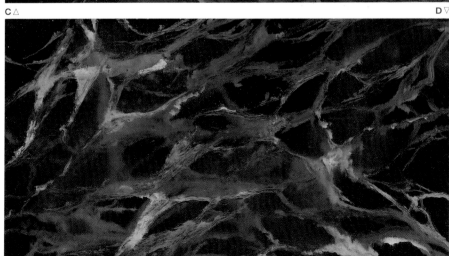

Preparation Cut hardboard [particle board or masonite] into tiles about 120 cm [4 ft] square. Prime it with acrylic primer, standard undercoat or thinned emulsion [latex] paint.

Cover your working area with newspaper or sheets of plastic. Paint over the tiles with white or off-white oil-based mid-sheen paint. When the surface is dry, sand it smooth with medium sandpaper. The finish should be not only smooth, but also opaquely white, so it will probably need as many as three coats of paint, each one sanded down. Smoothness matters with this marbling technique, because brush-marks or bumps left on the paint surface interfere with the opening-out movement of the glaze that produces the fossil shapes. Rub over the surface with the thinnest smear of raw or boiled linseed oil, just enough to give a faint sheen. This will stop the moving glaze from spreading uncontrollably.

FILLING WOODGRAIN If you plan to marble a table top and the wood is coarse textured and open grained, you will get much better results by filling the wood grain before painting. Use proprietary wood filler [wood putty], all purpose filler [spackle] or synthetic gesso, applying as many coats as necessary to level up the grain. Rub the surface smooth with sandpaper, then undercoat it and paint it with oil-based mid-sheen paint for a hard, fine-textured surface. Tabletops undergo closer inspection than floors, so it is worth taking extra trouble to get a first-rate finish.

Materials Two paint glazes, made by mixing one part white flat or mid-sheen oil-based paint with two parts white spirit [mineral spirit], and tinting with artists' oil colours or universal stainers [tinting colours]. The glazes should be as thin as milk, and dark enough to show up well on the white ground – test them on a corner of a hardboard tile.

You will also need a 75 mm [3 in] brush; a stiff stencil brush; white spirit [mineral spirit]; methylated spirit [denatured alcohol]; a marine sponge or some crumpled paper tissue.

Method Work on one tile at a time, laying it flat, face-up, on your protected work area. Dip your brush into one of the glazes, and with it dab a roughly chequered pattern over the surface. Then dip the brush into the other glaze and use it to fill in the gaps, not worrying too much about keeping the sections apart. Go over the whole surface with the sponge or paper tissue to remove some of the heaviest glaze and produce a crumpled-looking, slightly blended effect.

Now take up some white spirit [mineral spirit] on the stiff stencil brush, and flick this with your thumb to spatter the wet glazed surface quite thickly. In seconds, the glaze will start 'cissing' – little holes opening up and radiating outwards to suggest round fossil shapes. For more variety you can flick on some methylated spirit [denatured alcohol] at this stage – it also cisses, but produces rather different shapes. Small drops of water will leave neat rings. If you spatter on any extra large blobs that threaten to ciss rampageously, mop up the excess liquid quickly with a corner of paper tissue. See the photograph on page 177 for an idea of the effect.

This is a technique to have fun with – the difficulty is knowing when to stop. Do not overwork the effect. When you are quite satisfied with it, leave the tile to dry perfectly flat.

VARNISHING Once the marbled tiles are completely dry, varnish them with up to five-coats of clear gloss polyurethane varnish – thinned three parts varnish to one part solvent. Rub lightly with sandpaper after every coat except the first. When the tiles are finished, scrub a little water into the back and leave them overnight to adjust to the conditions of the room before laying.

This finish can of course be used on furniture as well as floors. For a superbly smooth finish on a tabletop, do not sand the last coat of varnish, but rub it over with powdered pumice, rottenstone or household scouring powder and a little baby oil or salad oil. Apply this mixture with a piece of felt or with a soft flannel cloth, using long strokes and following the direction of the grain underneath. Wipe it off with a damp cloth, and when dry, polish the surface with a soft, clean one.

TORTOISESHELLING

The technique of painting woodwork or walls to look like tortoiseshell is an example of intelligent manipulation of paints and varnish to create a desired effect. Confronted by a spectacular tortoiseshell stretch, rippling with tawny yellow, chestnut brown and shiny black, I doubt whether anyone but an expert in paint behaviour would be able to figure out how it was achieved. Yet once you grasp the technique, it is possible for the amateur to do, and goes fast enough to cover largish areas at a time. The secret is that the colours are laid into wet varnish, and the resultant 'spreading' is controlled by lightly brushing diagonally in two directions with a dry brush, creating the characteristic tortoiseshell markings almost auto-matically. This is not to say that you should tackle it mechanically, letting the paints do the work for you and repeating the same procedure unvaryingly across a surface. Monotony is always lifeless. Study examples of real or painted tortoiseshell before embarking on this finish. There are blonde tortoiseshells, leopard-spotted in translucent browns on an amber ground; red tortoiseshells, with a great deal of red-brown background; and darker ones inclining to black and dark browns, like the brown tortoiseshell described here. An expanse of tortoiseshell can look superb, but the finish looks best in small, confined spaces – tiny front halls, with a lot of doors, small studies, a bathroom or cloakroom.

Preparation   The ground for brown tortoiseshell should be a smooth bright yellow, mid-sheen oil- or water-based paint. A light, sharp yellow is best, tinted with chrome yellow and raw sienna artists' oil colours, because the subsequent layers of colour will darken the ground considerably.

Materials   Medium oak varnish stain; burnt umber and black artists' oil colours; two standard decorators' brushes 50 mm [2 in] wide and two small, flat artists' brushes about 12 mm [½ in] wide – one of each will do, but it means more wiping and cleaning; white spirit [mineral spirit]; clean rags; saucer.

Method   Using one of the large brushes, cover the surface with the oak varnish stain, working speedily and not too carefully. The varnish will probably bubble, but don't worry about this.

When the area is covered, use the brush to fidget the wet varnish into diagonal bands of zigzags, approximately 5 cm [2 in] wide. The varnish will go on 'moving' after you have done this, so that the bands will run into each other, creating an overall impression of movement. Dab some extra splodges of varnish – about the size of a walnut – along the diagonal rows. Position these fairly quickly and randomly, but not less than about 6 or 7 cm [2½ or 3 in] apart.

Now take the burnt umber and squeeze a blob onto a saucer. Dip one of the small brushes in it and make lively squiggles, like Arabic writing, maybe 2–3 cm [1 in] under the previous splodges. Keep working on the same diagonal, and again don't join up the squiggles or make them too regular, since the effect will look less natural this way.

Dip the second small brush into the black oil colour and dab small tadpole shapes in clusters here and there in the blank spaces between the other markings. You should have fewer black squiggles than brown ones.

STROKING Now comes the exciting part of the finish. Take up the dry large brush and, following the direction of the diagonals, very gently stroke it across the wet surface to make streaky graph-like peaks as the varnish and paints flow into each other; and then stroke even more gently back in the opposite direction. Repeat this two-way stroking operation on the other diagonal. Finally stroke a second time on the original diagonal – gently in one direction and then lightly back. In all, you will have brushed across the surface six times (you can soften more than this if you want). As you do so, you'll see the blobs and streaks magically opening out into the subtle, transparent markings of tortoiseshell. The colours will continue moving gently for a while after you have finished – until the varnish 'goes off' – and will dry glossy, as tortoiseshell should be.

BLONDE TORTOISESHELL For 'blonde' tortoiseshell, use a light oak varnish stain, or medium oak thinned with white spirit [mineral spirit] over the same yellow base colour; burnt umber – which thins to a rich red-brown when stroked – for the squiggles; and a very little black, or omit it altogether.

Panels

A tortoiseshell door, mantelpiece, or whatever, has to be completed in one go to avoid demarcation lines showing – unless the piece is divided into panels and surrounds that you can treat separately. If you have a large area – a wall for instance – you will need two people on the job. The convention is to divide the surface into tortoise-sized rectangles, outlined in white or black and worked separately, varying the flow of the markings. Masking tape helps keep a straight edge. Make sure each panel is completely dry before you start on the next one.

To create a tortoiseshell effect, the ground must be bright yellow mid-sheen oil-based paint, dry and sanded. Using a large decorators' brush, cover it quickly with dark oak gloss varnish stain (A). Don't worry if this bubbles.

With the brush, fidget the wet varnish into diagonal stripes of zigzags about 5 cm [2 in] wide. These will begin to run into one another almost immediately. Dab walnut-sized splodges of varnish along the diagonal bands, at random but a minimum of 6–7 cm [2½–3 in] apart (B).

Squeeze a blob of burnt umber on to a saucer. Dip a small artists' brush in it and apply curly squiggles along the diagonals, say 2–3 cm [1 in] under the previous splodges.

Dip another small brush into black oil colour and place small groups of tadpole shapes in the spaces between the other markings. There should be fewer black marks than umber ones.

Take a clean, dry brush and very softly stroke it across the wet varnish, following the direction of the diagonal bands – in the photograph these run from left up to right. Stroke back even more gently the other way – here, from right down to left. Now repeat this two-way stroking on the other diagonal, from right up to left, and from left down to right (C).

Finally, stroke once more back and forth along the first diagonal. You will find that the individual marks have been smoothed out into the subtle pattern of genuine tortoiseshell (D).

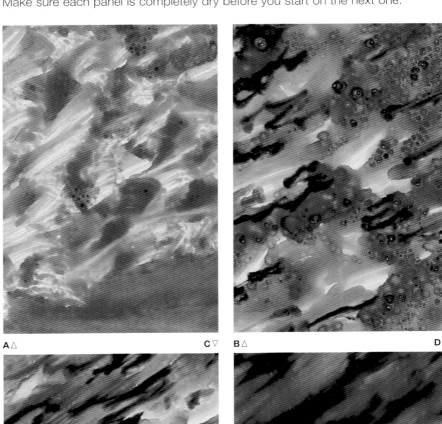

A △ C ▽ B △ D ▽

Floors

Floors always present a problem when decorating. They are rarely good enough to leave exposed just as they are, with no more than an occasional waxing to keep them in shape. Covering them is expensive, especially if one has to deal with stairs, passages and landings as well as main rooms. One alternative to carpet, matting, tiles and vinyl – as decorative as it is cheap – is to colour the boards with paint – opaque or transparent depending on the state of the wood – or with stains or varnish stains, which come in a wide range of non-wood colours as well as more traditional shades.

Fashion is on the side of the DIY decorator here. The trend is increasingly towards simple effects, painted chequers, bold stencilled borders, or a cool wash to give a bleached look. The fashion for 'distressed' paint has influenced the treatment of floors too, encouraging people to see it does not matter if paint wears down gradually and allows the wood texture to show through – in fact this adds homeliness and atmosphere. Pictures of Scandinavian interiors have demonstrated that diagonally set black and white chequers look excellent painted in matt, chalky water-based paint worn thin here and there to give a semi-transparent effect. Where Scandinavians used linseed oil paint, we would choose a matt emulsion [latex]. Either way the saving in time and effort, when compared with a serious traditional paint system, is considerable, as these paints are applied directly to the bare wood and varnished with a water-based varnish which goes on and dries very quickly. Transparent finishes that retain the natural wood texture and warmth are based on stains, which can be used to create marquetry-style effects.

There are floors in such poor shape that the best treatment is to paint them out, using opaque paint. Where boards have been crudely patched, stained black round the perimeter, or are noticeably battered, the easiest disguise is a dark colour overall – navy, red oxide, dark green or black – to which light relief may be added by way of stencils, rugs or a floorcloth (see page 145). Dark colours need a dark undercoat, and should be sealed with a suitably tough varnish. The new water-based acrylic eggshell paints could be a good choice; they are odourless, fast drying and to save still more time can be applied with a roller.

Light-coloured paint calls attention to defects, but if you crave the brightening effect of a pale floor in a dark room, you could achieve this by priming the boards with acrylic primer, painting over with a roller and a matt emulsion [latex] colour, and sealing with two coats of matt varnish. It is the varnishing that gives painted floors durability; a matt finish is less demanding than a glossy one.

Intricately patterned floors can look wonderful, but the decks will need to be cleared for action, most of which takes place on hands and knees. Stencils and templates are a help when executing any repetitive pattern (see page 141). Paint is a useful way of dealing with stairs. Wash them over in a driftwood colour to go

previous page The simplest floor treatment can be the most effective. Big painted squares of alternating light and dark colour cut across existing floorboards, cracks and all, creating a strong architectural presence and an exciting perspective. Here the squares have been lightly marbled to soften the contrast of such large chequers and also to suggest the marble pavement from which the idea derives.

opposite Combining elegance with simplicity, this Swedish eighteenth-century interior has all the ingredients that make the Gustavian style so appealing: delicately textured walls in faded ochre and blue, with trompe l'oeil panelling; bleached floor; 'sky' ceiling; painted chairs with simple red and white checks.

Faux marquetry can also be highly complex, involving multi-layer stencilling and painstaking brushwork. But notice how this elaborate design gains from the woody texture of the floorboards.

with Scandinavian style chequers on the hall floor. Or try painting and stencilling a stair carpet on a bare wooden staircase.

Plain paint, without trimmings, looks good when the colour is imaginative – try mixing your own. A glossy cadet blue or a sunflower yellow makes a practical and cheerful finish in a child's playroom, while matt, weathered-looking earth shades like raw sienna or Venetian red look warm and friendly on a sitting-room floor, scattered with rugs. No one would paint fine parquet, or wide old oak boards, but as a finish for the average scarred, beat-up softwood planking, paint is hard to beat.

MAKING GOOD & PREPARATION

Unlike furniture, a floor does not need to provide an ultra-smooth foundation for a painted finish. In fact, one advantage of using paint on a floor is that it will cover a multitude of sins, provided it is finished off with enough coats of varnish to build up a smooth, tough surface. Nevertheless, some filling and sanding down may be necessary to level the surface and disguise the worst blemishes.

NAILS & TACKS Nail down any loose boards and remove any protruding nails or tacks left over from previous floor coverings. Use pliers, a tack lifter or the forked end of a standard claw hammer. Obstinate nails can be punched down below the surface, using a 7 mm [¼ in] punch.

Stripping down You may need to remove dark, gummy varnish stain before you can put a finish on a floor. This tenacious substance contains black-coloured preservatives that seep into the wood beneath. Small patches can be removed by scrubbing with methylated spirit [denatured alcohol], but the only way to deal with large areas is by deep sanding (see overleaf), to remove the stained layer of wood. This can be very hard work, and takes a long time. If you have a floor that has been partially or wholly finished with varnish stain, your best move is probably to sand it enough to clean up the surface, and then paint it over completely.

Old paint usually responds to softening with a blowlamp or heat stripper [heat gun], scraping off the softened paint with a paint scraper and a shave hook for tricky corners.

Levelling up A painted or stained floor will look better if larger cracks and craters in the wood are filled. For a transparent finish, such as a stain or wash, use one of the proprietary fillers designed for woodwork [wood putty], since they expand and contract with the wood, and are thus less likely to shrink and drop out. Tint the filler to match the bare wood roughly, using water-based colours or universal stainers [tinting colours]. Alternatively, tint it with the wash or stain you are going to use on the floor. When the filler has dried, sand it smooth. Under an opaque, painted surface you

Sanded deal floorboards have been transformed by the imposition of a striking marquetry design in two colours, the palest tone being supplied by the wood itself. Designs like these can be carried out in coloured wood stains or paints sufficiently thinned to allow the wood grain to show.

can use putty for filling. The crack or hole must first be roughened and given a dab of primer or undercoat, to prevent the putty from shrinking and 'lifting'. Do not attempt to fill every crack and knothole, just the worst scars.

Sanding

If a floor is to be left *au naturel* and sealed, or given a transparent finish, it should first be sanded down, to remove accretions of dirt, varnish, paint or stain and to present a nice, clean blotting-paper surface. Power sanding machines do the job infinitely quicker than any small domestic sanding appliance, and can be hired from most do-it-yourself shops. The shop will advise you on how to operate them. Use a large sander for the main floor area and a small edge sander for borders and tight corners.

Preparation

Sand down the floor before you do any other decorating. Clear the room of every-thing moveable and keep it sealed, since wood dust clings. Sanders produce a lot of dust, so wear a face mask or scarf over your nose and mouth. Keep the machine on the move, so that you don't scar the wood. Starting from one corner, sand the floor in diagonal strips, each strip overlapping its neighbour by about 7 cm [3 in]. When you have been over the entire floor, sand along the other diag-onal in the same way. Lastly, fit a finer abrasive and sand the floor following the direction of the woodgrain. Vacuum up the dust as you go along, and finish the floor off by scrubbing with water and a little bleach. Allow to dry out thoroughly.

Failing a sanding machine the best course is to give boards a thorough scrub. I find a strong cream cleaner and a scrubbing brush do a good job. Rinse over with a mop and hot water and leave to dry thoroughly.

Sandpaper will rub away the odd scar or stain – wrap it round a sanding block for greater efficiency. Sand in the direction of the grain with long, smooth strokes, using coarse or medium, then fine, sandpaper.

Stairs

Cleaning old paints or stains off stair treads and risers can be a lengthy chore because so many 'amateurs' have been at work over the years, usually with every sort of paint and varnish stain, lying like an uninviting 'crust' over the wood. Getting the staircase back to bare wood is usually well worth the effort. In older houses especially, staircases tend to be well crafted and put together, using softwood that is straight-grained and relatively knot-free.

Once the stair wood is bare and clean, the stairs can be bleached (see Trip-Trap floor treatment page 135), scrubbed for an authentic eighteenth-century look, or stained with a dark stain to imitate hardwood. Stains and varnishes will need to be reapplied from time to time because they tend to wear thin paticularly when subjected to heavy foot traffic.

If at all possible, remove banisters and balusters, and organize for them to be professionally stripped to save time. Sanding these yourself is extremely labour-intensive.

Usually, with old stairs, the treads (where you step) rather than the risers have been worn down, often to the point where a 2 cm [1 in] tread has been worn away under foot traffic to a mere 1cm [½ in] thickness. Replacing these with new wood treads is a tricky joiner's operation, and looks odd, being both new and flat. But sensitive sanding can recreate something of the old, worn, 'hollowed' feel. The least attractive option is simply to tack new treads on top of the old. This does work but looks and feels wrong in an old building.

The taut graphic chic of black-and-white interior schemes is becoming increasingly popular, evoking shades of artists Aubrey Beardsley and Bridget Riley, black-and-white photographs and classic movies. The ingredients are simple – paint the walls and floor white, and furniture glossy black.

Transparent Finishes

WASHES

Bare wooden boards, cleared of layers of musty underlay and tacky carpet, are a sign of the times. People seem to want to get back to the architectural data of their homes, finding the honesty of this reassuring, the woodiness pleasingly natural, and the whole approach, of course, much less ruinous on a tight budget. Floorboards provide an excellent background to rugs and modern furniture.

Your first glimpse of the original floorboards, patched, spotted and riddled with nail holes, tends to be off-putting. But take courage – a preliminary sanding, followed by a thin water-based wash of an appropriate paint, finished with one of the latest tough and quick-drying water-based lacquers, will impose a civilized calm, without obscuring the woody grain itself.

Use thinned emulsion [latex] or Woodwash (see page 135), testing the effect in a corner. You want enough colour to even out knots and patches, but not an opaque coat. I brush on colour, let it settle, then rub back with rags (old towels are good) to show the right amount of grain.

Finish off with two or three coats of varnish (see page 132).

STAINS

Stains penetrate deeply into wood. They usually come in woody colours, but ranges of stains in fantasy, non-wood colours are also available.

Different media help the pigment to penetrate the wood – water, spirit, oil and varnish. Water-based ones are the easiest to apply, but tend to dry patchily. Oil-based stains are best if you require a very even colour, since they dry more slowly. Spirit stains dry very fast, so that you have to take care not to go over the same patch too often, or it will become darker than the rest. Modern varnish stains are quick and easy to apply and available in a good colour range but tend to be shiny when dry.

All stains should be applied over clean, bare wood that has been well-sanded and scrubbed. Follow the manufacturer's instructions. The exception is a coloured wax stain, which needs a coat of floor seal beneath it.

WAX STAIN To make a wax stain, melt beeswax or paraffin wax with artists' oils in a double boiler. Let it cool to a soft paste, rub it hard into the boards with a brush or cloth, then polish for a rich shine. Rub the surface frequently to keep it burnished, and remove the stain completely before applying another finish.

opposite Three options for softwood floor-boards are encapsulated here. Black-and-white painted chequers lend coherence to a patched landing floor. The steps retain an earlier dark stain and varnish. The foreground boards have been treated to a traditional Scandinavian lye bleach and soaping. To create a similar finish see page 135.

STAINS & STENCILS

One interesting decorative possibility is to use a dark wood stain to stencil an overall design on a light-stained floor. This gives a warm marquetry effect that allows the grain of the wood to show through.

Method

Apply the first stain over the entire floor, and leave it to dry completely. See pages 141–144 for stencilling techniques. Use simple geometric stencils. Dab the darker stain through the stencil holes with a lint-free rag or a brush. Do not take up too much stain at a time, or it may creep under the stencil and ruin the outline. This can be prevented by first pencilling in the stencil and coating the adjacent areas with shellac. When the stain is dry, wipe away the shellac – plus seepage – with a cloth dipped in methylated spirit [denatured alcohol]. The marquetry effect may be heightened further by carefully scoring round the designs with a sharp knife, or by outlining them with black felt-tip pen or paint, to imitate ebony inlay. Finish off by varnishing (see below).

VARNISH

Polyurethane varnishes (see page 214) are tough and easy to apply. They can be applied straight over a sanded wooden floor, as long as the wood is well seasoned. Any filling should be done with a compatible filler [wood putty] first. Choose matt, semi-gloss or gloss, depending on the degree of shine you want to achieve. Gloss varnish is slower-drying and tougher. Don't worry if a gloss varnish floor comes up too shiny when you would prefer a matt finish. The shine soon wears off underfoot. Acrylic varnishes do not yellow or discolour, and some are now tough and durable enough for floors, notably water-based lacquers (see page 214).

Method

Before you start work, make sure that the room is as clean and dust-free as possible. Apply the varnish with a clean brush reserved for the purpose, laying the first coat across the grain, then levelling it off with the grain. When the varnish is dry, sand the floor down before applying the next coat of varnish.

Polyurethane varnish is touch-dry in six to eight hours, but it is best left overnight before recoating. From the second coat on, it can be thinned with a little white spirit [mineral spirit]: three parts varnish to one part solvent. The thinned varnish can be poured into a container, and if preferred, swabbed on with a soft pad made from a wad of cotton wool [absorbent cotton] wrapped in a clean, lint-free cloth.

The more thin coats of varnish you apply, the better it will wear – two or three coats is the minimum, but allow for five on a floor subject to heavy traffic. Recoat the floor with varnish at least every year. Before recoating, make sure that the surface is thoroughly cleaned and dust free. A final coat of wax will improve the durability of the varnish.

A board floor carefully painted in brisk and bold chequers of grey and white is a clever choice for this small hallway with its eclectic mix of furnishings, from austere antiques to startling contemporary pieces.

PROPRIETARY FLOOR SEAL

Floor seal is a conveniently easy finish to apply, as it is thin enough to be swabbed on with a soft lint-free cloth. Not as tough as polyurethane varnish (see page 214), and slower-drying, you will need two or three coats of proprietary floor seal to build up a surface that will withstand much wear.

The first coat of proprietary floor seal should be carefully rubbed into the wood across the grain, and then successive layers of floor seal should be rubbed in the direction of the grain. Remember to sand the floor boards lightly between coats to achieve a smooth finish.

Maintenance

Like varnish, floor seal can be re-applied every year or two if it is wearing thin, but all wax and grease should be removed first by rubbing the floor boards with solvent-soaked rags or scrubbing with a mild sugar soap solution.

WAX

Wax smells agreeable, gives an incomparable shine and enriches the natural wood colour in a sympathetic way. But there is no getting away from the fact that it involves hard work.

Do not apply wax directly onto bare wood, particularly a softwood like pine, since it may allow dirt to become embedded in the fibres of the wood. Coat the surface first with floor seal. This will prevent the wax sinking in too far and will make raising a shine much easier. Swab the seal well into the woodgrain, and sand it down with fine sandpaper in the direction of the grain when it is dry.

The oldest, simplest form of waxing, using nothing more than beeswax and turpentine, is still to my mind the most pleasing, because of its delicious smell and its beautifully rich honey colour. It is now expensive for use on a large scale, and has always been a devil to apply and burnish, but for people who would like to try it out – especially on stripped pine, for which it is ideal – here is the formula. Beeswax can be bought from chemists [druggists] or craft shops.

BEESWAX POLISH To make beeswax polish, melt a chunk of wax with some pure turpentine, in roughly equal proportions, in a double boiler or an old can placed in a saucepan of water. Take care that neither the wax nor the turpentine comes near direct heat, since both are highly inflammable. Leave the mixture to cool a little, and while it is still soft (but not liquid), scrub it thinly but thoroughly into the surface with an old soft brush or a lint-free cloth pad. Leave it for several hours to harden completely, then rub it up to a shine with a clean soft brush – a shoe-cleaning brush will do. You will need to clean the brush often as it clogs up.

Modern waxes are considerably easier to apply, and contain silicones to make them tougher, and driers to speed hardening. Use a soft cloth to spread the wax thinly, and after a few hours drying, a soft brush to buff up the surface. End by polishing with a soft cloth.

LIGHTENING

This technique for toning down wood colour is helpful on knotty deal, or on any pine, which tends to go a hot orange colour if sealed or varnished after sanding.

Tinted white paint is brushed onto the wood and then rubbed off again, so that a residue is deposited in the cracks and pores. Use a flat white oil-based undercoat softened with a squirt of raw umber and dashes of ochre and black artists' oil colour or a greyish matt emulsion [latex]. With a stiff brush scrub this liberally over a small section of the wood, leave it for a few minutes, test to see if it is adhering, then rub it off with a rag. Rub against the grain quite firmly but not so hard that you remove all the paint, which should leave a distinct film of pale colour. Repeat this treatment over the entire floor.

BLEACHING

The smooth floors of bone-coloured wooden planks, which are such an attractive and distinctive feature in old Swedish houses, are the result of decades, if not centuries, of regular scrubbing and scouring with green soap and sometimes wet silver sand. Softwood, subjected to regular scrubbing, gradually whitens and leaves the harder sapwood slightly upstanding. There is no shortcut to attaining this weathered and worn effect, but a reasonable approximation can be achieved on a standard plank floor of pine or deal by rubbing in a tinted greyish white undercoat or emulsion [latex] paint.

Diluted emulsion colours can be brushed on and wiped off with an old towel for driftwood effects. Choose cool off-white to grey shades with a grey-green cast to counteract any yellowness in the floor boards. For the chalkiest, the driest and most powdery looking finish, however, a water-based paint with a high proportion of plastery filler gives the best results, and here I must admit to an interest, having devised a paint of this type, called Woodwash (see list of suppliers). It can be diluted with water to give the desired degree of transparency, yet it has sufficient pigmentation to alter the overall shade and even out knots and other blemishes in the surface colour.

TRIP-TRAP FLOOR TREATMENT

At last, after many attempts to fake the look with paints and varnishes across the decorating world, the secret of those pale, pearly wooden floors – a coveted ingredient of historic Scandinavian interiors – stands revealed. Imported from Denmark, quaintly christened Trip-Trap, this consists of a two- or three-part treatment for use on stripped or sanded softwood floorboards. It leaches out the yellow/orange tints that turn bright orange when varnished, and fades out the invariable knots. The result is cool, greyish, uniform in tone, with the natural grain cleanly visible.

Materials

Trip-Trap three-part system, sold in plastic 2.5 litre [5 US pints] tubs; large brush; mop and pail.

Method

Each stage of the system contains some lime, to aid 'greying'. It begins with the bleach, based on lye. This is brushed or mopped over bare boards, going with the grain, and left overnight.

Next, this is followed by 'soaping' (which is also a protective waxing) using the stage two mixture. This is mopped on and mopped off, changing water frequently, as the 'yellow' in the wood is swabbed off. Repeat this stage a few times. The soaping affords some protection underfoot, but probably requires topping up every few months to get rid of darker patches of wear under foot traffic.

The third part to Trip-Trap, known as Master Wax, provides extra protection in use, plus further greying of the wood. Follow the manufacturer's instructions.

Painted Finishes

PLAIN COLOUR

A priming coat is needed for an opaque finish as it helps paint go over wood smoothly, to cover better and to last longer. Give wooden floors, old or new, two coats of acrylic primer, which both primes and undercoats. If the top coat is to be a rich or dark colour, follow with a dark toned – but not matching – undercoat. This will show up any 'skips' in the top coat so that they can be quickly painted out before the paint has time to dry. One coat of the top colour may be enough for a plain paint finish, or as a ground for further decoration, although two may be needed in some instances.

PAINT Most types of paint can be used successfully on floors, because a good varnish finish (polyurethane varnish or water-based lacquers) will protect even soft-textured paints from being rubbed off. Matt emulsion [latex] paints are suitable, provided they are well varnished. I find their dry powdery surface an excellent base for decoration. The degree of shine in the paint is not really important, since the finish will be provided by the type of varnish you choose – matt, semi-gloss, or gloss. Undercoats or flat white oil paints have more opacity than gloss [enamel] paints, and are particularly suitable for painting floors. Professional decorators like flat white oil-based paint, tinted with universal stainers [tinting colours] or artists' oils, because of its pleasant brushing qualities and velvety texture, but frequently substitute standard undercoat or acrylic primer.

Method

Before you start work, clear and clean the room thoroughly. Seal it off as much as you can. Always keep one window open to let out the paint smells, which can be overwhelming in a confined space.

Like walls, floors should be painted a section at a time, using roller or brush. Choose a brush wide enough to help, but not so wide that it cannot be handled comfortably. The chief thing to remember is to plan your floor painting so that you end up at the exit, not boxed up in a corner surrounded by sticky wet paint.

It makes a great difference to the final result if you sand lightly between coats, to smooth new paint surfaces and get rid of any grit, crust or fibres.

When you have obtained the opacity of colour you want, leave the floor to dry out thoroughly. If you are not going to add any further decoration, all that is left is to varnish it – matt, semi-gloss or gloss, depending on the degree of shine that you require. See page 132 on varnishing.

A warmly coloured painted floor treatment in a small bathroom calls to mind Renaissance floor designs based on optical illusions (half close your eyes and the lozenges turn into piled 'blocks'). For this treatment to work, the floorboards need to be the same width throughout, and evenly spaced.

137

CHEQUERS

Squares of alternating light and dark colour arranged on the diagonal (at a 45° angle to your boards) provide an exhilarating and uncomplicated transformation for any painted floor, adding unpretentious dignity and a sense of perspective which both strengthens a space and fits in with most decorating schemes. Which is why, of course, its noble progenitor, the chequered marble pavement, became *de rigueur* in so many grand houses, especially, though not exclusively, in hallways and formal rooms. I think the painted version sits well with much less ostentatious decors, from bathrooms to garden rooms. The delight of it is that it offers light (because of the pale squares) without glare, structure (because of the dark squares) without oppressiveness; it creates a trick of perspective which never fails to expand your given space and yet can be made flexible enough, given a simple dark border, to fit the most meandering, crooked or simply cussed architectural details.

Preparation

Scale is the first question to resolve. Huge checks, which work beautifully in a ballroom or palatial foyer, can look overblown on a small irregular floor. But equally, small tile-sized squares are sometimes too busy for visual repose, as well as being a devil to paint.

A floor plan, measured to scale, will help determine the best chequer size, although some people can more or less gauge this by eye. A floor plan helps to take account of unexpected factors such as walls that slope off on a diagonal, hallways that narrow suddenly, nooks and so on, interrupting a precisely geometric plan. A dark border, in the same colours as your dark chequer, can accommodate all these irregularities, narrowing or broadening to suit the case but remaining visually credible. In this context, think of your chequers as a geometrically exact carpet or rug, set at the correct angle to the doors, but with an unobtrusive border that can assimilate structural oddities.

Method

When it comes to marking out I find the old LP sleeve or ply template useful for most situations – having an ingrained resistance to practising what I preach when it comes to serious measuring and graph paper, I have painted chequered floors successfully simply by tracing round one of these useful templates over and over again. Sternly practical readers should invest in an automatic chalk line, obtained from builders' merchants and specialist paint shops. This consists of thin string wound into a receptacle containing chalk dust, which becomes 'chalked' as it is released, depositing a chalk guide line when it is stretched between two points and plucked firmly.

What you do now depends on the type of paint used and the desired finish. If you want opaque chequers, apply primer or undercoat followed by the topcoat of your chosen pale colour. If you are going for the semi-transparent look apply the

opposite The sharp contrast of black-and-white floorboards, underlined with black paintwork, and splashes of warm red on cupboards and ceiling, makes a 'place' out of a landing space given over to clothes and books. Glossy black balusters are visually effective and also very low maintenance.

pale topcoat directly onto the wooden floor boards. Let the paint dry, then pencil or chalk in the main guidelines and fill in alternate squares with the dark shade, using a fat brush to fill in the squares and a fine pointed watercolour brush (No. 4 or 5) to give neat-edges. For a matt colourless seal use an extra pale dead flat polyuethane varnish applied according to the maker's instructions, or water-based acrylic lacquer (see pages 214-215).

FLOOR STENCILS

The most successful floor stencils I have seen kept quite close to effects created by more traditional types of flooring, using fairly dark and subdued colours and regular, repetitive designs. Apart from the practical consideration of not showing dirt and dust, there is an aesthetic or psychological point behind this preference. Visually, a room gains from being weighted at the bottom with a solid-looking floor – a delicate flowered porcelain effect on a pale ground may look pretty, but it can make one feel vaguely uneasy unless the other colours in the room have been chosen with care to balance the 'floating' floor. Study examples shown here, as well as traditional floorings and decide for yourself. Technically speaking, floors are stencilled in the same way as walls. See instructions on pages 73–76 on how to design, prepare and cut stencils for walls.

Preparation

The floor surface must be in fairly good condition for stencilling; it needs to be reasonably smooth if the stencils are to look crisp. Stencilled patterns look more dramatic and carpet-like over an opaquely painted ground, softer and less demanding over a semi-transparent finish. If you want an opaque ground, finish with a matt emulsion [latex] or undercoat plus a top coat of water-based eggshell paint. See page 137 for instructions on how to paint a floor.

Materials

PAINT The paints to choose for stencilling floors, as well as walls, are those that dry quickly, give maximum coverage and come in good colours. Most professional painters today use artists' acrylics (see pages 216-217) for all stencilling purposes, because they dry almost instantly, can be diluted with water to the required transparency, and avoid the health hazards posed by using spray paint in a confined space. The joy of spray paint was its soft yet clear image, but I find this can be matched by using acrylic colours very sparingly on a rounded mop brush or stipple brush. American readers may prefer to use japan colours thinned with white spirit [mineral spirit]. These have the advantage that the stencils dry almost as you do them, so there is little risk of smudging as you move across the floor.

A flat paint, either undercoat or standard matt emulsion [latex], will give excellent coverage for stencil floor designs.

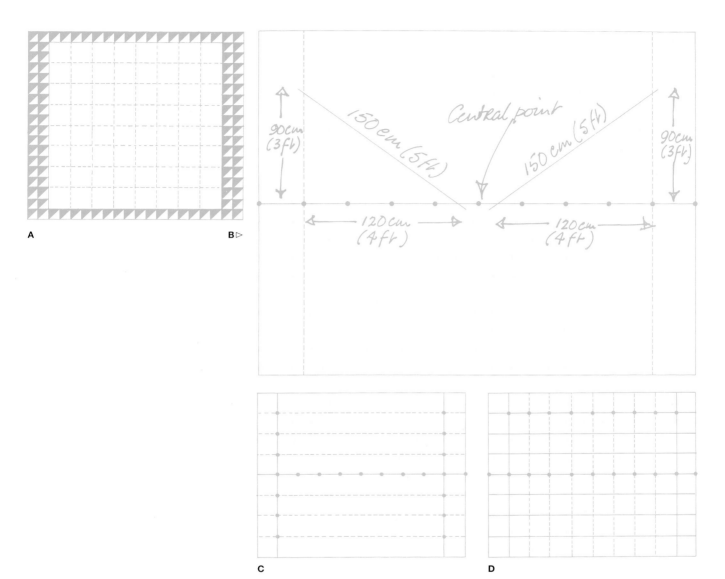

A

B ▷

C

D

To square off a floor design (whether for a chequered or squared, stencilled design) you will need a pencil, ruler and squared paper; chalk, ball of string and/or a long wooden batten; a set square.

Measure the room or floor space and draw it out to scale on a sheet of squared paper. Having decided on the size of the squares (or pattern blocks for stencils) mark these off in pencil along the sides of the floor plan, working outwards from the central point of each wall. You may have to adjust the size of the squares to suit the floor space – most simple patterns look best if they complete a run. A border (A) gives room for adjustment.

Find and mark the centres of two opposite walls. Using chalk and a long batten, or a length of heavily chalked string pulled taut across the floor and snapped in the middle, mark a straight line across the floor between these points. The centre of this line is the centre of the room.

Working from the central point, measure off the width of the squares in both directions along the line you have just drawn. Through the two outer points draw two more lines, parallel to each other and at right angles to the first line, running the length of the room. Check the right angles with a set square, or better still by the following simple method.

Measure 90 cm [3 ft] along one parallel, 120 cm [4 ft] along the central line. Mark these points and draw a line between them. This third line should measure 150 cm [5 ft], if it doesn't the angle is not a right angle (B).

Having drawn these lines with chalked string or batten, mark off the squares along them, as before. You are now in a position to draw in all the lines in one direction by joining up the points across the floor as shown (C).

Choose one of the outer lines (parallel to line one) and again mark off the width of the squares from the centre outwards. Complete the grid by joining the two sets of points as before (D).

above Painted floors can be delightfully carefree and animated in their design. This pretty stencilled floor was given a coat of white paint to provide a cool background to sprays of blue flowers. A delicate border echoes – and may even be actively inspired by – a profusion of pattern in a nearby collection of blue and white porcelain.

right The dazzling colours of a Swedish neoclassical interior are handsomely counterpointed by a stencilled floor scheme of dramatic simplicity. The brown octagons, which are the colour of the timber, and the black diamonds have been stencilled on a pale grey background. A matt varnish is best suited to a floor scheme like this.

BRUSHES A rounded mop brush or stippling brush, used in a round and round movement, gives the crispest definition, with a nice, textured look. If you are stencilling with more than one colour at a time, use a different brush for each colour.

OTHER EQUIPMENT Squared paper; chalked string or chalk and a straight-edge; supply of rags for mopping up; saucers for mixing paints; stencils or stencil-making materials.

Method Before beginning to stencil, square off the floor so that you have one square for each stencil position. Measure the floor and make a floor plan on squared paper. Mark out on the plan squares based on the size of your stencil. Use your plan to mark guidelines on the floor, using a chalked string or a straight-edge to help you position the stencils. For an all-over, regularly spaced pattern, square off the floor as shown [on page 141]. To plan a border, divide the wall lengths by the size of the motifs to calculate how many repeats will fit in. Chalk a guideline the length of the floor at the required distance from the skirting [baseboard], and mark off short lines along it at the central point of each motif. On each stencil again mark the centre of the motif and draw two lines at right angles through this point so that the stencil can be accurately positioned at each 'cross' on the guideline.

For instructions on how to mix colours and position and paint stencils, see stencilling on walls, pages 71–79. Stencilling floors is a strain on the back muscles, so it is best not to try to cover too much ground in each session. Also, because of the heavier pressure one tends to exert on the brush in this position, there is more likelihood of smudges and blobs. Have a good supply of clean rags or tissues handy to wipe these away as you go along, and clean the back of the stencil frequently. Carefully lift the stencil off the surface each time you use it so as not to slide it over the wet paint.

Leave the completed floor for no fewer than 24 hours before varnishing. The paint must be perfectly dry. Give it at least three coats of matt, semi-gloss or gloss varnish. Gloss varnish is always tougher.

MARBLED FLOORS

Painting a floor to look like marble adds a palatial air to any room. It is not as difficult as it sounds, because over a large surface the marbling can be done in a very loose and Impressionistic way and still look convincing. You will find the technique easier to handle if you divide the floor into squares, to imitate paving slabs.

At the other end of the scale, marbling the floor in pale, cool colours adds a look of space and light to small, confined areas like hallways and corridors. As long as it is given several protective coats of varnish, a painted floor stands up well to foot traffic.

FLOORCLOTHS

Floorcloths, 'painted carpets' of primed, painted and varnished canvas, were popular during the eighteenth and nineteenth centuries before being largely replaced by linoleum. In view of modern scepticism about the wearing qualities of paint underfoot, it is worth noting that in their day floorcloths were valued because they were both hardwearing and easy to clean. In darker colours, painted to suggest marble pavement or patterned tiles, sometimes stencilled in imitation of straw matting or even Turkey carpet, these floor coverings were thought especially suitable for hallways, dining rooms, corridors, and the upper servants' rooms in country houses, all areas which might expect hard wear. A seamless floorcloth was often made to fit a given space and the requirement for extra-wide canvas led to many floorcloth factories starting up near sail-making centres in sea ports and docklands.

Today the chief appeal of a floorcloth is surely aesthetic; it surpasses mass-produced vinyl floor covering by virtue of being hand-painted and retaining something of the pleasant texture of the canvas base. The design and colouring can be adapted to suit every decorating scheme. But it remains a practical proposition too – with periodic revarnishing, a floorcloth will last many years. (The durability of a floorcloth does in fact depend more on the varnishing than on the type of paint used.) Modern primer, paints and varnishes make the creation of a floorcloth a comparatively speedy process, as each stage is quick to dry.

The critical factor in deciding the size of a floorcloth is the amount of space you have available in which to work. A small floorcloth, say the size of a bedside mat, can be done on the kitchen table, as long as you have somewhere it can be laid out to dry between coats. A room sized cloth is best painted *in situ*, which of course puts the room in question out of bounds until the project is completed. The intermediate sizes are probably the biggest problem because the cloth should be stretched during priming and drying. One solution is to pin the cloth out on a reasonably flat stretch of lawn during a spell of fine weather.

Designs

These can be as traditional or as fanciful as you please. Geometric designs forming a regular grid are probably the easiest to execute and look handsome underfoot. Or you could cut down the work by stencilling a wide border and a central medallion against a plain coloured or spatter painted background (lapis lazuli looks excellent – see page 181.) Look through magazines for design and colour inspiration: chequered stone or marble, marquetry inlay, Roman mosaics, medieval tiles, flooring designs by architects like Robert Adam and William Chambers – all these sources could provide ideas and may be interpreted with stencils and paint. For colour and gaiety underfoot, copy blue and white Spanish tiles, or the motifs appliqued on an old quilt.

Furniture

F urniture has always been painted, usually to add surface colour and texture, sometimes to protect or conceal inferior wood, or to disguise crude workmanship. Each creative historical period has added some particular refinement of technique or decorative flourish.

There has never been a more beautiful plain finish than the old lacquer that the Chinese made from the sap of the lac tree. The 'japanning' techniques used by later European craftsmen to simulate lacquer are flimsy by comparison, although they do have a witty sophistication.

No painted furniture is more poetic in its fantastic decoration and tender colouring than that produced by the Venetians from the time of the Renaissance onwards, yet the very refinement of their gesso and tempera finish served the more prosaic purpose of disguising inferior woods and joinery. For elegance of a highly strung sort, French and English furniture of the late eighteenth century is unrivalled, its colours and decoration applied with taste, discretion and consummate technique. Regency craftsmen added the spice of wit, sparkling colours and a great deal of gilt to shapes that are a lively spoof of the Gothic and the Chinese. Later in the nineteenth century, painted furniture entered a brief new phase in England under the inspiration of William Morris.

Painting junk Such painted furniture belonged to the world of rich patrons, but alongside it evolved a democratic form – usually now called folk, rustic or provincial furniture. The workmanship is solid rather than refined, the shapes often clumsy, while the painted decoration itself tends to be bold and uninhibitedly colourful. It is often spirited, and like the decoration on Delft tiles or Staffordshire figures, skilful for all its apparent slapdashedness. Its brash colouring softened by time and use, much of this folk-style furniture is endearing, and at ease in modern homes.

Unless one is lucky, the chances of picking up an attractive old piece cheaply are getting smaller all the time. The only really inexpensive items around seem to be the boarding-house and office furniture of thirty years or more ago, often solidly made, usually of oak, but with a treacly varnished finish that looks unhappy anywhere. Painting them in the ordinary way makes them inconspicuous, but decorative finishes can transform them into really attractive, colourful pieces.

Painting furniture is tempting to try, because the preparation and work can be done in a small space without making too much mess or disrupting the household. In most cases the materials are cheap and easily available – filler [spackle], paint, universal stainers [tinting colours], varnish.

There is a decorative finish to enhance any type of piece and emphasize its attractive features while camouflaging its worst points. Ugly, coarse-grained wood texture is easily hidden by priming with the modern equivalent of the old Venetian

previous page Decorative painting is taken to new limits in this spectacular wall of fitted cupboards designed and executed by a London-based artist. Her mysterious vistas, framed in rich gilt and burnished mouldings are broodingly lovely, evoking the distant landscapes of Italian Renaissance paintings.

What looks like an antique cupboard packed with blue and white china is a complete fraud; the cupboard was made yesterday, of medium density fibreboard and deal, but has been given a lightly distressed paint finish and gilded to suggest age and class. The china collection is make-believe, painted in trompe l'oeil on the door panels which have then had chicken wire stretched across them to strengthen the illusion.

gesso, to build up a hard, poreless surface for paint. Large, looming wardrobes, sideboards or chests of drawers undergo a visual shrinking process when given a simple distressed finish in quiet colours that match or tone with the wall colour. Such outsize pieces are always improved by a matt or at most a semi-gloss finish because non-shiny surfaces seem to look smaller than glossy, reflecting ones.

Two important changes in the field of furniture painting over the past few years have been the steady rise in popularity of water-based paints and varnishes rather than the oil-based ones, and a marked preference for paint surfaces that have been crazed, crackled, rubbed away and otherwise 'heavily distressed'.

Acrylic, water-based media dry in a twinkling compared with their oil-bound relations. They are also healthier, being free from solvents like white spirit [mineral spirit]. The practical gains in terms of speed of application, odourlessness and easy clean-up are countered by an aesthetic loss: there is a certain flatness and stodginess of texture about standard emulsion [latex] water-based paints. There are, however, ways of handling and finishing them which give back some richness and texture, and this is where distressing plays such an important role (see page 165).

Selecting furniture for painting

Whatever materials or paint effects you have in mind, start by looking for items in good working order: drawers that slide, hinges in place, doors that fit, chairs that do not wobble. Choose a simple shape, an air of solidity, sensible proportions – in other words a piece with recognizable kinship to the classic models. Superfluous twiddly bits or gimcrack detail such as nasty handles can simply be removed, while stylish ornament can be made a feature of, with a suitable finish.

Furniture with built-in decoration – relief carving on panels, turned knobs or curlicues – can be painted, too. A fantastic Gothic-style piece responds to a folk approach using strong, contrasting colours, but keeping the finish quite matt to resemble the powdery texture of old paint. Offbeat colours are best: dull reds, maroon, pea green, murky yellows, faded indigo, bistre, all of which can be achieved by mixing raw umber into a basic tint. In total contrast, furniture with shallow relief carving, the sort that looks more pressed than carved and usually goes with 1930's shapes, looks surprisingly urbane and attractive if given a finish of that period – ultra-sleek creamy 'lacquered' paint achieved by patient rubbing down and varnishing. Good colours to use are cream, black and vermilion red.

Odd dining chairs can be given a visual link by painting them all in the same way. Spattering (see page 179) is a useful finish, a technique so simple that a child could tackle it quite effectively. Paint cane-seated chairs of almost any style in soft, matt blues and greens, with the caning itself painted in a trellis pattern. Use the same colours and patterns to give a French provincial charm to the most ordinary, battered kitchen units – useful again if you want to link up pieces with disparate finishes.

Furniture does not, of course, have to be hideous or in bad condition to qualify for decorative painting. But no one would be foolish enough to paint anything made of rare or expensive hardwood, or wood with attractive figuring. As a general rule, the best articles to paint are those of wood that looks better covered up, and these are usually of recent make. Sometimes an old piece may need painting to conceal unsightly repairs in wood that does not match, or to replace an old finish that has worn off – though be careful here, since old paintwork in tolerable

The richly decorated cabinet, with its fluted panels, massive iron hinges and locks, and splendidly battered and worn crimson paint finish, is an exceptionally successful repro piece. Limewashed walls, in vivid ochre, leaf-paned windows, and an upholstered Jacobean-style chair add suitable *gravitas*.

condition adds to the value of a good item. If you do repaint, make sure the technique and finish are appropriate to the piece, its age and style.

Small wooden items, such as picture frames, boxes, trays or hanging shelves are fun to decorate and one can afford to lavish more pains over a small thing that takes only a few minutes for each step. Marbled picture frames look chic, as do blonde tortoiseshell painted boxes. Trays and table tops look elegant covered with neat, formal stencil patterns. Fossilstone marbling makes an easy and convincing finish for table tops. See pages 116–119.

PREPARATION FOR PAINTING

Decorative finishes of the sort discussed in this section are wasted effort unless the surface beneath is prepared to a good standard. Surface imperfections, such as rough grain and unfilled scars or screwholes, will show through the finish you put on top, and detract from the overall effect.

Although giving a first-class finish to an old item of furniture usually involves painstaking preparation, extra time and trouble taken at this stage are well worthwhile since the result is an elegant piece that looks as though it comes from a professional studio, and comes up smiling after years of use.

Stripping down

The most important step is to take off the old finish and get back to clean, bare wood. Occasionally old paint is in good enough condition to paint over. Paint that has gone thin and chalky with time makes an excellent undercoat and small chips and cracks can be filled in with all-purpose filler [spackle]. But more often the old paint has been badly applied, sometimes straight over varnish, and is flaky, blistered and wrinkled. If you sand it down, wear a paper mask (as bought from a chemist [druggist]) or a scarf tied over nose and mouth, because old paints can contain lead, the dust of which should not be inhaled. Varnish should always be stripped or sanded down, to provide a good finish for painting. It is easily dissolved either with proprietary paint or varnish stripper or, in the case of a shellac finish like French polish, with methylated spirit [denatured alcohol]. It is often difficult to tell what the finish is, so try a little methylated spirit on the piece first, and if that fails to soften the finish quickly, progress to paint stripper. In any case, use proprietary stripper for smaller pieces, especially those with fine detail such as carving, fretwork and turned ornament, or on pieces that could prove to be made of superior wood. Unscrew hinged doors, remove drawer pulls and other metal attachments. Cover the surrounding floor with sheets of plastic, wear gloves, and apply the stripper with an old paintbrush, following the maker's instructions. When the top layers of paint have softened, which usually takes 10 minutes or so, scrape the sticky paste off large surfaces with a flat scraper, taking care not to scratch and scar the wood. Then clean up tricky surfaces with coarse, then finer, steel wool. It can take several applications of paint remover to work through many old paint layers. Small pointed knives or nail files, as well as matchsticks and toothbrushes, are handy for digging paint out of cracks or carving.

CAUSTIC Large pieces, covered with numerous layers of paint, can be cleaned with a strong caustic solution. This should be done out of doors, using rubber gloves and applying the mixture with the type of spatula sold for putting on oven cleaner. Loosen the paint layers with an old scrubbing brush. A hose is handy for rinsing off the sludgy dissolved paint. Removing layers of paint may take several successive applications, and the mess is considerable, but over a large area it is infinitely cheaper to use caustic than proprietary stripper. To make things easier for yourself, lay as many sections as possible flat before rubbing it on. This will concentrate its

Furniture painting can also be contemporary in style, as in this repro pine chest, which has been softened and distressed with layers of white and buff paints to blend with an overall neutral colour scheme. Simple wooden knobs, dark and varnished, make a gutsy contrast.

action, since it runs off vertical surfaces. Caustic leaves wood fuzzy and discoloured, but gentle sanding down with finer and finer grades of sandpaper will restore a smooth finish; alternatively, make use of a paint-stripping service.

Primer

Primer is the first coat of paint in a system. It should be used if painting new wood, as it counteracts wood's natural porosity, so subsequent coats of paint do not sink in. Of the various types available, the toughest is the traditional pink or white oil-based primer, sold for use on wood alone; it should be thinned three parts primer to one part white spirit [mineral spirit], applied liberally and brushed well into the wood. Aluminium [aluminum] primer goes over any highly resinous woods. Acrylic primer acts as a combined primer and undercoat. Metal has its own primers.

Knots in pine and deal should be sealed with patent knotting [knot sealer] before priming. Do not skip this; knots continue to exude resin for years, and unsealed ones may cause surface paint to crack and discolour. Use it according to the maker's directions, applying two coats – more if the wood is really raw – over each knot, dabbing it on with a rag.

Filler

Fill coarse woodgrain, cracks and scars to present an even surface. Use a proprietary woodwork filler [wood putty] or standard all-purpose filler [spackle]. Mix it to a creamy consistency and apply it with a brush. Apply the first layer with the grain; allow it to dry and then apply a second layer against the grain. When dry rub it down firmly, with the grain, using medium sandpaper. Coarse-grained woods like oak may need two applications to level them up.

Holes, dents or chips should be filled with a stiffer mix of filler, applied with a palette knife, left proud and sanded flat when dry. Serious holes should be filled with a harder substance such as plastic wood – follow manufacturer's instructions.

Sand down the primed, filled surface until smooth before going on to the undercoat. Apply a coat of shellac to any special piece, or one that will get a lot of handling, now – it improves the look and feel of the finish, giving a slick surface for paint. Thin with one part methylated spirit [denatured alcohol] to two of shellac.

Undercoat

Highly pigmented, oil-based undercoat does a good cover-up job on furniture, as well as providing the ideal flat, 'hungry' surface for subsequent paints. Apply one or two coats (thin it with a little white spirit [mineral spirit]), depending on the state of the surface beneath, as a primer. Under pale colours, white undercoat is fine, but under dark ones it will need tinting to something near the final colour.

Rub it down firmly when dry with medium then fine sandpaper. On large surfaces begin rubbing in a circular motion, and end by rubbing in the direction of the grain beneath; on smaller pieces, rub with the grain throughout. For a super-smooth finish, use a special quick-drying fine filler, which comes ready mixed, to level up any little remaining blemishes. Keep the lid on this, since it hardens quickly if exposed to the air.

The routine of primer, filler and traditional undercoat can be replaced by gesso or two coats of acrylic primer (see page 156).

Gesso

Gesso consists of whiting, a very fine chalky powder, mixed with water and bound with rabbit-skin glue. Kept warm in a double boiler, this mixture remains fluid enough to apply to different surfaces with a brush. Many layers of gesso build up a surface that can be rubbed down with abrasive paper to create a surface as fine, flawless and hard as porcelain; it is cheap to make, and versatile. Traditionally, it was used to prime wooden surfaces for painting or gilding, as well as artists' canvases. It not only provides an immaculate and 'thirsty' surface for paint, but, as cabinetmakers were quick to discover, helpfully disguises coarse-textured wood and hasty workmanship. During the vogue for 'japanning' in the eighteenth and nineteenth centuries, gesso was used to build up raised figures and other elements which, carved and gilded, are such an attractive feature of the style.

Framers, gilders and restorers still swear by traditionally made gesso as a primer and base. It takes a little practice to get the hang of making and applying gesso, but it is worth the effort for anyone aiming to achieve a high standard.

Watercolour in the form of gouache in gum arabic can be painted directly onto gesso. A coat of diluted orange shellac gives it the colour of old ivory, an excellent base for penwork. Or it can simply be treated as a superlatively smooth and strong primer/filler/undercoat for an oil-based paint system, in which case it is usual to seal it first with shellac.

Materials

Rabbit-skin glue granules and whiting, both obtainable from artists' suppliers; bowl for soaking the glue size granules; conical sieve; wooden spoon and some sort of double boiler on a hot plate.

Method

Soak half a cup of granules overnight in cold water to cover. They will swell and soften. Put this mixture into the top of a double boiler, over water which is just simmering, and add ½–¾ litre [1–1½ US pints] of water. Heat slowly, stirring to dissolve the glue, and when hot start adding whiting, sifted in through a conical sieve, stirring to blend and break up any lumps. The whiting should amount to between a third to a half of the total volume of the gesso, and the gesso should have the consistency of thin cream. The traditional test of consistency is to pinch a little between finger and thumb; if the mixture is just perceptibly 'sticky' as you separate finger and thumb, it is strong enough. If not, add more dissolved glue granules. On the other hand if the mixture shows up transparent rather than whiteish when painted on a piece of wood, it is short of whiting, and you should add more, stirring as before. Apply warm with a soft brush, avoiding brushmarks as far as possible, though these can be smoothed off with sandpaper when dry. A coat takes roughly two hours to dry depending on climate and heating. One coat must be absolutely dry before applying the next, which should be brushed on at right angles to the previous coat. Rubbing down between coats smooths and compacts the gesso.

Acrylic gesso/acrylic primer

People with less exacting requirements may prefer to substitute one of the modern, acrylic-based products, sold ready-to-go and drying much more quickly, though the final surface will not be as hard and fine-textured as traditional gesso. Acrylic gesso, sold by artists' suppliers, is convenient but expensive and many decorative painters use ordinary acrylic primer instead because it has many of the same properties when it is built up in layers and thoroughly rubbed down between coats. Acrylic gesso and primers are delightfully easy to use. Gesso adheres better and builds more rapidly if the surfaces are well sanded first to provide 'tooth'. Depending on the state of the original finish, sand the surface first with coarse, followed by medium sandpaper. Fill in any cracks and chipped veneer with wood filler [wood putty] or all-purpose filler [spackle], and sand it level when dry. Wipe over the whole piece with a rag dipped in white spirit [mineral spirit] to remove grease and dust.

Using an old brush – these plastery substances are hard on brushes – paint a thin coat of acrylic gesso or primer over the entire piece. Do not bother with the insides and unseen parts of furniture, but paint over all the previously finished surfaces, which usually include the edges of doors and tops of drawers.

The first coat takes about an hour to dry, subsequent ones somewhat less. Rub over the gesso or primer with medium sandpaper in the direction of the woodgrain, using firm pressure and long, level strokes. Dust off with a rag, and recoat, repeating the whole routine several times until you have built up a smooth, white, level surface over the whole piece.

Rub the gesso or primer down harder on door and drawer edges or they may not fit properly. If you are rubbing down correctly, the finish will be so fine and compacted that the original finish will just show through on sharp edges. Beginners tend to go too gently from a natural reluctance to remove too much of what they have just laboriously put on – the result you should aim for is a thin, level and very smooth surface.

The number of coats needed varies with the type and condition of the wood and its previous finish. For example, open-grained wood will require four or five coats, previously painted wood only two or three. Pieces that get a lot of handling, like chairs, should have several coats, and these should be rubbed down harder in between. You will need at least five coats of gesso if you are going to put transparent watercolour on top, to build up a white, shadow-free surface.

ALL-PURPOSE FILLER [SPACKLE] It is worthwhile using traditional or acrylic gesso or primer for special pieces of furniture. For less important items use all-purpose filler thinned with water to a creamy, brushable consistency. Apply the filler and rub it down in exactly the same way as acrylic gesso, although you will find that each stage takes longer.

Sanding down   Sanding between layers of filler, undercoat, gesso, paint and varnish smooths the surface, while providing 'tooth' for the next coat. Scrupulous sanding makes a difference to the final look and feel of a painted piece out of all proportion to the time involved. Professional work is always sanded, at every stage.

What we tend to call 'sandpaper' is, strictly speaking, abrasive paper, which may be coated with one of a number of substances such as glass, aluminium oxide or silicon carbide. These papers come in grades between coarse and fine, which are split into progressively finer subdivisions. The routine is to begin with a coarse paper and work down to a fine one. The finer you want your finish to be, the finer the grade of paper you must end up with.

When sanding a flat surface wrap your paper round a sanding block. This distributes your hand pressure evenly. Use firm pressure, and long, smooth strokes. Rub backwards and forwards in the general direction of the grain beneath, going gently over sharp edges, relief carving and turned detail.

To sand a narrow, rounded surface, such as a chair arm or leg, wrap a small piece of sandpaper round it, like a scratchy collar.

Wet-or-dry (silicon carbide) paper, as its name suggests, can be used in either condition. Use it dry over bare wood. For rubbing down paint and varnish, it should be used with soapy water to soften the abrasive action and prevent scratching. Mix pure soap flakes with water and pat the sudsy solution over the surface. Rub the paper smoothly with long strokes from edge to edge of the surface, following the direction of the grain and going easy on projecting areas. Test the surface with your fingertips for smoothness from time to time, and wipe off the soapy mixture to check your progress. When you have gone over the whole piece, wipe it dry with a clean, damp rag.

As an alternative to wet-or-dry paper you can use steel wool, also with soapy water, but throw away after use, since they rust up quickly. Like abrasive paper, steel wool comes in coarse to fine grades.

Painting Furniture

To produce a high-class paint finish requires patience – you need to linger longer over each stage. The aim is to achieve a sleek, level paint surface, thin enough not to obscure any carved or turned detail, flat and smooth enough for any decorative finish to glide into place. The more thoroughly you do the base painting, the better the finish will look and the more gracefully it will age.

PAINT

Mix your colours by hand, tinting paint as instructed on pages 216–221. This allows for much finer colour adjustments and is more convenient, since one can of paint plus the various tints takes up less room than an equivalent range of cans of bought colours.

Gloss [enamel] paints are not used in good quality furniture painting. Shiny paint does not provide enough 'tooth' for subsequent decoration, and it looks wrong, especially on old pieces. Any shine required is added later by means of clear or tinted varnish coats, rubbed and polished.

Flat white oil-based paint, tinted with artists' oil colours, is the one commonly used for furniture painting by professional decorators and restorers. Relatively soft-textured, it needs several coats of varnish as protection. Flat paint protected with matt varnish is the ideal finish for large, vividly decorated country-style pieces that look brash given a gloss finish. A cheaper, quicker-drying alternative to these is standard oil-based undercoat, which dries with an attractive chalkiness and can be tinted in the same way. Being soft-textured, it will need adequate varnishing. Mid-sheen, or eggshell, paint is also used in furniture painting, especially under glaze work. It is more durable than flat oil or undercoat, and gives a nice smooth surface for lining, stencilling and other applied decorations. Recently a water-based eggshell paint has been introduced which has the added advantages of drying speedily and being low-odour.

Emulsion [latex] paint and acrylic colours are widely available, easy to use and quick-drying, giving a pleasantly chalky texture close to that of the aged lead paint found on many old country pieces. Use matt emulsion to paint any piece that would look best with a simple, rustic finish, and acrylic colours for any decorative painting on top. This gives a quick and passable imitation of the old 'gouache over gesso' decoration. Varnish renders an emulsion finish as durable as any other. Use two coats of clear matt varnish to give protection while retaining the flat, lean look.

opposite Against vibrantly coloured walls, vividly painted furniture looks particularly stunning. A 'brushily' finished armoire holds its own here against yellow limewashed walls and a floor of provençal terracotta tiles. Colour contrasts deliver a visual charge, and blue and yellow are a proven combination.

Brushes Use a standard paintbrush on large pieces. On small, delicately detailed ones, a brush with soft, fine bristles, such as a glider, helps the paint to flow on smoothly. Use a pointed sable watercolour brush (No. 3, 4 or 5) for fine decorative work.

Method After tinting, mix the oil-based paint thoroughly with white spirit [mineral spirit] to a thin cream consistency – about one part white spirit to about four of paint. Leave each paint coat plenty of time – say overnight – to dry hard, before applying the next. Most of the troubles that arise in painting come from applying paint before the surface beneath is hard and dry. You will need between two and five coats of coloured paint to provide a good finish, or a ground for subsequent decoration. More but thinner coats give a professional appearance, and rubbing down is crucial. Use medium-grade sandpaper for the first coat, fine wet-or-dry paper with soap and water for the following ones.

APPLYING EMULSION [LATEX] PAINT Although emulsion can be applied directly to bare wood, it tends to sink in and raise the grain. It is better to apply primer first, rubbed smooth when dry. You will need two or three coats of emulsion [latex] paint over primer, three or four over bare wood, each sanded down with medium sandpaper.

To capitalize on the inherently dry texture of this finish, apply further decoration in acrylics straight on to the emulsion [latex] ground. Be warned, however, that once a colour is brushed on to the emulsion [latex] surface, it is pretty permanent. You can apply a barrier coat of clear matt varnish, but this means some loss of texture. However, you can always paint out a real disaster area with a couple more coats of emulsion [latex] and start again.

GLAZES AND WASHES For how to make and apply these, see pages 222–227. Although tinted glazes are traditionally used in furniture decoration, their slow drying time means that they are often rejected in favour of quicker-drying tinted varnishes. Acrylic scumble is another option.

TRANSPARENT PAINT

For a special richness, an inimitable depth and glow unmodified by white pigment, you can make a sort of transparent paint, or tinted varnish, by combining a varnish finish with a tinting agent. Discreetly used, this is an easy way to give depth of colour to a painted wall or piece of furniture; it can also create the effect of an aged patina of dusty colour.

It is essential that both varnish and tinting agent are of the same composition – oil being mixed with oil, water with water. Dissolve the tinting agent in the appropriate solvent, then mix it thoroughly with some decanted varnish, and test on paper before use.

Raw umber, burnt umber, and burnt sienna are all colours that age a piece effectively. Layering varnishes tinted with slightly different tones of the base colour – orange-red, brown-red or crimson-red over base red for example – creates a complexity of tone that can be very pleasing.

Application

Wipe the surface with a rag moistened in white spirit [mineral spirit] or in vinegar. Brush on the transparent paint like varnish (see page 163) thinly and rapidly.

SHELLAC

A spirit varnish, soluble only in methylated spirit [denatured alcohol], shellac comes in various colours ranging from orange (also called button polish) to clear white. It is most frequently used in French polishing, but because of its imperviousness to most solvents and its quick drying time – an hour for one coat, a little less for two – it is often used in furniture restoration and painting as a barrier between different stages in the work. It is also used in high-class work to seal surfaces after priming and filling and before undercoating. At a later stage, it can be applied after painting but before glazing or decorating, so that the glaze or applied decoration can be rubbed down, or even wiped off altogether, without fear of disturbing the coat beneath. In effects involving media and colours of possibly conflicting ingredients, a coat of shellac is a useful insurance against what the textbooks sinisterly describe as a 'breakdown' of the paint system.

Do not buy too much shellac at a time since it does not keep well. For this reason, try to buy it from a shop that has a quick turnover of stock.

Brushes

Reserve a special brush for shellac – it should be soft-bristled. After use, wash it out in methylated spirit [denatured alcohol], and then in warm water with a little ammonia added, not soap or detergent. If the bristles harden, they can be softened before use by dipping again into methylated spirit.

Application

Manufacturers frequently recommend shaking shellac before it is applied, but this in fact creates bubbles that will show up on the finish. It is better to tip it into a saucer, add one part methylated spirit [denatured alcohol] to two of shellac, and stir gently. This thins and blends it.

Shellac should be used in a dry, warm atmosphere – in damp, draughty conditions a white bloom will appear on the surface, although this usually fades as the shellac dries. In damp weather, close the windows and heat the room up slightly.

Shellac can be awkward to brush on, drying so fast that one brushstroke is half-dry before the next overlaps with it, which creates build-ups of colour and a patchy look. Charge the bristles quite generously with shellac, press out the surplus against the inner sides of the can. Lay it on in the middle of the surface and with quick strokes draw it out toward the outer edges, trying not to overlap. Smooth it out by brushing from edge to edge, lightly and fast. A little patchiness in the final result is not too serious – correct the worst mistakes by rubbing down gently with fine steel wool and a little soapy water.

Varnish as a barrier coat

In place of shellac, you can use a coat of clear acrylic or varnish to seal off a surface or finish. This is tougher – shellac is not water- or alcohol-proof – and somewhat faster drying.

VARNISH

Recent years have seen such a proliferation of new types of varnish that even professional decorators are confused, let alone those of us wanting to select the appropriate protective seal for anything from a painted wardrobe to a little penworked box.

Painted surfaces look better and last longer when treated to between one and three coats of an appropriate varnish. Varnishes can be divided into three main types: oil-based, resin-based and acrylic. Oil-based varnishes are tough, traditional and slow-drying – 12 to 24 hours. Most familiar to DIY painters are resin-based varnishes, comprising polyurethanes, which come in matt, midsheen and gloss finishes. These are the workhorse varnishes, tough, fairly slow-drying (four to five hours) with a tendency to darken and yellow over time. Professionals recommend them for surfaces that can expect hard wear. Alkyd varnishes are related to polyuerathane varnishes but more refined, giving a sensitive patina, and are as near to colourless as a traditionally formulated varnish can be while still affording reasonable protection. The most popular of these are matt (absolutely no-shine) and eggshell versions with drying times of two to four hours. These are the products professional painters choose for finishing furniture, woodwork and in some cases walls. See pages 214 and 234 for product details and suppliers.

Newest of all are the acrylic varnishes, water-based, low-odour, colourless and extra fast-drying (1 to 1½ hours). They dry rapidly and do not yellow. They do, however, have some disadvantages. The varnish is as yet only available in gloss and mid-sheen, both with a distinct shine; they are a little awkward to brush out smoothly, though the manufacturers have brought out a special nylon brush to make them easier to apply. They do not take to burnishing and smoothing as readily as the polyurethane varnish, but are useful for rapid finishing of woodwork and furniture projects.

The elegant graphic lines of a small occasional table, in a good-quality hardwood, needs no paint effect to enhance it. Stripping back to the raw wood and varnishing, oiling or French polishing (depending on the wood) underline its sleek shape sweetly and appropriately.

Preparation

The basic drill remains much the same with all types of varnish. Surfaces to be varnished should be dry, well dusted, clean and free of fingermarks. Get rid of these by wiping the surface with a rag moistened with white spirit [mineral spirit]. Sandpaper leaves fine particles – dust these off with a brush. The ideal conditions for varnishing are as warm, airy and dust-free as possible. Any adhering dust, grit and hairs can later be smoothed off with abrasive paper, but prevention, where possible, is better than cure. When varnishing large areas such as woodwork, roll back the carpet, take down curtains and blinds and mass furniture under a dust sheet. Large single pieces should be tackled in a garage or garden room, standing on a dust sheet. For small items of furniture, where a perfect finish matters most, rig up a temporary plastic tent to make an ideal microclimate for drying coats of varnish as and when they are applied.

Brushes   Special varnish brushes have fine bristles which help to brush most varnishes out smoothly, with fewer brushmarks (see page 231). Some painters find foam applicators help in applying varnish smoothly and quickly over larger areas. For smaller items, soft artists' oxhair brushes are useful. If you are working in different media, it saves time to provide one brush for each, clearly marked. This also keeps brushes in better shape – a mixture of different solvents and cleaning processes beats the life out of a brush. Brushes can be stored overnight by slotting through a cardboard lid into a jar of the appropriate solvent.

Applying varnish   Varnishes are usually applied with a more loaded brush than one would use when painting, with the varnish applied copiously to the middle of a surface and brushed out smoothly in all directions. The aim is to avoid brushmarks and bubbles, the results of slapdash handling; varnishing should proceed calmly and patiently under a good light if possible, to avoid 'skips'. With awkward pieces it pays to think through the procedure first. With a chair, for instance, turn it upside down and begin on the legs.

Check the drying time with the manufacturer's instructions. Several thin coats of varnish give better results than one or two thick ones. Two to three coats are usually needed, with more for special pieces or lacquer effects. It is customary to thin the first application with the appropriate solvent (20 per cent or so) to float it on extra smoothly.

Rubbing down, an essential concomitant of effective varnishing, begins after the second coat is hard dry. Lightly rubbing down clears off surface imperfections and gradually creates a finish that is clear and silky. Fine wet-or-dry paper, used with a little water as lubrication, or aluminium oxide paper, is a popular choice. Some people swear by fine steel wool, but this deposits lots of tiny particles, which must be dusted well before recoating. Gloss varnishes can take more rubbing down than the rest, and this can also usefully soften the hard shine they create. But all varnishing is improved by patient smoothing.

In case the process of applying varnish described here sounds tiresomely perfectionist, it might be worth mentioning that eighteenth-century japanned pieces customarily had 30 coats of varnish (or shellac) and oriental lacquer at least 40 coats of 'lac'.

Multi-layered varnish finishes   Traditionally, some complex decorative paintwork, marbling and graining for example, was treated to a sequence of varnishes; first gloss, for clarity and toughness, then eggshell for a more subdued sheen, or matt, if a flat effect was the aim. Sometimes the decorative paint effect on furniture was finally waxed and polished with a soft cloth for a soft lustre.

POLISHING OR BURNISHING

It is traditional to give any varnished work a last going over with fine abrasive powders such as rottenstone, powdered pumice or French chalk to work up a texture of baby-skin delicacy. The process is not difficult. Using a pad of firm but soft material, preferably felt or flannel, dip it into a light oil (salad oil or baby oil), then into the powder, and gently rub the surfaces in a circular motion until all is silky, compact and immaculate. Rinse off with a damp sponge or cloth and when dry, rub briskly with a soft clean cloth for a superior final lustre.

QUICK COLOUR

Finger printing delivers a fascinating mark, like an oyster shell with a pearl in it, to give interest to small items, such as picture frames, or larger pieces, like wooden chairs. This simple decorative ploy is charming, but the pieces must be varnished.

There are going to be occasions when short cuts are not just a help but a necessity – you might want to decorate a box, tray or frame quickly to give away as a present. This is where modern superquick-drying paints come in useful. Acrylic colours dry so fast and immovably that you can complete the basic colouring of a piece in a few hours.

This is the routine for painting a piece in a tearing hurry. After basic filling and tidying of cracks and scars and rubbing down – a process that cannot be rushed – give the piece two or three coats of acrylic primer. This takes a couple of hours to apply and dry. Then paint a base coat of one of the water-based paints, matt emulsion [latex], artists' acrylic colour thinned with water or one of the excellent casein paints [milk paints] (see page 212) which have exceptional covering power. Decoration can be painted straight onto this base using artists' acrylic colours. When the decoration dries, give the piece whatever antiquing it may need by sponging a thin wash of acrylic colour over the whole surface. Then apply two coats of thinned polyurethane varnish, matt, semi-gloss or gloss as required. If you are really pushed, use a fast-drying acrylic varnish. Rub the first down lightly with fine steel wool and polish the second with rottenstone or scouring powder. Finally polish the piece with a soft cloth.

If you cannot spare the time for a second coat of varnish, try polishing over the first one with floor or furniture wax.

Finger printing

Easy as it sounds, finger printing (actually thumb printing) involves pressing your thumb into wet vinegar glaze to leave a mark that looks even better repeated on a regular grid. Only the vinegar glaze (see pages 185–187) has the proper consistency to leave a little dark pearl sitting in the middle of your shell-like thumb prints. It looks more comtemporary in black-and-white rather than the woody tones associated with this old grainer's standby.

Varnish is essential to bring up the effect of the finger-printed furniture. It must be an oil-based polyurethane varnish or a shellac, since acrylic varnishes will smudge the vinegar glaze.

Paint Finishes &
Decorative Flourishes

DISTRESSING

The lead in the taste for distressed furniture seems to have come from the USA where people with an eye have been collecting old, battered, painted country-style pieces for many years now, and putting them together in modern as well as rural interiors where their well-worn surfaces and colours add a comfortingly human dimension to a room. In Australia the McAlpine Collection of bush furniture, toys and artefacts, simple yet vigorous, has led to a new appreciation of the resourcefulness of early settlers in the outback. Furniture manufacturers have picked up on this trend rapidly, introducing distressed finishes into their more avant-garde ranges of kitchen furniture and fittings, partly to make them look old and atmospheric, and partly too, no doubt, to hide the fact that a fair proportion of them are made not of timber but of one of the substitutes such as medium density fibreboard (MDF).

Distressing has been the most popular finish over the past decade for all painted furniture or units, kitchens in particular, as shown here. It lends an aura of age, use and 'lived with' charm to characterless modern materials, like MDF or cheap whitewood. A distressed effect is easy to simulate.

The appeal of distressed finishes to amateurs is that they are easy to do, fast and visually effective in a rugged, understated style that suits the way most people live today. Distressed surfaces are decorative just as they are, but they can also provide a foil for applied decoration, painted lines, stencils or designs painted on freehand or with transfers. They can be further 'antiqued' with coloured washes, tinted varnishes, or simply with dark boot polish. The simplest distressed finish is achieved by rubbing back, which creates a time-worn look.

Rubbing back

The rubbing back technique concentrates on the areas that would get the most handling, such as leading edges, doors, the area around drawer handles and door knobs. Remove all handles, knobs and fittings first, for easier access to the parts you want to concentrate on. On a wooden piece the usual approach is to apply the chosen base colour directly to clean, bare wood (all varnish, wax or lacquer must be removed for a good grip), brushing on sufficient coats to build up a dense colour – two are usually enough. When dry, the paint is rubbed back with fine wet-or-dry paper softened with soapy water, until the bare wood surfaces again here and there. Don't rub too fast or hard, or you may take off the top layer of wood too. When the effect satisfies you, let the piece dry then go over all the surfaces with a flat varnish. If the contrast between paint and exposed wood looks too raw, soften this by rubbing or brushing a suitably 'dirty' wash of thinned acrylic tube colour, in raw or burnt umber, over the whole piece. This can be done before or after varnishing. Use a rag to even it or lighten some areas. Alternatively, if the paint looks too matt and chalky, a rub over with boot polish will add depth, warmth of tone and a subdued shine when buffed with a soft cloth.

Over mixed surfaces, such as MDF panels framed in deal, the simplest solution is to apply two coats of matt emulsion [latex] in different colours to both surfaces, rubbing back the top coat carefully just before it is quite dry to reveal the paint colour beneath, rather than the underlying material. An electric sander speeds this.

Rubbing back over wax

Wax can be used as a 'parting agent' to stop the second coat of paint from covering the whole of the first one. The effect is similar to the one described above, but easier to control. Woodwash, a densely pigmented, water-based paint does a good job of this finish, but any water-based paint can be used. You will need an ordinary wax candle, and pads of medium and fine steel wool.

Brush the base colour densely over clean, bare wood and let dry. Rub the candle over areas you want to show through the top colour, applying the wax thickly where you want streaks and gashes of contrast, or rubbing lengthwise across the whole surface for a light speckling of colour. Brush the second emulsion [latex] colour on top and let it dry. With the medium steel wool followed by the fine steel wool, rub firmly but not too forcefully across the waxed areas and you will find the base colour surfacing cleanly. This is a rustic finish, suited to simple shapes and strong, folk colours – red-brown, dark blue or green, ochre yellow. If you are planning further painted decoration, use artists' acrylic colours, and remember that these too should be rubbed back sensitively when dry to remain in keeping with the distressed finish.

Woodwash takes a pleasant burnish when rubbed down all over with steel wool, and this can substitute for varnishing, especially when the piece is waxed and buffed. But furniture that gets a lot of handling should be varnished with either flat or eggshell varnish.

ANTIQUING

Antiquing with paint, as distinct from the roughing up of furniture with bunches of keys, chains and dropped bricks that restorers use to match reproduction pieces to time-scarred antiques, is of interest to anyone who paints furniture, because it is a process that not only ages a piece in a trice but makes it look more convincing. Imitating the complex patina acquired over years of use is an effective way to restore character to a refinished old piece and to enrich the appearance of a newer one. It should be done with some understanding of the way in which wear and tear occur naturally on painted surfaces – abrading the finish on parts that get the most handling and along exposed sharp edges, while darkening the parts that collect dust or grime. This is not to say that antiquing should make a piece look dirty; if it appears grubby and smeary, the technique has been misjudged. Properly handled, it is more like subtle shading in half-tones, emphasizing structure and modelling, and delicately softening paint texture and colour. It is no exaggeration to say that any piece of furniture newly painted by a professional will have been 'aged', 'distressed', or 'dirtied down' by one means or another, not simply to counterfeit age and wear but to soften the raw, blank look of new paint. Antiquing gives painted finishes a 'lived-in' look and 'atmosphere'.

A combination of techniques, sparingly applied, gives a more convincing effect of age and patina than any single one pushed to the limits. Methods include shading with neutral, earth-coloured glazes distressed in some way, a light spattering of brown or black dots, or patches of crackle glaze here and there; alternatively, give varnish a final rub with rottenstone and leave some of the dusty powder behind in corners and carvings. Brash new gilding looks better rubbed back and aged. Hard painted lines or stencils can look more appealing discreetly rubbed away in some areas. An isolating coat of bleached shellac over the paint finish allows you to experiment with various antiquing effects, and rub away the ones you don't like, without affecting the finish itself.

ANTIQUING GLAZES & WASHES

For antiquing effects, glazes and washes are usually tinted with the duller earth colours, but grey or much-thinned black is sometimes used. A little of the ground colour of the piece can be added to the antiquing glaze to soften the contrast. Glazes are usually thinned to transparency, applied overall and then gently manipulated as they begin to set, to create a softly shaded effect.

Materials

OIL-BASED PAINT GLAZES These give the most subtle and controlled patina. A glaze containing flat white oil-based paint (see pages 222–225) will be slightly opaque: for a completely transparent one, blend artists' oil colour with a little linseed oil (see note, page 184) and a lot of white spirit [mineral spirit]. Artists' oil colour, rubbed on neat from the tube and then mostly rubbed off, can be sealed successfully with shellac.

WASHES For instant antiquing on flat or well rubbed-down finishes, use watered-down acrylic colour or gouache (see page 227 for recipes). Washes allow less time for adjustment, softening – or second thoughts. So begin cautiously with a dilute mixture of colour, sponging or wiping it on with a rag, and softening at once where required by wiping off the wash again. Though a little tricky to control, the drying speed of such washes is a point strongly in their favour. Fix with shellac or a spray varnish.

COLOURS Tint the glaze or wash with earth colours – raw or burnt sienna, raw or burnt umber, plus a speck of black. Raw umber is the standard antiquing colour, because it ages and softens almost every other hue without muddying it. It is a safe standby when in doubt. Raw sienna adds a warmer tinge to glazes applied over cold colours. A speck of black with each intensifies their effect. A little rottenstone mixed with the glaze medium or with polyurethane varnish makes a very convincing, dust-coloured antiquing liquid. The tint of the glaze or wash should be a couple of tones darker than the base colour.

OTHER EQUIPMENT Soft brush; rags or a marine sponge; fine steel wool. Optional: shellac; brush for shellac.

Method

APPLYING A GLAZE With a soft brush, cover all the surfaces of the piece thinly and evenly. The longer the glaze is left to dry before blending and rubbing down, the heavier the antiquing effect. Heavy antiquing looks better on rustic-looking pieces – for this effect, leave a glaze overnight. Light, urbane furniture needs a much gentler nuance of colour, achieved by leaving the glaze until just tacky, and then rubbing it down.

opposite Old or newly distressed? These days it is hard to tell, but it hardly matters when the final result looks like this attractive rustic dresser, whose original pine surfaces warmly emerge here and there from a much rubbed subtle green paint. Note the clever juxtaposition of formal objects with country pieces.

Rub the surfaces gently with a pad of fine steel wool so as to lift the glaze from the parts that would get most wear and tear, while leaving it like a dark bloom over the rest. Rub down harder on places like chair arms and backs that get worn naturally. Rub away, too, over the centre of flat tops, sides and drawer fronts. Any prominent mouldings or raised carving should be rubbed down hard on the highest points, leaving the glaze darker in the recesses. The glaze should blend very gradually from highlight to dark, without streaks or smears or sudden transitions. Even where you have rubbed most of it away, just enough will remain embedded in the minuscule flaws of the paint finish.

As you work, stand back from time to time to judge the overall effect. Go gently when rubbing over any applied painted decoration unless you want it to emerge slightly worn and tattered. If not, you should apply a coat of clear varnish or thinned shellac first.

DISTRESSED ANTIQUING GLAZE The glaze can be finely dragged, sponged or stippled over the paint-finish to give more texture than the method described above (see pages 45–52 and 56–60). Rub down a distressed glaze in the same way, when drying or dry, to soften it.

APPLYING A WASH A wash should be sponged on with a rag or sponge, left to dry for a moment or two, then rubbed with lint-free rags bunched to make a soft pad, and finally blended with fine steel wool. It works best over a flat and slightly absorbent paint finish.

Varnishing

You should protect the finish with varnish, as described on pages 162–163. Antiquing is usually done before the final protective coats of varnish. Over antiqued paint the most suitable varnish is matt or semi-gloss – if you use gloss you should rub it down well, to dull it. Use a clear varnish, unless you wish to emphasize the antiquing tone further, in which case you can add a little of the same tint to the varnish.

On a special piece, use a rottenstone rub and polish for a very fine finish (see page 164); allow a little of the dusty powder to remain in cracks and recesses.

Instant antiquing

For an immediate softening effect, which works especially well over dry-looking matt emulsion [latex] or other water-based paints, there is nothing to beat old-fashioned boot polish, in light or dark tan or black, wiped on with a soft cloth, rubbed in, then briskly buffed up with a soft cloth to an agreeable gentle lustre. The one disadvantage is that the wax must be cleaned off with white spirit [mineral spirit] and soft steel wool, before repainting at a future date. Coloured waxes are also available in intense jewel tones (see pages 212–213).

CRACKLE GLAZE

The varnish on old painted pieces owes its mellowness not only to the warm depth of colour the varnish acquires, but also to the fine network of crazing that develops as it ages. Paint often ages in the same way, with a layer in a different colour showing through the crackled top coat. These time-worn effects can be created almost instantaneously with crackle glaze and craquelure (see page 173). Crackle glaze is a commercial product, colourless and somewhat sticky, which can be applied between contrasting colours of emulsion [latex] to create a strongly cracked surface that lets the base colour show through. It can be used over an entire piece, or on isolated patches in conjunction with the rubbing back effect (see page 166) for variety and texture.

Materials

Crackle glaze can be obtained from artists' suppliers and other specialist shops, in bulk, or in 500 ml [1 US pint] containers, enough to crackle an area of 7m², [21 sq ft]. Apply with a standard 25 mm [1 in] brush between two coats of emulsion [latex].

This French panelled door shows an unusually subtle and striking use of a crackle glaze finish, the 'alligator' effect offering an excellent background for 'picking out' stencils. Crackle glaze is best handled on horizontal surfaces – take doors off hinges and lay flat.

Method To produce a good crackle, the glaze itself should be brushed out thinly and evenly overall. Use random brushstrokes, radiating out every which way; the cracks follow the brushstrokes and regular ones look monotonous. When the glaze is dry the top coat of emulsion [latex] can be applied in the usual way. Once the water in the top coat activates the crackle glaze the top coat becomes volatile; this can make it awkward to control, particularly on a vertical surface. The solution is to apply the top coat on horizontal surfaces only, one facet of the piece at a time, laying it on thickly and quickly, but taking care not to rebrush once cracks start appearing, or the whole surface skids and smears.

On a large or fiddly-shaped piece this becomes a tedious business, compensated for, however, by the unfailing excitement of watching the crackle appear. Cracks continue to spread and open for some time, so leave each facet to dry out thoroughly before moving the piece round to tackle a new one. The thicker the top coat, I find, the bolder the crackle. Firms using crackled finishes commercially spray on the top coat, thus cutting out a good bit of waiting. A hairdryer helps speed up the process. Obviously you can have fun playing off the two emulsion [latex] colours involved. Don't underestimate the subtle effectiveness of overlaying browns, greys and creams, as well as the dramatic primaries.

above left Using a subtle colour contrast, a crackle glaze finish can deliver an interestingly distressed effect, adding punch and excitement to the simplest picture frame. Here, I used a smoke-beige water-based paint over a white base coat, with a layer of crackle glaze sandwiched between. A touch of instant gilding wax adds glamour.

above right Craquelure is a two step finish which cracks the varnish only, creating fine cobwebby lines that only show up once the surface is rubbed over with artists' oil (see page 216), or coloured wax see (page 212).

Sealing   Crackle glazed surfaces must be sealed, otherwise any water that gets to the surface will start it sliding and moving again. Use a coat of bleached shellac followed by oil-based varnish. Water-based acrylic varnish will activate the finish.

FINE CRACKLING

An American correspondent suggests a different method of crackling top coats of matt emulsion [latex], which gives a finer and more even 'crazing', similar to the craquelure described below. Because she intends an antique effect she customarily base-coats a piece in a raw umber shade (sludgy green/brown) of emulsion. When dry she covers this with an even coat of animal glue size (preferably rabbit-skin glue) dissolved thoroughly in hot water and kept warm in a *bain marie*. When this has dried she recoats the piece in her chosen final colour of emulsion [latex] which, as it dries, becomes finely crazed in a random, natural-looking fashion.

CRAQUELURE

Often confused with crackle glaze, this is in fact a two-tier varnish system, with a fast-drying varnish applied over a slower-drying one, or water-based over oil-based. Marketed together, these varnishes can be found in most artists' suppliers; they are expensive, but they give a nice fine, cobwebby craquelure which looks handsome when burnt umber tube oil colour is rubbed into it to bring up the finished effect (the craquelure remains invisible in the transparent varnish until this final step).Water-based craquelures are perhaps the easiest to use, as are those with two step finishes.

Preparation   The craquelure effect is set off to best advantage by pale base coats, cream, ivory, grey, or pastels. The varnish adds its own warm tone, so this should also be taken into account. I find it a usefully flattering finish for any piece with applied decoration, because it helps to blend colours, soften contrasts and create a mellow finish.

Materials   Water- or oil-based craquelure varnishes; varnish brush; artists' oil colours in burnt or raw umber; shellac; polyurethane varnish, for final sealing.

Method   Successive varnishes are applied to a clean, painted surface, which should be smooth, dry and dusted. Follow the maker's instructions as to which varnish goes on first. Using a varnish brush cover the whole surface with varnish A, checking the piece against the light to ensure there are no 'skips'. Set the piece aside for approximately 45–50 minutes. Now recoat with varnish B (crackle varnish), again taking care to avoid missing out patches. Set aside for half an hour, or longer. You should begin to see fine, superficial cracks forming a network over the surface. You can now leave the piece to dry naturally, overnight, or give it a blast of hot air from a hairdryer. In my experience the varnishes can prove a touch temperamental, one craquelure coming up clear and even and another less so for no apparent reason. But one point needs emphasizing – the top coat of the craquelure varnish must be allowed to dry hard before you go to the next stage, the rubbing in of dark artists' oil colour. Once hard dry, it can be safely treated to an application of artists' oils in burnt umber or raw umber, straight from the tube, rubbed in gently with a soft rag. The colour can be applied quite freely to the surface, and rubbed back again with the cloth until the dark craquelure seen against the rest of the surface has the degree of emphasis you like. Leave the piece to settle down, overnight. Rub clean with a wet rag, then coat with shellac. When this is dry, recoat with polyurethane varnish, flat or eggshell . Take care not to let the piece get wet before applying the varnish as the finish is not permanent until it is sealed.

SPATTER ANTIQUING

Spattering is an elegant way to antique a slender, shapely piece of furniture in light or medium colours, giving artful shading and emphasis that never looks crude or overworked. With a little experience, one soon acquires the knack of producing an even and controlled shower of colour without creating a mess that does not go all over the room.

Another trick, often used in combination with a heavily rubbed, or dragged, glaze, is to use just a scattering of spots in a strongly contrasting colour – brown or black – to suggest an aged freckled look.

Method

Make up a thin antiquing glaze or wash as on page 168. Spatter it with a stiff brush, practising first over a large piece of scrap paper. The spattering should not be too uniform. When it is dry, you can apply a second coat, concentrating on the parts that you want deeply shaded. When the whole surface is quite dry and the colour sufficiently softened, the spatter coats can be blended a little by gently rubbing down with fine steel wool.

FRECKLES For a coarse, random spatter, use a little black or sepia drawing ink. If it is permanent ink, either use it over a barrier coat of varnish or shellac, or dilute it a little with water so that blobs and mistakes can be wiped off easily with rags. Diluted Indian ink, blotted as it falls, leaves faint grey rings that look most convincing on delicate pastel finishes. Take a little ink up on your brush, and knock it on a stick with a quick, jerky movement to direct the spatter where you want it. Spatter (sparingly) the surface on a previously antiqued piece of furniture, to add contrast and texture.

VERDIGRIS

One of the current darlings of the decorative effects trade is the painted imitation of verdigris, the vivid blue-green patination that occurs on copper and bronze when these metals are exposed to weathering. Verdigris is a flattering and undemanding finish for many materials, from wrought iron to wicker and wood, and for objects as varied as flower pots and fireplace surrounds. For all its undoubted elegance, it is gratifyingly quick and easy to apply and is best done in water-based paints. The method suggested below uses emulsion [latex] paints, but you could also use acrylics.

Materials

Depending on the size of the object, you will need a quantity of standard matt emulsion [latex] paint in a sludge or khaki colour for the base coat; small quantities of emulsion in blue and green for the stipple colours – a turquoise and sharp lime green work well together; a standard decorating brush to apply the base colour, and a rounded brush, such as a rounded fitch, for stippling; flat polyurethane varnish if protection is needed.

Method

Coat the piece with one or two coats of base colour to give a solid cover and let dry. Tip some of the turquoise stipple colour into a saucer. Dip the stippling brush into the colour, then work the colour up into the bristles by pounding them onto waste paper (this also blots up surplus moisture).

When the stippling on the paper gives a soft, clear impression, not a wet splat, the brush is ready. Using a light, jabbing movement, 'pounce' a fine dusting of colour over the entire surface, leaving a ghost of the base colour showing through. Pile the turquoise colour on more densely over any relief mouldings, and work it into crevices.

Next, with a rinsed dried brush repeat the process with the sharp lime green emulsion, covering some, but not all, of the turquoise colour. The green acts as a sort of highlight, intensifying the effect. The whole secret of this finish is to use a drier brush than you think possible.

For a chalkier, crumbly look wash over the whole finish with thinned white emulsion [latex], brushing on and wiping off with a rag to leave white deposits. To even up a verdigris that looks patchy or blotchy, simply stipple over lightly with some of the base colour.

Verdigris also gains from a discreet contrast of gold; gilt cream (see page 208) is easy to apply and looks well. Shine looks incongruous on this finish, so if you need to varnish, choose a pale flat polyurethane varnish.

Using the same technique, but different colours, metallic effects like pewter, even rusty iron, can be simulated effectively. A little metal (bronze) powder in the final varnish adds sparkle (see page 204).

A verdigris finish is a quick and easy means of creating the rich blue-green patina of a weathered copper surface on small household objects such as this slim candlestick.

MARBLING

Traditionally, marbling would have been used on parts of a piece that might plausibly have been made of real marble – the top of a table or commode, for instance, to fill in small recessed panels on the front of an armoire or cabinet. On such pieces, verisimilitude in marbling was the aim and a painter would often combine several different 'marbles' of contrasting colour and formation to enrich the overall effect.

A different and freer approach to marbling grew up in the seventeenth and eighteenth centuries for decorating the sort of furniture that might loosely be classified as 'provincial'. The best examples of this cruder but more boldly decorative use of the technique come from northern Europe – Germany, Holland and Scandinavia in particular. Provincial painters were not fettered by precedent or anxious to be 'correct' and, lacking first rate examples to study at close quarters, they would often work from the copy of a copy, a process that inevitably tends to blur the original and leads to something more individual and – sometimes – more picturesque.

Latterly, marbling has become fashionable again as one of the painted finishes used to ennoble certain types of furniture that benefit from a highly decorative finish. When deciding which furniture to marble, consider its suitability, style and period. Painted finishes are a merciful disguise for plywood or blockboard, but it would be a folly to paint over mahogany or satinwood. Vigorous marbling, decorative swags and floral motifs look handsome on a nineteenth-century dresser but less convincing on a 1950s bedside table.

Preparation

The piece should have the usual sequence of undercoats – primer followed by one or two coats of undercoat and one or two coats of base colour. The base colour sets the tone of the finished piece so it should be chosen to fit in with the decorating scheme. Eggshell or mid-sheen paint is best, as it is both durable and smooth enough to give a good surface for marbling. All paint coats should be rubbed smooth when dry.

Materials

Transparent oil glaze [glazing liquid] or acrylic scumble; universal stainers [tinting colours] or liquid tinters; whiting (optional, see page 38); boiled linseed oil (see note, page 184); paper, rag or polythene bag; painters' dusting brush for softening; artists' pointed sable or lining fitch for 'veining'.

Method

Brush over the area to be marbled with a thinned transparent glaze [glazing liquid] – oil or water – to give a surface with enough 'flow' to allow marks to be softened out realistically. If the glaze is drying too fast, add a little solvent. Some professionals add a little powdered whiting to the glaze to add body.

This fantasy marble panel was produced with two glazes made of thinned oil paint. The first glaze was tinted with grey and the second with indigo. This sample was then spattered with red oxide while wet to give random but pleasing textures which looks handsome as a table top panel, or for a bathroom cabinet finish, or bath surround.

VARNISHING Allow 24 to 48 hours for the piece to dry and then seal with two or three coats of clear semi-gloss varnish. For an ultra-smooth finish, gently smooth over the final varnish coat with fine grade wet-and-dry paper lubricated with soap and water. Alternatively, rub over gently with fine grade wire wool. A final light waxing can be an embellishment, giving the dull lustre of real stone.

FANTASY MARBLING

Dissolve artists' oil colour in white spirit [mineral spirit] in a flat saucer. Scrumple paper, rag or polythene, dip in colour and dab in a deliberately random fashion over the wet glazed surface. Go over these marks with the softening brush for a natu-ralistic and attractive effect, gently stroking the colour into the wet glaze, applying only a very light pressure, so that it blurs and softens a little. 'Softening' is the key to successful marbling effects, and can be practised first on a spare sample board. The aim is to give a slight cloudiness to the crumpled prints, resembling 'sedi-mentary veins' in real marble. Change direction of the softening brush as you go so the blurring does not get too uniform.

IMITATION MARBLING

For a closer imitation of 'real marble', you can add a second or third 'scrumpled' layer of colour, using varied tones (look at a real piece) to give depth and richness. Finish up by painting in 'veins' of a more distinct and positive sort, using a fine pointed brush or lining fitch, or a goose feather if you can get hold of one. If this is done before the wet glaze has dried hard, the veins, which should always 'go somewhere' and intersect as in the real stone, may not need softening. However, softening will help to make them more convincing. Use the dusting brush again, gently brushing out the veins in all directions.

177

For a Swedish porphyry finish, the piece is first covered with an opaque coat of bitter chocolate matt emulsion [latex]. When dry, this is spattered lightly with coral red emulsion or acrylic thinned with water. The colour is flicked onto the surface by running a finger briskly across a loaded (but not too charged) brush. Considerable base colour is left showing.

A second spatter coat of pale pink covers more of the brown base and lightens the whole effect. The spatter need not be even; indeed, it looks more convincing like this.

The last spatter coat is a pale grey, not too evenly flicked. This porphyry finish is a splendid foil to gilding and gains enormously from final varnishing – follow instructions for varnishing marble (see previous page).

SPATTERING

Spattering – the name decorators use for showering a surface with flecks of coloured paint – is one of the easiest and most artful ways of distressing a painted surface. Since the colour is broken up into such tiny particles, it never looks heavy or clumsy, as can happen with brushed-on glazes.

Use it to give a rich flick of extra colour to a plain painted surface. A heavy spatter of bright green over turquoise, for instance, creates a vivid blue-green with far more depth and vivacity than if you had mixed the two colours together in the pot, or even brushed the green over the turquoise in the form of transparent glaze. A fine spatter of black over a red, mock lacquer surface adds the merest suggestion of texture without obscuring the glossy colour beneath. Spattering in a neutralizing umber or black will tone down or simply add a texture to whatever is beneath.

COLOURS Keep in mind the principle that complementary colours of the same intensity, viewed at a distance, neutralize each other. Thus, two spatter coats of roughly equal density, one of red and one of green (or orange and blue, or purple and yellow), will appear softened to an indeterminate neutral.

Preparation

The snag with spattering is that it makes a bit of a mess over a pretty wide area – especially if you are trying it for the first time. Ideally, take the piece into the garden, if it is a fine day. Indoors, cover the floor with newspaper, rigging some more up to form a protective screen behind.

The ground coat should be a flat oil paint, or an acrylic eggshell paint with the appropriate oil- or water-based universal stainers [tinting colours].

Materials

PAINT You can spatter with any kind of paint or glaze, as long as it is thinned to a watery, flickable consistency. If you are experimenting, the water-based colours – gouache or acrylic – are a good idea, since they can be wiped off quickly with a damp sponge. Gouache is particularly good for spattering several coats one on top of the other, and can still be washed off. It will, however, need extra heavy protective varnishing.

BRUSH The best type to use is a long-handled stencil brush. A stiff, round hogshair brush or a fitch are good, too. You can also use an old artists' brush, with about half the bristle length sliced off to leave it stiff and straight-ended. Swedish painters used a bunch of small birch twigs.

Spattering is done by passing your finger or a metal blade (a knife, ruler or comb) over the painty bristles. You can get very even spattering by rubbing your paint-laden brush through a medium-mesh, round wire sieve. For spattering as fine as mist use a 'diffuser' [atomizer], which can be bought from artists' suppliers (see page 234). For a much heavier spatter effect, try using a stencilling brush (see page 231) which can simply be scrubbed across a wide-toothed comb.

OTHER EQUIPMENT The appropriate solvent for the paint; paper or a board so that you can practise your technique; rags; paper tissues; saucers for mixing colours.

Method Having made a watery thin paint, pick up a little on the bristle tips of your stiff brush. Then pass your finger steadily over them, releasing a few bristles at a time. Experiment on sheets of white paper – with a little practice you will find that you can aim your coloured spray quite evenly and accurately from a short distance away. Avoid overloading the brush, as this gives a heavier spray, with some blobs that might start to run. If they do run, blot them up quickly with a corner of paper tissue.

Very fine spattering dries almost immediately, heavier coats should be left to dry before applying further colours. Finish off with varnish.

SPATTER PRINTS Spattering can be used quite differently over templates to leave negative prints. This technique was a favourite in the heyday of hobbies, the mid-nineteenth century, when use was often made of the elegant lacy outlines of that beloved Victorian pot-plant, the common fern. Fern fronds, dried flat, still make ideal templates, arranged into patterns with plainer leaves as borders. You can also try cut paper, doilies or any other decorative shapes. Spattering for this technique is most easily done with a diffuser [atomizer]. Spray paints are too difficult to control.

Early examples imitated marquetry, using dark spatters over colours like red-brown or golden-brown. This looks pretty with fern patterns, which then appear in relief against a dark ground. Another good combination is olive green over a light or golden brown ground. For a more imposing effect, suggestive of inlaid marble, try the spatter colour mixtures suggested for porphyry (see page 178) over templates fixed to a grey or cream ground.

Materials You can make up the spatter paint with oil-based colours as for porphyry, but for a softer, mistier spray, use acrylic colours in water (other possibilities are coloured drawing inks). You will also need a diffuser [atomizer]; leaves or other shapes to spatter round and a jam jar or similar container; Blu-Tack.

Method Whatever type of colour you use, it should be poured into a container and stirred thoroughly. Arrange your leaves and secure them in position with a piece of Blu-Tack, then place one end of the diffuser [atomizer] in the paint, and blow hard through the other, mouthpiece, end. Blowing creates a vacuum that forces the

For a lapis lazuli finish, first spatter a base coat of vivid ultramarine emulsion [latex] lightly with a pale blue thinned emulsion or acrylic wash.

The second lapis spatter is a deep blue-black and covers more of the base colour.

A spatter of lemon yellow brings the ensemble to life. For fun, and to suggest the 'fool's gold' often found in lapis, the finish has also been flecked with gold metallic paint, done at the last stage. Like porphyry, this is a finish improved by careful varnishing and rubbing to create a smooth lustre.

contents of the jar to rush up the tube. If you point the angle formed by the two sections toward the surface to be spattered, and puff, the paint will flow over it in a fine mist of colour. Practise on sheets of paper laid flat and propped up vertically, to get an idea of how to control the spray.

Leave the spatter to dry, remove the templates, and touch up any 'skips' in the spatter by stippling in dots of the same paint with the tip of a small stiff brush. Use a fine sable artists' brush and the same paint to add further detail such as leaf veins or vine tendrils.

GRAPHITING

Graphite represents the search for a finish that combines the softness of a 4B pencil with the elegance of antique Japanese lacquer, and gives a subdued metallic lustre to furniture, woodwork and walls. It can be achieved by adding a small quantity of graphite powder (available from artists' suppliers) into a varnish coat. Sophisticated, with a distinct pewtery sheen (emphasized by buffing with a soft cloth once the varnish has dried), a graphite finish is simple to apply and costs next to nothing.

By varying the colour of the base paint and the tint for the varnish, you can achieve a wide range of different tones and still retain the characteristic 'soft pencil' look of graphite. Mixed into a clear, semi-gloss polyurethane varnish and applied over a pale grey base paint, the effect will be pewtery grey, with a quiet lustre. Added to a deep-blue-tinted varnish and applied over a mid-grey paint, the resulting colour will be a softly metallic deep blue. The amount of graphite depends on the degree of lustre you are after – more graphite equals more lustre.

Graphite is not lead and does not present a health hazard provided it is used sensibly and care is taken not to inhale the powder. Wear a mask.

Once you have the colour and lustre you desire, apply a clear coat of semi-gloss varnish to prevent the graphite in the previous coat from being disturbed by rubbing or cleaning later on.

Preparation

Cover surfaces with a base of good quality flat or mid-sheen paint. Any varnished finish tends to emphasize roughness or imperfections, so spend a little time beforehand getting a smooth, even finish on the wood.

Materials

170–225 g [6–8 oz] of powdered graphite should be ample; a good-sized tin of clear semi-gloss polyurethane varnish; artists' oil colours or universal stainers [tinting colours] for tinting the varnish; a long handled artists' brush for mixing; a 50–100 mm [2–4 in] wide flat varnishing brush for applying the varnish; rags; solvent; a spoon for adding the powder; a small container or paint kettle.

Here a polyurethane varnish mixed with graphite has been applied over a charcoal base paint on a modest kitchen chair.

Method   Tip a little varnish into the container. If the varnish is to be tinted, add a little of the desired colour or colours, mix well and try out on a small section of the wood to judge the effect. When the right tone has been reached, spoon a little graphite powder into the tinted varnish, mix well and try it out again. Sample patches can be wiped off again with a rag and solvent. Once you have the effect you are after, use the same procedure to mix up a much larger quantity of the mixture. You may need to use a whole tin of the prepared varnish mixture if you are planning to cover the walls of an average sized room.

Give the room a good clean before starting work as dust and grit tend to settle on varnish while it is drying, and while they may not show up much, they do make the finished surface less pleasantly smooth to handle. The temperature in the room needs to be warm – 21°C [70°F] – for the varnish to handle well.

Apply as you would a standard varnish, in light but even strokes, brushing out smoothly but quickly to avoid runs. Check carefully against the light as you go for 'skips' in the varnish coat. Leave to harden overnight in a warm room. Once dry, gently buff with a soft cloth to increase the sheen. A second coat of varnish can then be applied to seal the finish.

ROSEWOOD GRAINING

The simplest version of rosewood graining consists of dragging a thinned brownish black glaze over a rich brownish red ground. Well varnished, this looks fine over large areas. The other, more complicated version involves more preparation and final coats of transparent colour, but the reward is a glowing intensity of colour, with something of the depth of natural wood. This longer method is described below.

Preparation   The finer the painted surface the more convincing the finish. To imitate the dense, fine-grained texture of rosewood, most cheap wood or veneered boards will need preliminary filling. Use proprietary filler [wood putty] or all-purpose filler [spackle], watered down to paint consistency, or acrylic gesso (see page 156). Two or three coats may be needed, depending on the wood texture and type of filler. Finish with two coats of acrylic primer, also sanded when dry.

Materials   **FLAT RED PAINT** Oil-based paint tinted with four parts alizarin crimson, two parts burnt sienna and one part vermilion artists' oil colours mixed in white spirit [mineral spirit], with a teaspoon of liquid drier (optional). Alternatively, a good red acrylic colour sealed with shellac.

TRANSPARENT RED PAINT The same artists' oil colours as above mixed into three parts clear gloss varnish thinned with one part white spirit [mineral spirit].

DARK GLAZE Four parts raw umber, one part burnt umber and one part black artists' oil colours, mixed in equal parts of gloss polyurethane varnish and white spirit [mineral spirit]. Add a little boiled linseed oil, about an eighth as much as the white spirit (measuring in tablespoons helps with these sums), also ½ teaspoon of liquid drier. (NB: Linseed oil is sold either raw or boiled. Never attempt to boil it at home.)

OTHER EQUIPMENT Orange shellac; methylated spirit [denatured alcohol]; brush for shellac; 50 mm [2 in] decorators' brush for the red paint; dragging brush or dusting brush (see page 232), or other paintbrush for streaking the glaze; wet-or-dry paper; very fine steel wool; a soft cloth dipped in solvent or vinegar, for removing grease.

Method

RED GROUND Apply two coats of flat red paint (see 'Materials' on page 183). Mix more paint than you need for one coat and store the remainder in a jar sealed with clingfilm [Saran wrap]. Follow the flat paint with two or three coats of the transparent red paint. Rub down all but the first two coats of paint using wet-or-dry paper and soapy water for the finest, smoothest surface. Now give two coats of orange shellac diluted half and half with methylated spirit [denatured alcohol]. This seals off the red body colour, allowing more play with the dark glaze.

GLAZE Before streaking, wipe down the red surfaces with a cloth pad dipped in vinegar or white spirit [mineral spirit] to remove grease and fingermarks. Dip the brush bristle tips into the glaze and test on a piece of paper for colour and consistency. More burnt umber will make a warmer colour, but remember the red base is going to show through the dark streaks. Streak the glaze on by drawing the bristles firmly over the red ground to give even, dark, fairly parallel stripes. Cover the whole surface in this way. You will find the glaze easy to manipulate, drying slowly enough to allow bits to be gone over again until the graining effects looks right. Don't aim for a ruled regularity – a little build-up of glaze on corners, or where strokes overlap helps give a naturalistic effect. Leave glaze to dry and harden for 24 hours, then smooth in the direction of the graining with fine steel wool and soapy water. This leaves a dulled, sleek surface.

VARNISH Apply two coats of clear gloss varnish. Rub the second coat over with steel wool and soapy water and polish with a soft cloth when dry.

QUICK METHOD Fast rosewood graining for less precious pieces requires only three coats of flat red paint, followed by the dark streaked glaze brushed over the red ground and two coats of clear gloss varnish. The transparent and shellac stages can be left out altogether from the rosewood graining method.

A detail of a once plain tool box given the rosewood graining treatment. Over this was added gilding, using decorative stencils and metallic powder, in an elaborate pattern taken from an Ottoman textile.

VINEGAR PAINTING

This intriguingly named technique (also known as putty graining) is one of many devised by busy country craftsmen of the nineteenth century to meet the increasing demand for 'fancy graining' on furniture and woodwork. Compared with the convincing wood effects produced by master grainers, vinegar painting was a wild parody, but it was quick and easy to do, and the materials were few, cheap and handy. The irony is that to modern eyes the early American pieces in this vigorous style, with their bold patterning, often look more attractive than the top-class work.

It remains a beguilingly simple method of decorating large, flat surfaces rapidly, and looks prettiest in purely decorative colour mixtures: black on white, dark over light blue, dark over light green, or any of these colours over off-white. It is a technique that one can really have fun with, since the vinegar medium takes clear, bold impressions of almost anything that comes to hand – a cork, a roll of modelling clay [modelling dough] or the putty traditionally used, crumpled paper or fingerprints. The more playful and bizarre the effects, the better they look, especially on large pieces like chests and dressers, where tight, repetitive patterns could look monotonous. For small things like trays, boxes or table-lampstands, elegant little patterns can easily be built up with close-printed impressions made with a cork or a blob of modelling clay.

There is plenty of time to experiment in the 15 or so minutes before the colour dries, and if you do not like what you have done, you can easily wash it all off again. Vinegar-painted pieces, like all those finished in watercolour, need thorough varnishing as a final protection and to bring up the finish.

Preparation The piece to be vinegar-painted should be finished in flat paint, in the required colour, and when dry rubbed smooth with fine wet-or-dry paper and soapy water. Mid-sheen paint can be used instead, but it should be rubbed down thoroughly to cut the sheen.

Materials Vinegar and sugar (the traditional grainer's alternative to vinegar and sugar was flat beer – by all means use that if you have it to hand); a squeeze of detergent; dry powder colour: if you cannot get artists' quality powder pigment, children's poster colours will do; two jam jars; standard decorators brush; sundry objects with which to make patterns: for example, a cork, modelling clay [modelling dough] or putty, cardboard cut into comb shapes, a rag or crumpled paper.

Method Mix half a cupful of malt vinegar and a squeeze of detergent in one jam jar. Put some powder colour and a little sugar in the second. Add a little of the vinegar and blend it to a paste, then pour in the rest and mix the whole lot together thoroughly.

A △

Malachite is one of the most impressive-looking decorative stones, with its vivid colouring and instantly recognizable markings. It was a favourite with the Czars, who had a soft spot for gilt consoles with malachite tops. The stone is rare and expensive, which has encouraged painters to develop a *faux* version. Surprisingly perhaps, malachite is quite a simple finish to do; the most important thing is to have some visual references to consult – photographs of a large slab of stone – to get the hang of its markings. The stripy, interlocking curves need to be done boldly and decisively; there are no fuzzy or indeterminate areas in a piece of malachite.

Malachite comes in a range of greens and blue-greens. The glaze shown here (A) has been made up of viridian green, mixed into an oil glaze. The glaze is thicker than usual – 60–70% transparent oil glaze [glazing liquid] to 30–40% white spirit [mineral spirit]. The base colour used here was a pale turquoise vinyl silk emulsion [latex] from a commercial range.

The base colour is covered with the blue-green glaze, brushed on with a standard brush. Then with the special fan brush, the characteristic curving stripes are described in the wet glaze (B). Some painters use the torn edge of a piece of cardboard instead, pulling this through the wet glaze to make random stripes.

The finish looks more convincing if the malachite colour varies a little here and there. Make up variations on the basic glaze by mixing it with a little white or yellow. With a fine brush, add touches of these to some of the thicker stripes. Mix up a much darker version of the basic glaze by adding more viridian, and use this to darken some of the finer stripes. Soften lightly across the stripes, to make 'peaks' (C). Varnish with polyurethane varnish.

B △   **C** ▽

Test the colour on a piece of paper. Hold it vertical for a minute or two – if the mixture runs in 'curtains', it is too thick – dilute with more vinegar and test again.

Before you get to work on your piece in earnest, spend a few minutes experimenting with different effects: brush a little mixture onto it and try stamping, combing and cross-combing (for a woven effect), dabbing with crumpled rag or paper or printing with a roll of modelling clay [modeling dough] to leave delicate whorls.

When you have hit on an effective combination, wipe the surface clean again with a rag moistened with plain vinegar. Then brush the vinegar mixture over a large area and begin making your patterns. Its slow drying-speed leaves enough time for patterning an area as large as a dresser door or the side of a chest, but if the colour begins to dry out and gets harder to work, simply brush more vinegar mixture over it, and start that bit afresh. The real problem is knowing when to stop, and being sufficiently disciplined to impose a coherent design over the whole piece. Brushed out finely, the vinegar solution makes a pleasant semi-transparent wash in itself, which can be used to create restful areas among the patterns.

Varnishing   When the vinegar paint is quite dry, in about an hour, varnish it overall with clear semi-gloss or gloss polyurethane varnish (not water-based)– two or three coats on a piece that will not get much handling, four or five on a piece that will. Rub down the last coat lightly with wet-or-dry paper lubricated with soapy water, followed, if you like, by a rub with rottenstone and oil (see page 164). Polish it with a soft cloth for a mellow shine.

MALACHITE

This is a bold, vivid finish that looks handsome as a table top, and gives a precious look to smaller objects such as lamps or obelisks.

Preparation   The base colour is a clear pale greeny blue. It can be painted in two coats of oil- or water-based eggshell, or three of vinyl silk emulsion [latex].

Materials   Transparent oil glaze [glazing liquid]; white spirit [mineral spirit]; artists' oil colours in viridian, oxide of chromium green, yellow ochre, white; a fan brush, from specialist suppliers, to create the distinctively contoured stripy curves; a fine sable (No. 2 or No. 3) brush for fine detail; softening brush.

Method   Mix up a light, vivid blue-green glaze with the two greens, using transparent oil glaze [glazing liquid] and white spirit [mineral spirit], to a single cream consistency. Put blobs of all the oil colours on a plate. With the fan brush dipped into the glaze start drawing in scalloped curves, like chinoiserie 'clouds', as shown. Overlap these, irregularly, until the surface is covered. With the fine brush, mix a little of the various oil colours into the basic glaze and touch in patches or strips of more vivid green or paler blue green. These can be gone over again with the fan brush to blend them, or gently softened in all directions with the softening brush for a hint of blur – not too much because this is a clearly marked stone.

Use the fine brush to 'tweak' the jags on the scallop shapes into little wispy peaks. Leave it to dry for 24 hours. Finally, varnish with one or two coats of mid-sheen polyurethane varnish.

TORTOISESHELLING

The tortoiseshell finish described on pages 119–121 is a stylized effect especially suited to larger surfaces, with its strong directional-flow and slightly exaggerated markings. For furniture the whole effect needs scaling down and simplifying if it is to be a background for further decoration. There are several traditional methods of achieving the rich tones and varied markings of the natural shell, in which varnish stain is a key ingredient. Other 'fantasy' tortoiseshell finishes can be achieved with oil glazes.

STAIN VARNISH TORTOISESHELL

A bold and stunning finish, streaky black and red tortoiseshelling was often found on early American japanned pieces. It looks superb under gilt decoration, raised or flat, and is best used on furniture, not on walls, where it would be overpowering.

The technique is based on the standard one for tortoiseshell. Where possible, paint a horizontal surface, laying cupboards and so forth on their backs or sides on the floor. It is possible to work on a vertical surface, but you will not have the same level of control, and it is considerably less comfortable.

Paint one surface at a time and try to see each surface as part of a whole, so that the black and red streaks carry on parallel over drawer fronts and doors.

Use dark bronze powder for gilding on top of it, antiqued with earth-coloured glazes (see page 168), but reserve this finish for suitably aristocratic pieces.

Preparation

The ground should be smoothly painted with a strong, opaque orange-red. American readers can buy japan colour in just the right shade; otherwise, it can be achieved by tinting flat or mid-sheen oil-based paint with universal stainers [tinting colours] or artists' oil colours in raw sienna and scarlet.

Materials

Dark oak gloss varnish stain: this is an essential ingredient – nothing else has the right consistency to stop the streaks running all over the place; black artists' oil colour; pointed artists' brush; 50 mm [2 in] decorators' paintbrush; a wider, clean, dry decorators' brush; white spirit [mineral spirit]; paper tissues.

A variety of tortoiseshell finishes are shown here: old red and black (top), which makes a striking, dramatic finish; shades of amber and brown (centre), dabbed onto a pea-green base to make 'islands', creating an elegant and unusual veneer; and blonde tortoiseshell over metal leaf (below), creating a lustrous effect.

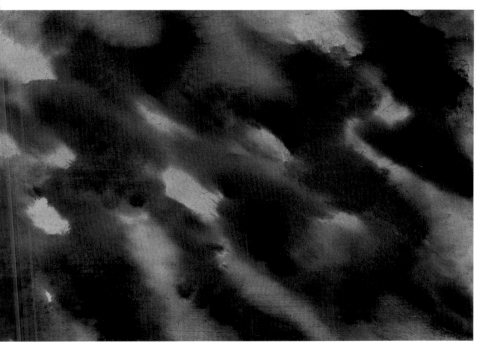

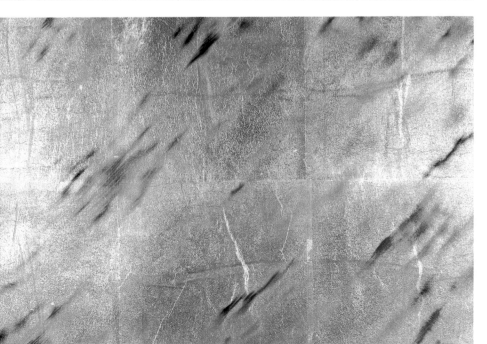

This rich effect is an excellent choice for a precious finish on small items, such as picture frames, mirrors and boxes. It looks especially glamorous applied over gold or silver base (here, gold), for which less expensive Dutch metal and aluminium transfer leaf are perfectly acceptable substitutes.

Method   Dilute the varnish stain, about one part white spirit to two parts varnish. Paint this over the surface. It will bubble excitedly. Fidget the brush diagonally over the wet surface, or dab with crumpled paper tissue, to distress it and remove any surplus varnish. Mix a little varnish stain into the black oil colour, and streak it into the wet surface with a pointed artists' brush, using a sideways rolling motion and jerking it a little as you go, to produce highly irregular black streaks roughly 5 cm [2 in] apart, which follow a parallel course in the same direction as the diagonals.

Leave to harden for just a minute or two. Then with the tips of a clean, dry brush, stroke the black streaks gently in the direction in which they were painted, teasing them out to give wispy ends. Some of the wet black will flow out over the red. Now stroke the streaks in the opposite diagonal direction. This opens them out and merges some together. Do not go on until all the original red has been darkened over. The colour ratio in this technique should be about three-fifths of the surface black and two-fifths thinned black fading into shaded red. Leave the finish to dry hard before applying further decoration.

Varnishing   Further varnishing is not mandatory, but for a more alluring surface, varnish, rub down and polish in the usual way (see pages 168–169). Do not rub down the tortoiseshell surface itself, or you may leave scars.

OIL GLAZE TORTOISESHELL   This effect imitates the furniture created by the French cabinetmaker, Boulle, in which a transparent veneer of tortoiseshell was laid over a green or red ground, usually in conjunction with polished wood and a good deal of ormolu for contrast. The same method is used for both green and red tortoiseshell, although the base and glaze colours are different.

The approach used here differs from the standard tortoiseshell as the colours are laid into a thin coat of transparent oil glaze, which dries more slowly than the varnish stain, allowing more time for adjusting, improving or correcting.

For green tortoiseshell, the surface should be given two coats of a mid-green eggshell or vinyl silk emulsion [latex] paint. The green colour should not be too bright but naturalistic; a cool pea green, obtained by adding a little white or cerulean blue to pea green, is about the right shade of green. The golden shellac will warm the overall hue at the end.

Materials   Transparent oil glaze [glazing liquid]; white spirit [mineral spirit]; artists oil colours in burnt umber, raw sienna, burnt sienna, and black; a standard paintbrush and soft fitch to apply initial glazes; fine No. 5 or No. 6 watercolour brush for smaller details; softening brush; white plate for mixing colours.

Method Thin oil glaze with white spirit [mineral spirit], tint with a little burnt umber, and brush out evenly over the whole surface to be tortoiseshelled. Tip some of this basic glaze into the middle of a plate, put dabs of the other colours round the rim, and mix these into the glaze as you go along.

Start with the lightest islands using some of the basic glaze warmed with raw sienna and burnt sienna. Dab at random on the diagonal over the surface. Soften. Mix up a darker glaze with more burnt umber and dab this on top of or in between the first patches, still at random. Soften, to blend some areas into each other. Mix a brown-black glaze with burnt umber and a dot of black. Use the watercolour brush to make a few little dark streaks, squiggles and blotches here and there within the previous 'islands'. Soften.

Leave to dry, then coat with orange shellac thinned with methylated spirit [denatured alcohol] or with a mid-sheen varnish lightly tinted with raw sienna (burnt-umber) artists' oil colour.

For red tortoiseshell, paint the surface with two coats of a scarlet red eggshell or vinyl silk emulsion [latex]. The method is as given for green tortoiseshell on the previous page. The materials are as for green tortoiseshell but artists' oil colours should be in burnt umber, burnt sienna and black.

TORTOISESHELL OVER
METAL LEAF On small objects – boxes, frames, trays – where a rich effect is not going to be overwhelming, tortoiseshell mottling over shiny metal leaf looks beautiful. Aluminium leaf makes a cheap and satisfactory substitute for the traditional silver leaf, while Dutch metal can pass for gold. The object to be leafed should have as smooth a surface as possible.

Materials Aluminium [aluminum] or Dutch metal transfer leaf – as many sheets as you need to cover the object, with a little over; goldsize, on which to apply the leaf; dark oak gloss varnish stain; burnt umber and black oil colours; 50 mm [2 in] decorators' paint brush; a wider, clean dry decorators' brush; pointed artists' brush; cotton wool [absorbent cotton].

Method See pages 206–207 for how to apply metal leaf. When it is dry, smooth and burnished, give it a coat of bleached shellac. When quite dry, it is ready for tortoiseshelling, which is done as described on pages 119–121. Do not fret if the overlapped squares of leaf are discerned through the final finish – this is hard to avoid and has its own appeal. But do smooth off any irregularities in the leaf. For a darkly glowing effect, try doubling up the technique – just enough of the silver shows through to give cool depth, like moonlight filtered through cloud.

LACQUERING

True Oriental lacquer ware, made from the milky sap of the lac tree, must qualify as the most painstaking finish ever devised. Built up through as many as 40 separate layers, each rubbed and polished smooth with a paste of oil and bone ash applied with the fingers, it is the hardest, most lustrous surface imaginable, so rich to the eye that it looks at its most handsome unadorned.

Not surprisingly, when examples of this superb craftsmanship reached the West, European craftsmen were soon earnestly trying to imitate the prized imported wares. More confusion arose when an identically named but intrinsically different resin, 'lac' made from secretions of an insect, *Coccus lacca*, reached the West. After processing, this became 'seedlac', which we now call shellac, an ultra-fast-drying resinous varnish differing from other varnishes in being soluble only in alcohol. By combining paint with shellac, Western craftsmen came up with a variety of technically incorrect, but aesthetically pleasing, pseudolacquers, which they called japan. Wooden pieces were smoothly primed, painted and decorated, often lavishly gilded, and finished with many coats of shellac, to simulate the depth and richness of the Oriental wares. Japanned wares bore a superficial resemblance to their eastern models, but as time passed and innovators added further refinements, the pieces developed a style and charm of their own.

The lesson to be learned from studying examples of old lacquer and japanning is that it is quite possible to emulate their warmth of colour and patina by painting a piece in suitable colours, decorating it with Oriental-inspired motifs, and finishing it with as many coats of varnish or bleached shellac as you have the patience to apply. The result may be only a pastiche of a pastiche, but it is still extravagantly pretty. The more effort you put into it – gilt or bronze powder decoration, streaky tortoiseshell ground, stencilled or hand-painted scenes, tinted varnishes – the more sumptuous the final result. At the opposite extreme, you could explore a modern, starkly simple lacquer effect, relying on brilliant glazed colours and many coats of rubbed-down clear gloss varnish.

Furniture of a plain, strong shape is the best choice for these gorgeous lacquer treatments. Modern-style lacquer looks especially good on dining chairs, cabinets and coffee tables. The wood beneath does not have to be anything special: the tattiest veneered blockboard by the time it has been gessoed, decorated and varnished to the nines is adequate, so long as the structure is sturdy enough to stand up to wear and tear. The tender loving care that goes into creating this finish, demands decent joinery and careful preparation. I once did a 'japanned' finish on a little reproduction desk, in a hurry, for photography. I skimped on the preparation and as a result the lovely pond-green finish is chipping off in places. Therefore, if you want to achieve a truly authentic eighteenth-century finish, the moral is, spend as much time on the surface preparation as they did.

below A cheap wooden box has been given the works with modelling paste, gold paints, bronze powders, Dutch metal transfer leaf and chinoiserie designs.

bottom The top of this eighteenth-century lacquered table has been given a witty contemporary trompe l'oeil treatment, then topped with coats of shellac for further shine.

Preparation   Fast-drying acrylic gesso greatly improves the surface of open-grained or inferior wood and adds to the final appearance of your handiwork. Unless the wood you are working on is fine-grained and smooth, in which case it need only be under-coated, give the piece four or five coats of acrylic gesso, or all-purpose filler [spackle] watered-down to paint consistency (see pages 154–156). When it is dry, rub each coat down with medium steel wool or medium sandpaper. Aim for bone-hard smoothness. When the last coat of gesso is dry, brush shellac, diluted with one part methylated spirit [denatured alcohol] to two parts shellac, over the piece.

Materials for black lacquer   Flat black oil-based paint, bought at any ironmongers or hardware store; burnt umber artists' oil colour; gloss polyurethane varnish; brush; wet-or-dry paper.

Method   The first two or three coats should be of flat black paint, the last one rubbed down with wet-or-dry paper and soapy water. For the subsequent two coats, mix five parts flat black paint with one part burnt umber and half a part gloss varnish. Rub these two coats down in the same way.

At this stage the lacquer may be gilded or otherwise decorated.

VARNISHING If you want a warm black, add a little burnt umber artists' oil colour, or dark oak varnish stain, to the last of your two or three coats of protective polyurethane gloss varnish. Each coat of varnish should be rubbed down and the final one polished with rottenstone (see page 164) – for a higher lustre, wax it and polish with a soft cloth.

Materials for red lacquer   Flat white oil-based paint; vermilion artists' oil colour or universal stainer [tinting colour] or, for American readers, orange-red japan colour, to colour the ground coat; white spirit [mineral spirit]; gloss polyurethane varnish; crimson and burnt sienna artists' oil colours for top coats; wet-or-dry paper.

Method   Mix the red oil colour, stainer or japan colour with just enough white spirit [mineral spirit] and flat white paint to give a little body and flow without making the colour too chalky. Paint the piece with two or three coats of this, rubbing down with wet-or-dry paper after the first two. For the next two coats, make a rich transparent paint by substituting gloss varnish for the flat white paint, and adding a squeeze of crimson and burnt sienna oil colours. This changes the effect of the opaque vermilion beneath quite astonishingly. A fast-fix version of this red lacquer effect uses a water-based paint (Really Red Woodwash, available from Paint Magic shops) as a base, which is then shellached with button polish to give a deep red-orange tone, antique glazed and finally varnished with polyurethane varnish.

VARNISHING If the red is too bright, it can be softened before final varnishing by applying a thin burnt umber wash or glaze, or by spattering it with sepia or black ink. Alternatively, your two or three coats of protective gloss varnish – thinned three parts varnish to two of white spirit [mineral spirit] – could be tinted, as above, with a little burnt umber artists' oil colour or dark oak varnish stain, and rubbed down and finished in the same way.

Other lacquer colours

As well as the classic black and vermilion, japanned furniture exhibited a wide range of colours – white, sharp yellow, olive, chestnut, blue and purple. The glow and brilliance of the final effect is greatly enhanced by brushing on a tinted varnish or, even more subtle, a glaze, in a slightly different tone of the ground colour. This can be brushed solidly over the ground, or dragged on with a brush in fine stripes, so that the two colours interact more vibrantly. Thus a ground of flat yellow – made by mixing Indian yellow into flat white – is sharpened by a glaze of chrome yellow or yellow lake; a blue ground of cobalt in flat white is made brilliant by glazing with Prussian blue or ultramarine. Spattering lightly 'antiques' effectively.

DECOUPAGE

Decoupage (cut out, in French) is simply a clever decorative short cut, that gives the appearance of lavish surface decoration by means of pasted-on coloured paper images. It is rooted in Italian *arte povera*, or poor man's art, of the seventeenth and eighteenth centuries. Threatened commercially by the deliciously exotic imported oriental lacquer ware, and also by japanning, Italian craftsmen (ever responsive to style and fashion) devised this relatively rapid and highly effective simulacrum, using printed images, where chinoiserie mingles with idealized rustic lovers, flowers, and other elements, which were hand-coloured before gluing in place. At first glance, heavily varnished to 'lose' the cut paper silhouettes, these have much of the gaiety and brio of their seriously costly equivalents. At second look, they are charmingly different, with a lighthearted appeal of their own. Genuine *arte povera* pieces are collectibles, with a ready market.

Self-taught craft

But this is an area of decoration where anyone can safely have a go, and where the most deft-handed work, and imaginative assembling and pasting, can transform a painted item into something colourful, pretty or chic, without years of art school training. Most of the commercial decoupage I have seen is the work of self-taught craftspeople who have taken time to learn this decorative skill, which is not to suggest that a painted box, pasted with a cut-out flower motif, or a gleeful monkey, will be saleable. As with all simple notions, attention to detail when pasting-on the coloured paper images in imaginative groupings and overlaying the

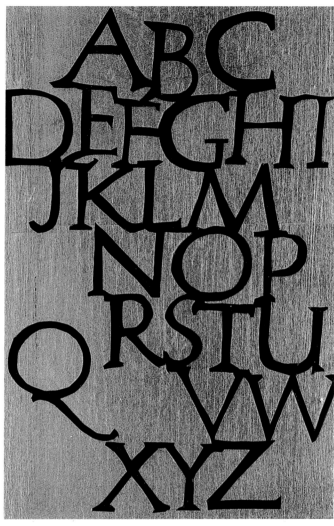

Decoupage is still appreciated as a decorative means with wide design possibilities. There is no lack of printed images available via books, photocopies, magazines. Recent trends incline towards a naturalistic play of fruiting branches, or higgledy-piggledy lettering, which break new ground decoratively.

layers of clear varnish, care in finishing, and an eye for appealing arrangements, make all the difference between heavy-handed decoupage work and something elegant and individual.

The first flush of interest in decoupage was highly 'pretty', majoring on flowers, butterflies and cupids; all the images were readily available in books of decoupage motifs. This led to a 'sameness' that devalued the craft.

New developments

Recently, there has been a distinct move in decoupage circles towards less colourful motifs – black-and-white prints, or one-colour *Toile de Jouy*-type motifs look fresh and appealing. There is also more use of decorative detailing, such as coloured or gilt 'lining', craquelure varnish finishes and hand-painted lettering. All these, lining especially, require practice, and a confidently free brushwork that looks professional.

LINING

Lining in a contrasting colour is used to trim painted furniture, to underline and strengthen its contours and to draw attention to decorative details. Traditionally the lining decoration used depended on the type of furniture to be painted. On curvy French and Italian provincial pieces, wide bands of watery thin colour edged table tops and chair frames. On the whippet-slim pieces by such eighteenth-century designers as Robert Adam, the lining had a calligraphic tautness. But it was on coachwork, the supreme test of a painter's skill, that lining displayed the utmost in slender precision – all of it executed freehand with a control and accuracy born of years of practice and experience.

Wide decorative edge lining looks tremendous even when painted quite crudely, but to paint immaculately fine lining freehand, you require confidence, practice and a steady wrist. However, there are ways of cheating to get a similar effect which are worth experimenting with. Applying an intervening coat of clear varnish or thinned white shellac allows botched lines to be wiped off and redrawn. A straight-edge used with a lining fitch or a fine sable brush enables one to produce satisfactory straight lines on flat surfaces; I have even known professional decorators who simply use a felt-tip pen.

Preparation

Lining is applied toward the end, after the glazing has been done, but before antiquing (see pages 167–170). This makes for crisper definition. The smoother the paint surface, the more fluently the painted lines will flow. If you are unsure of your brushwork, apply a barrier coat first (see page 161) before lining.

Materials

PAINT AND BRUSHES For transparent, watery edge lining, use artists' gouache or acrylic colour diluted in a little water. To help paint to stay put, add a drop of detergent. This effect is best suited to matt-finished pieces.

For fine lining, professional decorators generally use artists' oil colour dissolved in a little white spirit [mineral spirit] and mixed with clear varnish for body. Indian ink gives fine, distinct black lines but should be applied over a varnish barrier coat since it can be very difficult to remove. If you do have to remove it, wipe it off with a rag moistened with methylated spirit [denatured alcohol].

For broad edging lines, use a No. 6 sable artists' brush, for fine lines, a No. 3 sable brush. Professional decorators often use a swordliner (see page 231), because the curved, tapering bristles give greater control.

OTHER EQUIPMENT You will also need the appropriate solvent for your paint; rags or cotton wool [absorbent cotton] swabs; a saucer for mixing colour; a notched piece of card (optional), to keep a measured line even; a lining fitch; felt-tip pens; a straight-edge.

Method Make sure that the piece is placed at a convenient and comfortable height, and that the surface is stable. A low table, with solid legs, makes an ideal platform for painting most items.

Test the paint mixture on a board, to get the feel of your lining brush, and to check that the paint flows nicely and that the colour is sufficiently intense. Do not overload the brush, or your neat line may blob if you press harder. The thickness of the line depends on your hand pressure as well as on the width of the brush itself. Stand a little way back, hold the brush quite far up the handle, and draw with a steady, relaxed sweeping movement, your eye travelling ahead of your brush. Hesitation leads to wobbles and breaks in continuity.

Correct any mistakes after you have reached an obvious break but before the paint hardens. If the paint has set, leave it to dry thoroughly, then gently rub it away with fine steel wool and retouch lines with a light hand. Rubbing down will soften less than perfect lining.

EDGE LINING Chunky folk pieces often look good with really emphatic edge lining, anything from 12 to 25 mm [½ to 1 in] wide. It is the easiest kind to do, because you can use your little finger to guide the brush. Use a notched card to make little paint marks all the way along before painting, to keep the width of the band even. Slight variations do not matter.

Water-thinned paints produce delicate faded-looking lines, appropriate to antique pieces, but take care when retouching them, because thin colour builds up fast if you go over the same spot too often.

Along straight edges a helpful 'cheat' is to set a boundary of masking tape at the requisite distance in from the edge. Peel it off immediately after painting each section, for a clean edge. To keep the old and faded look, the paint should be matt, but not so thick it builds a raised line, and the piece can be finished with matt varnish.

FINE LINING This is usually painted a little way inside the edge of a piece, following the curves of a chair back or the taper of a flat chair leg. A chair back is best tackled with the chair laid on its back at normal table height, where it can be approached from three sides. Paint the inner surfaces first so that you won't smudge one line as you lean across to tackle another.

It is no good pretending that it is easy to paint a fine line freehand. However, confidence quickly grows with practice. Give the surface a coat of thinned shellac or clear varnish first, and strike out boldly in the knowledge that mistakes can be wiped off with cotton wool [absorbent cotton] moistened in solvent once you have completed the section; touch up the fine lines when they are dry.

BAMBOOING

Bamboo was one of the key materials in vogue during the eighteenth-century fashion for chinoiserie. Cheap and commonplace in the Orient, bamboo was both scarce and expensive in the West. It was not long before craftsmen were producing imitation bamboo from turned and carved wood. Made, as a rule, of inferior wood, this was painted in increasingly fantastic colours.

Most imitation bamboo kept to certain conventions. Prominent knots at the intersections were emphasized with painted lines in one, two or even three colours, and the same colours were used to add the little eyes and tapering spines characteristic of natural bamboo. The hand-painted detail would sometimes be done in discreetly complementary colours – grey-green on yellow buff, for instance – sometimes in flamboyant contrasts like pink on white, or black and gold on vermilion.

Bambooing adds colour and fantasy to a simple painted piece, breaking up uniformly coloured surfaces in a decorative and witty fashion. First candidates are are any pieces in turned imitation bamboo. Choose emphatic colour schemes for the elegant shapes that can take it – black, red, cockatoo pinks and greens – with bambooing in lighter, contrasting colours. For pieces with only a little turned bamboo decoration – on chair backs and legs, round table tops and drawers – stick to neutrals and discreet colours: sepia on buff, green on yellow, dark green or brown on green and any middle-tones on cream.

Any simple, rounded wooden moulding can be smartened up with a stylized bamboo treatment. Frames on mirrors, or screens, simple bedsteads, small tables with plain, round legs – once your eye is receptive, it is easy to pick out pieces that will gain from this treatment.

Bambooing can also be used to freshen up those spotted turn-of-the century pieces, made of real bamboo varnished and scorched to produce a brown mottling. It would be a pity to paint fine examples, but there are many inferior pieces that would look all the better for cleaning, rubbing down and painting in a restrained colour combination.

There are two main techniques for bambooing (see opposite). The first, picking out in colour, can be used only where the bamboo knots, or knobbly joints, are present – either on turned wood or genuine bamboo. The decoration consists of picking out the knots with fine lines and adding painted eyes and spines.

The second technique is bamboo striping, which can be used on plain round mouldings, with graduated rings – in tones of the same colour – painted one on top of the other. Pieces painted in greyish-white, bamboo-striped in pink, blue, green look fresh and pretty. Shades of sepia on a straw-coloured ground, echoing natural bamboo colours, look especially effective on plain round mouldings. Over dark colours, paint bamboo striping in light, sludgy colours like white tinted with raw umber, raw sienna or yellow ochre.

A turn-of-the-century junk-shop find, bamboo-striped in tinted and thinned varnish. The wicker surfaces are painted freehand in different shades of blue-green.

Preparation A sleek ground coat, applied over a smooth surface (see pages 152–157). Use at least three coats of undercoat or flat oil-based paint, tinted to your chosen colour, thinly applied and gently rubbed down with fine wet-or-dry paper and soapy water.

Materials For picking out in colour, choose fast-drying paints with good opacity, such as acrylic or japan colours. Flat oil-based paint tinted with universal stainers [tinting colours] or artists' oils can also be used, but will take many hours to dry.

For bamboo striping, use fast-drying transparent paint made by tinting clear varnish with artists' oils or universal stainers [tinting colours], dissolved first in a little white spirit [mineral spirit]. The proportions of solvent to varnish are about half and half for the palest stripe colour, ranging to one teaspoon of solvent to one table-spoon varnish for the darkest tone. The palest stripe should be transparently thin; over a dark colour it must contain some white pigment to show up sufficiently.

You also need fine, pointed sable artists' brushes, No. 3 and No. 6, for painting details; a square-cut oxhair artists' brush for stroking on transparent colour and, for bamboo striping, two standard decorators' paintbrushes or fat soft-bristled artists' brushes 12 mm [½ in] and 17 mm [¾ in] wide; rags; saucers for mixing.

Picking out in colour Mix up a little paint in a saucer, opaque enough to cover the ground colour, but thin enough to flow smoothly from the brush.

With the No. 6 brush, paint a neat band of colour round each knot. Fine spines and speckled eyes may be painted in with the No. 3 sable brush. The spines should be painted with two curving lines joining to form a delicate spike, not more than a third of the bamboo section in length. In nature the 'eyes' appear either side of the spine, slightly oval dots, surrounded by tiny freckles of colour. Paint a few sparingly on the more prominent sections, placing them asymmetrically.

Bamboo striping The widest stripe is painted in the lightest tone of your transparent paint, usually about 25 mm [1 in] wide, using the wider brush. Centre it over the bamboo knot (or where a knot would be), and paint a smooth ring of the thinnest possible colour around it. Paint all the wide rings on the piece, and wait a moment for them to dry. Now tint the paint a few tones darker, and paint a second narrower ring in the centre of the wide ones, about 12 mm [½ in] wide. Then make the remaining paint dark and, using the No. 3 brush, paint in a slender central ring, about 6 mm [¼ in] wide. You can also use this darkest tone to paint in eyes, and for lining on chair backs and table legs. When dry, you can brush or drag on a darker tinted varnish.

Varnishing When completely dry, give the whole piece two protective coats of clear matt varnish. To add a soft sheen, give it a light coat of soft, colourless wax.

PAINTING IN WATERCOLOUR

One unexpected spin-off of the current interest in fast, water-based paint for furniture is a revival of the gentle art of decorating furniture with flowers and motifs in watercolour, practised by young ladies in the eighteenth century. Experienced furniture painters often use watercolour in its simplest dried form, the little blocks or pans one associates with school art classes. Others will find it easier to work with gouache colours dissolved in gum arabic, a clear fluid with a gluey consistency which brushes out smoothly and as transparently as needed, but which can be overpainted with less risk of 'lifting'. Two points need emphasizing in connection with watercolour decoration. First, a pale base colour – cream or ivory, or a gentle pastel – is best suited to transparent decoration, as it will not affect the colours used over it to any great extent. On mid or darker shades it is first necessary to 'white out' the motifs, with white acrylic tube colour, or acrylic gesso. Secondly, because the watercolour is so fine and fragile, it is essential to seal it immediately on completion, before proceeding to any antiquing or further varnishing. Use a clear spray varnish for this, just on the watercolour work itself.

Materials

Gouache colours, which come in a wide colour range and are available from most artists' suppliers – they are very concentrated, so small tubes go a long way; gum arabic, sold in small bottles; white paper, or a white plate for mixing colours; brushes – soft, pointed watercolour brushes are esential, in fine, medium and fatter sizes, and one soft, flat-ended brush is useful for petals; a can of clear spray varnish, which can now be obtained in 'green' formulations, without aerosol; chalk. You will find that sable brushes are the most resilient, squirrel is satisfactory, and synthetics are cheap but apt to lose their shape.

Clean brushes well, and never leave them standing in a jar of water; to preserve their shape run them over a cake of soap before twisting back into a point after cleaning. Wash out soap before reusing.

Motifs and designs

Watercolour is perfect for floral subjects, and there are innumerable sources of inspiration for these, from botanical prints to postcards and stationery, painted china, chintzes, wallpapers and borders. In some ways it is easier to transpose from existing designs than it is to copy nature, but this is up to you.

Other appealing subjects might be seashells, feathers, birds and butterflies or cherubs. Simple lines look soft and pretty when painted in watercolour, perhaps just as an outline, or crisscrossing to form a lattice. Rococo curlicues and scrolls, and blue-and-white chinoiserie motifs are other possibilities. A browse round the postcard section of a good museum should give you lots of ideas, cheaply. But don't aim too high to begin with: choose a simple motif and leave the design understated.

opposite Watercolour decoration over a chalky gesso base creates the attractively worn and 'threadbare' effect of this small panel of birds and foliage.

Method First chalk in the main outlines of the design. Then begin by painting the midtones: pink, for rose petals, mid-green for leaves, for example. Next add darker accents, a touch of crimson (always diluted in gum arabic on either paper or your plate palette) or for leaves, a green 'dirtied' with raw umber or burnt umber. Tip a little gum arabic into the middle of the plate, with your dabs of gouache around the rim, and play with different combinations and intensities of colour. For highlights mix a little white into the mid tones; highlights should be added sparingly at first, since the white will tend to make the colours more opaque. Next stand back, half-close your eyes and decide whether you have the balance right – perhaps the pink roses need a little warmth of tone, a nuance of burnt sienna. Or the leaves might enjoy a faded yellowish tone. Add details such as leaf veins, thorns and stamens with a fine brush. A delicate shadowing around a motif, in one of the umbers much diluted in gum arabic, will help throw it into relief. Bear in mind that painted decoration of this kind is properly playing a supportive role, not clamouring for any attention. It should enrich a piece visually, but not compete for primacy. Effective watercolour decoration can be done in tones of one colour.

When the decoration is thoroughly dry to the touch, spray varnish to seal it. Then wash over with an antiquing colour or finish it with craquelure (pages 173–174); both effects help to 'tie in' the decoration to the background and enhance a piece of furniture, suggesting a look of casual elegance. On the whole this sort of work looks best given an unobtrusive varnish finish, in matt or eggshell.

GILDING

Something of a mystique surrounds the art of gilding – understandably, in view of the expense and fragility of true gold leaf, and the elaborate technique involved in traditional water gilding. The current price of gold leaf certainly puts it outside the reach of amateur furniture decorators – there is no fun in experimenting with a material so expensive that every mistake hurts.

Other ways of adding a rich metallic gleam to a painted surface use lesser metals in the form of transfer leaf or metallic powders. These are cheaper, easier to apply, and can be boosted with various professional tricks to give a pleasing suggestion of the real thing.

Fake gold materials look best treated in a throwaway fashion, distressed to let red ground colour show through and then antiqued with a raw or burnt umber wash or antiquing wax. Delicious effects can be obtained by using aluminium leaf or Dutch metal transfer leaf as a luminous ground for tortoiseshell finishes – a treatment that makes smaller objects like picture frames and boxes look precious. The simple gilding techniques described here are not so costly as to be inhibiting and can be confidently undertaken by any reasonably deft-fingered person.

Nothing becomes a handsome old painted piece so well as details picked out in burnished gold leaf. Gold on white is a favourite neo-classical mix, especially contrasted, as here, with dark green.

203

METALLIC POWDERS

Though it has the sultry glow of antique gilding, this obelisk is new plaster covered with Dutch metal transfer leaf. The secret of its allure is distressing, which reveals some of the red base and a burnt umber rub.

Also confusingly known as 'bronze powders', metallic powders are available in a wide range of colours from silvery white to rich bronze gold – and look attractive when several colours are used together. Use them for stencilling, freehand decoration or spattering. They can be applied straight over a tacky surface, usually painted in a dark colour such as black or red to set off the metal, or over motifs filled in with a sympathetic colour, say yellow ochre or Venetian red, which enriches the metallic finish.

Metal powders tarnish, so should be varnished for protection. They look effective shaded with tinted varnish or antiquing glazes, to suggest patina and modelling. Knocking back the metallic gleam in this way makes the untreated areas, paradoxically, shine more brightly.

Neatness and patience are the chief requirements for handling metal powders. They are so light and clinging that some care is needed to stop them from going where they are not wanted.

Warning: Always wear a mask when working with fine, powdery materials – especially metallic ones.

Preparation Surfaces for powder decoration should be covered with opaque flat or mid-sheen paint. Rich, dark colours set it off best – brownish red, black, dull green, chestnut or fake tortoiseshell. The ground colour must be left to dry completely hard, without a hint of tackiness.

Nervous practitioners might like to give the surface a coat of clear semigloss varnish or thinned shellac; this not only allows more scope for correcting mistakes but will encourage even drying in the varnish subsequently used as a size. This barrier coat should be rubbed down lightly with very fine steel wool, and wiped clean with a rag moistened with white spirit [mineral spirit].

METALLIC POWDER STENCILS

This way of using metallic powders produces great subtlety of shading and highlight. Stencils and metal powders were traditionally used for lacy borders, but also make effective all-over patterns and large single motifs. The stencils should be neatly cut, since any raggedness shows more with powder than it does with paint, and should be small enough to be easily controlled. Press them flat before use – ironing with a warm iron over paper flattens them quickly.

Materials Stencils (see pages 73–79); metal powders; clear semi-gloss or gloss polyurethane varnish; small pieces of silk, velvet or chamois leather; varnish brush; small brush for shading; square-tipped artists' hogshair brush, for floating on colours; artists' oils, or japan colours for tinting varnish; saucers or plastic jam jar lids; paper to hold excess powder; rags; masking tape; spray adhesive holds stencils well.

Method   First varnish the entire surface with semi-gloss or gloss varnish. Leave this to dry until there is a just perceptible 'tack' left – if you press the stencil on a corner it should come off with a faint pull but leave no mark. The tacky varnish will act as a size or adhesive for the metal powders.

Tip a little powder into a saucer or jam jar lid – if you are using more than one powder, use a separate container for each one. Place your stencil on the varnished surface, masking off the surrounding area, if possible, with paper fixed with strips of masking tape. The stencils should cleave tightly to the surface or powder may seep underneath.

Wrap a piece of velvet or chamois leather round your index finger, adjusting it so no creases appear. Dip the covered finger into the powder, then rub it on a piece of spare paper to remove the excess – very little powder is needed at any time. Place your finger on what is to be the highlight of your stencil design and, starting from there, rotate it gently, to polish in the highlight. From there work outwards, lessening the finger pressure so that the solid highlights blend to a softer bloom at the edges. When you need to pick up more powder, use the surplus on your spare paper first.

Use a different piece of fabric for each powder colour. Pale colours can be shaded with a darker one – use the lighter shade as highlight, and blend the two colours gently into each other for a modelled effect.

When your motif is completed, lift up the stencil and move it along to the next spot; repeat in the same way until the design is complete. Leave the varnish to dry hard – this usually takes about 24 hours. Then wash it gently with soapy water and a rag to remove any loose powder. Any powder that has landed on the wrong areas can be rubbed off patiently with a cotton bud dipped in a little household scouring powder.

FLOATING ON COLOUR When the powder stencilling is dry and clean, brush on a barrier coat of bleached shellac, to give yourself leeway for experiment.

Floated colours are made by mixing a little artists' oil colour with clear polyurethane varnish. Apply this tinted varnish smoothly over the metallic motif with a soft, square-tipped artists' brush. Keep the colour intense in, say, the deeper folds of petals or the crease of a leaf, and thin it out over the rest. The effect should be very smooth and a little melodramatic. It does not matter if the floated colour goes over the edges, since being transparent it will scarcely show over a dark ground colour.

Use this technique with raw or burnt umbers or siennas, if you want to add richness to metallic decoration without too strong a contrast. Finish with many coats of bleached shellac.

TRANSFER METAL LEAF

This consists of squares of leaf mounted on sheets of waxed tissue, which come in booklets. It is much easier to handle and lay than loose leaf, which is so light and fragile that it readily disintegrates. The most suitable types for use on furniture are Dutch metal – an alloy that closely resembles gold in colour and gleam – and aluminium. The latter is considerably cheaper than silver, and can be coated with button polish (orange shellac) to imitate gold, or shaded with a little umber to suggest aged and tarnished silver.

Transfer leaf can be applied over small or large areas, as fine line trimming, and on raised or carved surfaces as well as flat ones. Once laid, it can be etched through with a sharp stylus or pointed instrument to reveal the paint colour beneath. It is not particularly difficult to lay – provided the degree of tackiness is right (see facing page), and the size accurately applied, it goes on as easily as any other type of transfer.

Preparation Cover surfaces with opaque flat or mid-sheen paint. The ground colour must be left to dry completely hard. You might like to give the surface a coat of clear semi-gloss varnish or thinned shellac, as you will be able to correct mistakes more easily. Rub down lightly with very fine steel wool, then wipe clean with a rag moistened with white spirit [mineral spirit].

Materials   Dutch metal or aluminium transfer leaf; quick-drying goldsize or 'Wundasize', and soft artists' brush in suitable size for applying it; soft cotton wool [absorbent cotton]; orange shellac [button polish] or diluted Indian ink.

Method   Use chalk to sketch out your design. Colour in the areas you intend for gilding or leafing, using ready-made red gesso or red casein paint [milk paint] for Dutch metal, and cobalt blue casein for silver/aluminium leaf. When dry, cover these areas thinly with goldsize or 'Wundasize'. The great advantage of the latter is its flexibility – it is ready for leafing after 20 minutes, but it is still tacky enough to work with up to 24 hours later. For standard gold size, follow the maker's instructions.

The leaf is more lustrous when laid at the right time – if the size is too wet, it will tend to look dull. The time this takes depends on the conditions in which you apply it and the type of size used; the way to be sure is to test it. Extract a sheet of waxed paper with leaf attached from the booklet, and turn it leaf side down on the sized area. Rub over the back quite firmly with a pad of cotton wool [absorbent cotton] or your fingertips. Then lift the paper off gently – if the tack is right, and your pressure even, the leaf will be stuck to the sized portions. Lay the next sheet to slightly overlap the first, and repeat the procedure, continuing until you come to the end of the design. Carefully brush off any loose metal with a soft paintbrush. Repair any 'skips' in the leafed surface by pressing on scraps of metal while the size is still sticky. When the size has dried, rub the surface with cotton wool [absorbent cotton] to smooth it and remove any loose bits, taking particular care with the overlaps.

To turn applied aluminium leaf a convincing bright gold, give it one or two coats of orange shellac, which dries in less than an hour. Brush diluted Indian ink over it for a soft, silvery finish. Shading and antiquing can be added by applying raw or burnt umber oil colour mixed into a little thinned varnish.

APPLYING METAL LEAF OVER CARVING Over raised or carved areas, such as picture frames, paint the surface first with red, blue or ochre casein paint [milk paint]. When that is dry, apply the goldsize and wait for it to become tacky. Then apply the leaf to the prominent areas of the carving, not attempting to cover every crevice, but just to suggest gilding worn and weathered over the years. This selective use of leaf used to be known as 'parcel gilding' and has always been a sensible economy – no sense in wasting gold where it will not show. When the size has dried, any surface patchiness can be softened by rubbing down very gently with fine steel wool to reveal a little red, blue or yellow underlay here and there.

Varnishing   Finish off by varnishing the whole surface with clear semi-gloss polyurethane varnish (see pages 162–163).

opposite left Squares of copper transfer leaf, cut to the size of a postage stamp and applied on a regular grid, give great glamour to a red-glazed wall.

opposite right A contemporary picture frame is enhanced by delicate craquelure and decoupage (see pages 173 and 194) over a silvery metal leaf finish. The effect is simple but elegant.

METALLIC PAINTS, CREAMS & PENS

These are the easiest metallic finishes to apply, come in a good and convincing range of colours, and are useful combined with transfer leaf and metal powders, where their particular texture acts as a foil to the bright gleam of leaf and the soft but rich bloom of the powders. I find metallic paints handy for fine, brushed-on detail, twigs, stems, and leaves, such as might form part of a japanned scene. The creams are excellent for patching gilt frames quickly or for adding a smooth band of gold, silver or whatever to a painted piece. I would avoid using either over a large area, where their effect begins to look artificial.

Metal paints

These are available in both solvent- and water-based forms and should be applied with fine watercolour brushes, or lining brushes for line decoration. Metallic gouache colours are especially effective used over a dark base, so that the base 'ghosts' through to give a shaded effect. Practise this on a spare card or board first, painted in the same colour as the object to be finished. Being water based, metallic gouache is fast drying, and makes cleaning up quick and easy, but it must be sealed with shellac on completion, and before brushing over an antiquing wash of say, diluted acrylic, which would simply wipe it off again. Solvent-based metallic paints are a shade cruder in effect, but their consistency makes them especially useful for fine lining or details. Also, they do not require special sealing (see manufacturer's instructions). Rubbing back with finest steel wool when dry always softens new gilt decoration.

Gilt creams

Unbeatable for an instant touch of metallic lustre, these can be applied over virtually any finish with fingertips or with a flat, soft artists' brush. The brand I use has the disadvantage that it needs its own special sealant but this is a small hiccup set against its splendid ease of application and pleasing texture. A small jar lasts an impressively long time.

Metallic felt pens

Metallic felt pens have their place in the panoply of new tools and materials designed to make specific tasks easier. They can be used, sparingly, to add a touch of helpful richness where their neatness and direct results are effective and suitable. Picture framers use them with rulers for gold lines round mounts. They are also suitable for 'lining', on painted furniture, but rub them over lightly with fine wire wool for an aged effect, and spray with varnish to fix before proceeding to other treatments. Metallic felt penwork looks richest applied over strong colours. A Greek key pattern, for instance, bordering a mount, has real impact if you paint in a band of terracotta, dark green, royal blue or black first, and then ink in the pattern on top. The more mixed your media, the more convincing it looks. Use antiquing wax to 'age' the effect.

METALLIC VARNISHES

No sector of the paint scene has benefited more dramatically over the past few years than what we loosely call 'the metallics'. Time was when metallic varnishes were limited to gold and silver, and the resulting finish was thick and pasty with only a hint of a metallic gleam when looked at in the right lighting conditions. These early metallic varnishes also tended to darken noticeably over time. In fact, the only reason for buying second-hand frames and objects treated to these decorative effects was the hope that underneath one might discover a layer of real gold or silver leaf which some poor soul had decided looked shabby, and would be improved by a nice quick coat of metallic varnish.

The situation today has radically changed. Metallic finishes now comprise of a wide range of cutting-edge products, from emulsions [latex] with their soft radiance and reflectiveness of metal foils, fast-acting gold size, a gamut of metallic waxes which make adding a quick lick of gold, silver and copper fast work, and more recently, new metallic varnishes which do the job in one, bestowing a reflective pearly lustre on painted surfaces, while at the same time adding their quota of protection and durability.

Metallic varnishes open up interesting new possibilities for the DIY decorator. Obviously, they can be used as a varnish 'plus' over painted furniture and accessories to boost the painted finish – used in this way they are most effective when applied over pale or pastel base colours, including white, silver, grey, cream and stone. When used for this purpose, the metallic varnish should be applied with a fine bristle brush, in rapid movements without too much overbrushing because this may cause streaking. Another option is to use the metallic varnish to stencil over a matt base to create a subtle textural contrast reminiscent of damask or brocade. Maybe to extend this idea over an entire room would be too much but it could be used to great effect as a single 'panel' and focal point behind a bed or across a chimney breast. This technique can be carried out successfully over any oil- or water-based matt paint but is most effective where the base paint is extra-matt, like suede paint (see pages 210-211). If the metallic/matt contrast it too subtle, the metallic varnish can be tinted a few tones darker with liquid tinters (see pages 216–217) for a more emphatic contrast of colour plus texture. To stencil with metallic varnish, use a spray adhesive to fasten the stencil to a section of wall and apply the minimum of varnish with a domed brush and a stippling action.

All metallics – metal leaf excepted – obtain their 'gleam' from 'bronze powders', the confusing generic name for the whole range of powder pigments from gold and copper to silver, aluminium and pewter, and they now include a new extended range of reflective colours which are both lustrous and light-refracting. Although these new metallics are expensive, they work well when used as 'accents' on furniture or wall panels which make them attractively affordable.

Metallic finishes are currently very fashionable. A layer of metallic or pearly lustre is easy to apply to any paint surface, and enhances furniture, and even walls.

Fundamentals

WALL PAINTS: WATER-BASED

Type	Composition	Appearance	Solvent
Standard Matt Emulsion [latex flat paint/latex flat enamel]	Pigments and synthetic resins – usually PVA, co-polymer or acrylic polymers	Solid matt appearance – cheaper brands may have a slight sheen. Gives a thick, slightly 'plastic' coat	Water
Vinyl Silk/Satin Emulsion [latex velvet, eggshell, low-lustre, satin finish paints]	As for standard matt emulsion but with more binder added to give extra sheen and washability	A definite sheen (satin emuslion has more sheen than vinyl silk)	Water

WALL PAINTS: OIL-BASED

Type	Composition	Appearance	Solvent
Flat Oil Paint [alkyd flat paint]	Pigments, drying oil, alkyd resin	Perfectly flat, uniform film with no brushmarks	White Spirit [mineral spirit]
Oil-based Eggshell mid-sheen paint [latex velvet, eggshell, low-lustre satin finish paints]	Pigments, drying oil, synthetic alkyd resin	Smooth, opaque surface with a dull sheen	White Spirit [mineral spirit]

TEXTURED COATINGS

Type	Composition	Appearance	Solvent
Suede Paint	Pigments, synthetic resins and texturing agent	Matt 'soft' finish which gives texture and movement to the wall surface	Water
Impasto	Pigments, acrylic resins and high-build texturing agent	High-build water-based paint that can be used to create 3-D paint effects. Off-white finish as sold, can be tinted	Water
Marmorino	Marble dust, lime, additives	2 layers 1 mm (1/16 in) applied by steel float gives hardness over most bases. Finishes can be either rough, like weathered stone, or smooth as marble	Water
Stucco Lustro	Marble dust, lime, additives	Designed to give marble-like smoothness. Apply with a steel float in two layers 1 mm (1/16 in) thickness	Water
Metallic Paint	Metallic pigments, acrylic resins, acrylic binder	Offers metallic lustre over a variety of different coloured base paints	Water

Paint technology has changed radically over the past decade as the industry has moved away from oil media to water-based, mainly acrylic and polymer substitutes. The impetus for this revolution in paint manufacture came from evidence that oil media, specifically solvents create serious health risks, and prolonged exposure results in allergies, headaches and respiratory problems. Oil media are banned in many European countries and states in the US, but remain available for 'specialists'.

Uses & Advantages	Disadvantages
Cheapest and fastest drying finish for walls and ceilings. Re-coatable in about four hours. Widely available in a vast range of colours. Can be tinted with universal stainers [tinting colours]. Two to three coats needed	Too absorbent to be used as a base for decorative glaze work apart from stencilling. Can mark unless protected with varnish. Wipeable. Not suitable for bathrooms or kitchens due to condensation
Fast-drying, re-coatable in approximately four hours. For walls only. Can be used as a base for decorative glaze work. Is less likely to mark than standard matt emulsion and is wipeable	Not as hard-wearing as oil paints so not for use on woodwork. Less coverage than matt emulsion, requires more coats

Uses & Advantages	Disadvantages
Can be used for most interior finishes, such as walls and woodwork and gives the best flat finish available	Slow-drying. Limited availability. Expensive and more of a professional's paint. Shows scuff marks so not suitable for heavy-use areas
As a finish for interior walls, woodwork and furniture. Ideal as a base for translucent glaze work with oil glazes	Takes 12–16 hours to dry and requires careful brushing on and laying off. Slow-drying. Limited availability. Expensive and more of a professionals paint

Uses & Advantages	Disadvantages
Use alone for a slightly textured finish for walls. This paint reflects light to recreate the soft brushed effect of suede	Marks easily, but scuff marks can be wiped off with a damp cloth
Can disguise minor imperfections in a wall surface, such as fine cracks, or can be used to 'soften' artex surfaces. Also used for 'relief' stencils	Would need to be evened out with a second layer, if an even surface was required at a later date
Available in white only but can be tinted or colourwashed to highlight the rough finish. Final waxing with colourwax gives more depth and lustre. Offers a more 'stony' effect than stucco lustro	The smooth finish requires a degree of practice. For a highly polished surface, stucco lustro is preferable to marmorino
Designed to give marble-like smoothness and polish. Applied with trowel in two coats, each 1mm (¹⁄₁₆ in) thick	Application requires skill. Keeping coats extra thin can be tricky, can 'crackle' if layers are too thick
Good reflective qualities with a soft finish	Requires a toning base coat. Over-brushing can lead to streakiness

TRADITIONAL WALL PAINTS

Type	Composition	Appearance	Solvent
Soft Distemper	Whiting, glue size, powder pigments	Totally non-reflective, soft, matt appearance. Exceptional coverage and clear pastel colours. Blotting paper texture	Water
Limewash	Slaked lime putty, glue size, water and pigments	Absolutely matt appearance. Gritty texture, beautiful colours achievable. Translucent when wet, dries to an opaque finish	Water
Casein Paint [milk paint]	Casein, pigments, ammonium carbonate catalyst	Matt in appearance with less 'plastic' finish. Good coverage. Clear colours	Water

WOOD PAINTS (WOODWORK, FURNITURE, FLOORS)

Type	Composition	Appearance	Solvent
Acrylic Eggshell	Pigments, waterborne acrylic emulsion [latex]	Smooth, opaque surface with sheen. Similar qualities to real eggshells, i.e. brittle, chalky	Water
Coloured Acrylic Varnish	Water-based acrylic resins and pigment	Coloured varnish for bare wood that dries to a durable, slightly shiny finish	Water
Oil Gloss [enamel] **Eggshell Paints**	Pigments, oil-modified resin	Tough, shiny, hard-wearing film. Available in different sheens, i.e. eggshell/gloss/high-gloss finish	White Spirit [mineral spirit]
Flat Oil Paint	Pigments, drying oil, resin	Flat, uniform film with no brushmarks	White Spirit [mineral spirit]
Floor Paint	Polyurethane, resin	Glossy finish available in textured/non-slip format or smooth finish	White Spirit [mineral spirit]
Wood Paint	Pigments, acrylic, resin, filler [spackle]	Diluted, yields transparent stain. Used neat gives solid matt coverage	Water

STAINS & WAXES

Type	Composition	Appearance	Solvent
Water-based Stains	Acrylics	Colours the wood allowing the grain to show through	Water
Spirit/Alcohol Stains	Spirit-soluble pigments in shellac solutions	Colours the wood allowing the grain to show through. Matt appearance before varnishing	Methylated Spirit [denatured alcohol]
Coloured Waxes	Colour suspended in paraffin wax	Available in a range of colours, can be buffed to a soft sheen and used over painted or unpainted surfaces	White Spirit [mineral spirit]

Uses & Advantages	Disadvantages
Chalky finish not achievable with ordinary emulsion [latex]. No sheen whatsoever. Good for older residential properties because it allows walls to 'breathe'. Successive coats improve colour and finish	Not washable. Cannot be re-coated with oil-, water- or emulsion-based paints so needs to be scrubbed off before changing the wall finish
Used internally or externally on porous wall surfaces. Allows walls to 'breathe' and provides some mould resistance because it is an alkali. Loves 'damp' situations	Cannot be re-coated with oil-, water- or emulsion-based paints
Versatile. Popular with professionals. Often used as base coat under metal leaf and on furniture	Relatively expensive. Ammonium content can cause health problems in confined spaces

Uses & Advantages	Disadvantages
As a finish for woodwork and furniture. Ideal base for translucent glaze work with water-based glazes. Fast-drying. Re-coatable in approximately four hours	Brushmarks can be a problem, use a synthetic brush for best finish. Less coverage than oil media in same category. Requires priming with acrylic primer
Colours and seals the surface in one, so offers a one-process finish	Not recommended for heavy-use areas such as floors, unless sealed with heavy-duty varnish or lacquer
Use as base for translucent glaze work with oil-based glazes on woodwork or furniture. Extra hard-wearing and flexible in use	Slow-drying – re-coatable in 16 hours. Limited availability and colour range
Gives elegant high-class finish on woodwork, with a rich and smooth texture	Slow-drying – re-coatable in 16 hours. Limited availability and colour range
Hardwearing finish for rough floors i.e. concrete	Available in limited range of colours, usually dull grey, red and green
Extra quick cover and fast-drying. Versatile finish for furniture and floors. Polishes up with wire wool	Relatively expensive used neat but cheaper when used diluted as a stain

Uses & Advantages	Disadvantages
Advantage over oil-, white-spirit-based stains is non-yellowing and colour fastness. Speedy application. Wide colour range. A quick fix for sub-standard softwood	Needs to be varnished. Colour can be disappointingly weak, requiring more coats. Surface requires gentle sanding down as technique tends to raise grain
Available only in wood-coloured stains not primary or pastel shades. Brittle	Strong odour in confined area
Speedy application. Colour that can be controlled by rubbing off, or adding more wax. Gives shine and colour in one move. Excellent over painted furniture to add depth and movement	Cannot be sealed. Varnish recommended under waxes to protect paint finish

GLAZES & VARNISHES

Type	Composition	Appearance	Solvent
Emulsion [latex] **Glaze**	Polyvinyl acetate co-polymer or acrylic polymer	Milky white fluid which dries to a clear finish. Available in matt, eggshell or gloss	Water
Acrylic Scumble Glaze	Extender	Non-yellowing, clear, translucent glaze tinted for achieving decorative effects on walls and furniture	Water
Oil Scumble Glaze	Long oil alkyd/linseed oil	Shiny, clear glaze medium for making oil-based glazes. The 'old style' painters standby	White Spirit [mineral spirit]
Acrylic Varnish/ Lacquer	Water-based acrylic resins	Cloudy when liquid, dries clear. Available in matt, eggshell and gloss	Water
Shellac [button polish, white/bleached polish and knotting]	Natural shellac in methylated spirit [denatured alcohol]	Transparent lacquer. Pure shellac is yellow/brown; button polish is orange, as is knotting, For clear finish, use white/bleached shellac	Methylated Spirits [denatured alcohol]
Metallic Varnish	Water-based acrylic resins	Milky white with addition of metal filaments which dry to a translucent metallic silvery sheen	Water
Polyurethane Varnish	Clear or pigmented polyurethane	Clear, some yellowing and darkening over time. Available in matt, eggshell and gloss	White Spirit [mineral spirit]
Carriage Varnish	Long oil alkyd varnish modified with phenolic medium	Extra pale high-gloss varnish	White Spirit (mineral spirit)
Yacht Varnish	Phenolic tung oil complex modified with alkyd resin	Extra pale high-gloss varnish	White Spirit [mineral spirit]

PRIMERS

Type	Composition	Appearance	Solvent
Acrylic Primer	Acrylic resin and pigments	Available in white and grey. Use white under pale colours, grey under deep or strong shades	Water
Aluminium Wood Primer	Solvent-based	Highly reflective silvery finish	White Spirit [mineral spirit]
Stabilizing Primer	Water- or solvent-based	Sealant for 'powdery' surfaces	Water
Tile/Melamine Primer	Water-based acrylic blend of resins	Quick-drying acrylic primer that will adhere to tiles and melamine surfaces, allowing you to finish in the paint of your choice. Available in white	Water

Uses & Advantages	Disadvantages
Originally a seal for wallpaper this is now used as a sealant for wall finishes, the advantage being its totally matt appearance, speedy drying time and waterproof finish	Not as durable as a full-scale varnish. Limited availability
Fast-drying cuts 'open' time but shortens job. Shine can be knocked back by coating in emulsion glaze	Milky look when wet means tinting needs samples and comparisons when wet and dry. Needs to be worked fast and methodically. Dries with sheen
Mixed with colour and solvent makes a slow-drying glaze for decorative effects. Ideal for effects where you require a long 'open' time. Very receptive to decorative markings	Discolouration occurs over time when exposed to heat or direct sunlight. Hanging pictures leave pale shapes when removed from walls, as do rugs on glazed floors
Replacing oil-based varnishes for all uses in the home, including sealing floors. Will not yellow or darken. Fast-drying, easy application	Acrylic varnish is suitable for walls, furniture and woodwork. Acrylic lacquer is best for floors
Fast-drying isolating coat between paint layers and under applied decoration. Can be tinted to create high-gloss lacquered surfaces. Use in french polishing	Easily marked by water/alcohol. Brittle finish. Needs application with fine brush. Highly flammable
Used as a decorative finish on woodwork, furniture and walls. Can be used on floors if sealed with appropriate varnish. Adds lustre plus protection	Can streak with overbrushing. Use with a fine brush
Widely available. Responds well to sanding back for superfine finish	Yellows and darkens when exposed to light. Use over darker, brighter shades only
Varnish for interior/exterior finishes. Dazzling depth and shine for lacquer effects. Stronger than shellac but needs understanding in use. Very tough	Limited availability. Requires expert application and much rubbing back between coats
Toughest varnish available. Used to waterproof as well as add a high-gloss finish to boats	Slow-drying: cannot be re-coated for 16 hours. Will discolour, use over dark colours

Uses & Advantages	Disadvantages
Quick-drying, general purpose primer/undercoat for wood, MDF, hardboard [particle board or masonite], plaster and emulsioned walls. Good if walls are to be painted with much darker or lighter paint than previous product	Not advisable on metal, plastic or loosely bound surfaces, such as powdery plaster. Needs smoothing after each coat
For use on resinous softwoods, hardwoods to prevent stains from seeping through to the paint finish. Can look good in some contexts as a metallic finish	Limited availability from specialist trade outlets
Useful primer for certain situations. Can be used to seal limewash and distemper prior to finishing with ordinary emulsion [latex]. Also for powdery surfaces such as cement, plaster, brick and stone	Limited availability from specialist trade outlets
Allows unlikely partners to bond i.e. emulsion [latex] over melamine. A short-term solution, nevertheless	Recently developed product so availability erratic. Does the job but needs protective varnish as well

MAKING COLOURS

Although paint stockists can mix most of the colours that you are likely to require, learning how to mix your own precise colours and tones is an excellent way to develop a sense of colour – probably the definitive step toward becoming a successful decorative painter. With a small stock of concentrated pigments and a tin of basic white, or coloured, paint you can mix up most colours you are likely to need as you require them.

Type	Composition	Appearance	Solvent
Powder Paint (artists' quality)	Finely ground pigments	Matt colours, vivid, clear (unless mixed with white) and intense	Water (for water-based paints; can be mixed with oil to tint oil-based paints)
Poster Paints	Powdered pigments, not so finely ground as artists' quality powder paints	Matt, rather thick colours, not so vivid or rich as powder paint	Water
Universal Stainers [tinting colours]	Concentrated colours bound in high boiling point solvent which is compatible with oil-, water- and white spirit- [mineral spirit] based paints	Very strong, matt colours, clear unless mixed with white spirit [mineral spirit]	White Spirit [mineral spirit], water
Artists' Oil Colours	Highly refined pigments bound with linseed oil	Rich, varied and finely differentiated colours, matt if thinned with white spirit [mineral spirit], otherwise the oil gives some sheen	White spirit [mineral spirit]
Students' Oil Colours	As above, but generally cheaper mixes	As above	White Spirit [mineral spirit]
Watercolours	Pigments in a gum base, available in tubes and in semi-solid form in pans	Sharp, clear, translucent colours	Water
Liquid Tinters	Concentrated pigments in liquid form	Thick liquid to be added with dropper	Water
Gouache Colours	Concentrated colours in a water base	Particularly sharp, clear and fresh matt colours of great staining power. The white-pigmented base gives more opacity than ordinary watercolours	Water
Artists' Acrylics	Pigments in a water-soluble polyacrylic base	Watercolour-clear when thinned; juicy impasto used neat. Matt colours, a little less vivid than gouache	Water
Signwriters' Colours [bulletin colours]	Pigments in quick-drying varnish medium	Matt, intense, opaque colours	White Spirit [mineral spirit]
Japan Colours [US only]	Pigments in quick-drying varnish medium	Similar in texture and appearance to signwriters' colours	White Spirit [mineral spirit]
Casein Colours	Pigments in casein medium	Matt, powdery, opaque, very intense but hard colours unless mixed with white casein paste	Water

Pigment, or raw colour, is available in many forms – as loose powder, compressed blocks or cakes, or bound with oil, varnish, and other media in tubes, jars and tins. One rule to bear in mind is that like should be mixed with like – thus you mix solvent-thinned pigment with solvent-thinned paint, water-thinned pigment with water-thinned paint. But there are exceptions – universal stainers [tinting colours], for instance, can be used with both media.

Uses & Advantages	Disadvantages
Used to tint oil- or water-based paints, or varnishes. Dark colours stain wood. Pale colours make lovely washes	Cannot be used by themselves as they are tinters not paints. Can be difficult to dissolve completely – need to be soaked first, in water or oil, depending on the paint to be used
Cheap, easily soluble colours, used mainly by children. Can be mixed with water-based paints	Limited range of colours in rather crude shades, thick pasty texture. Not easily mixed
Cheap, highly concentrated colours that mix easily with both oil- and water-based media. Limited colour range, but intermixing gives greater colour possibilities	Rather hard colours that tend to need a touch of their complementary colours to soften them. No raw umber in some ranges
Decorators use these for a lot of smaller scale decorative painting because the colours are excellent, comprehensive and the texture is fine. Can be used thinned with solvent or oil, or mixed into clear varnish	Not cheap. Relatively slow-drying compared to acrylics
As above	As above but fewer pure colours
Can be used for small-scale tinting of water-based media	Expensive and difficult to mix. Not waterproof – need sealing with shellac
Use to tint or modify all emulsion, acrylic paints and glazes. Will not affect performance or drying time	Dropper clogs up. Needs cleaning from time to time
Really beautiful colours, especially in strong pastel range. Ideal for colouring water-based paints and colourwashes. Mix easily. Concentrated, so a little goes a long way. Used often in past to decorate furniture, on a gesso ground	Expensive. Not waterproof – needs sealing with varnish
Amazingly quick-drying, so stencils or painted decoration can be finished in one session. Can be used diluted with water for a transparent effect, or in a special acrylic medium for transparency with body, or straight from the tube for thick, opaque cover. Once dry, acrylics are waterproof and permanent	Expensive. Less rich textured than oil paints. Less mellow colours too. Dry so fast they need constant wetting in use (a retarding medium is available). There tends to be wastage because of this very rapid drying time
Very opaque, thick colours, so give good coverage with one coat – ideal for floor stencils. Large colour range	Not so rich or mellow as artists' oil colours. Need varnishing to bring out the colour. Available only from specialist suppliers
Rapid-drying, good flat texture and excellent colour range. Ideal for furniture decoration and any stencilling; use thinned with solvent and with clear varnish – to bind colours and improve adhesion	Give reasonable opacity when thinned, but not full coverage. Though touch-dry in less than half an hour, must be left considerably longer before applying second coat or this dissolves the first
Use thinned with water only (about one part colour to two parts water) for a colourwash, or added to white casein paste or other water-thinned paints for creamier and pastel shades. Dry very quickly, excellent opacity and therefore economical to use. Hard finish	Must be left for some time and sealer applied before painting on second coat. Tend to solidify if not used up quickly. Unpleasant smell. Limited availability

REDS

Burnt Sienna + Alizarin Crimson

+ Cadmium Scarlet =

Raw Sienna + Cadmium Scarlet =

Venetian Red + Cadmium Scarlet =

PINKS

Burnt Sienna + White =

Mixed Pink No 1

Mixed Pink No 1 +

Yellow Ochre = Mixed Pink No 2

Mixed Pink No 1+

Black +

Cobalt = Mixed Pink No 3

Crimson + White =

YELLOWS

Yellow Ochre + White =

Lemon Chrome + Chrome + Burnt Umber =

*These bright colours cannot easily be mixed, but may be bought from artists' suppliers

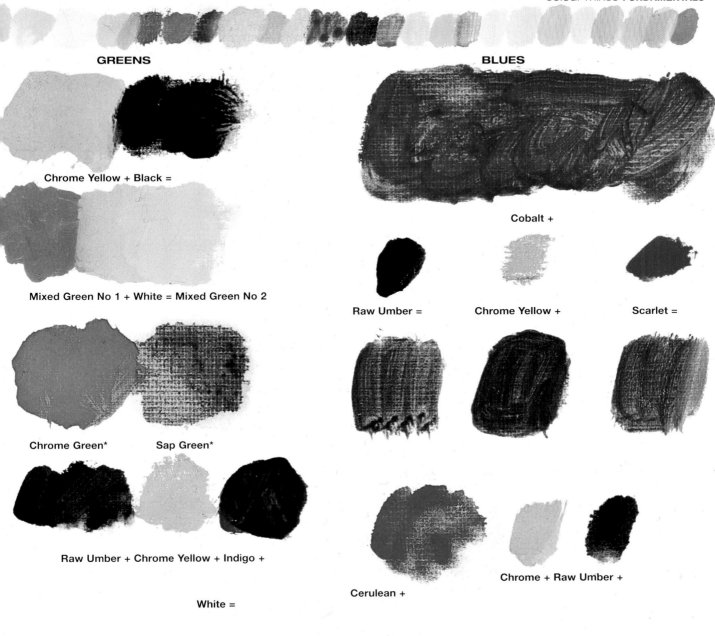

GREENS

Chrome Yellow + Black =

Mixed Green No 1 + White = Mixed Green No 2

Chrome Green*   Sap Green*

Raw Umber + Chrome Yellow + Indigo +

White =

BLUES

Cobalt +

Raw Umber =   Chrome Yellow +   Scarlet =

Cerulean +

Chrome + Raw Umber +

(varying amounts of) White =

COLOUR MIXES

If the ability to combine colours inventively is a largely instinctive process, knowing what to mix with what to get a specific colour is something you pick up as you go along, making notes of happy combinations you come across. Here are some rough indications of how to get what decorators call 'good' (that is, gutsy, lively, distinguished) colours. It would take a book to go into the subject in depth, but half a loaf is better than no bread and you may find these notes helpful.

Don't be frightened of experimenting with colours. But don't mix large quantities while you are experimenting; a few spots of likely shades on a plate or sheet of paper can be worked together with a fingertip to give a good idea of what they look like when mixed. Once you know you are on the right lines, it's safe to proceed with larger quantities.

Don't run away with the idea that there is only one way to get a particular colour. If your requirements are not too precise, if you are after a warm earthy red rather than the exact shade to match a piece of fabric or an old tile, there are probably half a dozen or more ways of arriving at a colour in that general area. Most interesting colours in decorating are, literally, mixed-up ones, but there are exceptions, generally in the pure and paler shades: for example, a mix of cobalt blue, white and a tinge of yellow does not give quite the same cerulean tint as the paint of that name, nor do cobalt, chrome yellow and white give quite the lettuce green of chrome green. But it is nevertheless sound practice and training to begin with a fairly limited standard range – such as the universal stainer [tinting colour] range plus raw umber and crimson – and see how far you can get by combining these in various proportions. Some decorators swear that they can get all the colours they want this way. Others insist that some shades can be prepared only from bought pigment. But you can always add these special colours to your collection as you need them.

DIRTY, OR OFF-WHITES Raw umber plus white gives a cool greenish grey, a very safe colour. A spot of yellow ochre warms it, a dot of black intensifies it – easy on the black, though, as a little goes a long way. Yellow ochre plus white gives a warm cream, which is lightened to ivory by adding more white. A dot of umber shades it to parchment. White plus ivory black gives a cool grey, known as French grey.

PINKS You can make good pinks by mixing burnt sienna with white. This gives delectably warm, but not sissy pinks, like faded cottage walls. Adding more white lightens them, a little yellow ochre (earth colours are mutually compatible) gives an apricot cast, a touch of cobalt and black takes them toward terracotta. Venetian red and white also make a good strong pink. Use the crimson reds to get sky blue pinks, because they contain a little blue.

REDS It is rare to find a really good commercial red, they tend to be too brash and hurtfully bright. But it is easy to mix your own. Composite reds always work better on walls, floors, woodwork and furniture than pure ones, in my experience. Burnt sienna, alizarin crimson and a little cadmium scarlet, vermilion or bright red stainer give a magnificently vital, rich but not hard red with a brownish cast. More crimson makes it deeper, cooler, more sienna makes it earthier and browner, more vermilion brings it nearer to old lacquer. Raw sienna mixed with scarlet gives a soft, warm orange-red. Venetian red, red oxide and Indian red are all good strong sympathetic slightly brownish reds. Add a dash of cadmium or one of the other red reds above to make them brighter and less earthy. A spot of green softens red red; umber will help to age the red tone.

YELLOWS Yellow ochre and Indian yellow are both warm friendly earthy yellows, with a creamy tone when mixed with white – nice wall colours. Chrome yellow is a hearty, sunflower colour with more orange to it. It is also the best, most opaque, one for mixing other colours, but you can also use cadmium yellow. For the sophisticated yellow often used for lacquer wall effects, try a glaze of mixed yellows: lemon chrome (or cadmium lemon), chrome and a touch of burnt umber, over primrose: white tinted with chrome yellow.

GREENS Yellow ochre mixed with lamp black gives a strong, drab olive green much used in the eighteenth century, on woodwork and furniture. Adding white to this produces a Dijon mustard colour. Cobalt and chrome yellow again give a green of olive tone. Indigo, chrome yellow, raw umber and white give strong greens paling to duck egg green as one adds more white. Some greens cannot be successfully mixed, and must be bought as tube colours. The sharp, light yellow-greens are a case in point. Chrome green is the juiciest but sap green is another good one.

BLUES Cobalt is the blue most used by decorators, a nice clean but soft blue, less strident than ultramarine and Prussian. A little umber dulls it, chrome yellow warms it, a spot of red knocks it back. I like indigo, a very distinguished blue, darker than cobalt, with purply sloe-berry overtones. Mixed with the above colours it gives similar, but moodier effects. To make the ethereal cerulean/thrush egg blues, best start with a bought cerulean, adding a spot of chrome and raw umber, or yellow ochre, to give the greeny cast, and then lots of white. For a terrific, vibrant stained-glass sort of blue, with green tones, use ultramarine or Hortensia, but don't try to get it in one, use a tinted glaze in one tone over a ground coat of another. To make a very pure violet, mix ultramarine and crimson, rather than Prussian blue and scarlet, which both contain yellow.

GLAZES & WASHES

Glaze is a word that crops up repeatedly in this book, as it is a key ingredient of many decorative finishes, for walls, woodwork and furniture. Broadly speaking, a glaze is a semi-transparent film of oil or acrylic-based colour, while a wash is a semi-transparent film of colour diluted with water. There are subtle visual differences between the two; oil-based colour tends to be richer, sleeker and more transparent, while colour in water is fresher, purer, still diaphanous, but 'brushier' looking. Both can be used over painted surfaces to soften, enrich, and otherwise modify the colours beneath.

Glazes, being slower drying, are more easily manipulated than washes. Classical painting used oil glazes routinely, to float delicate tints on hair and skin, deepen shadows, suggest the fragility of flower petals, the lustre of pearls. In the decorative field, the concept of colour seen through transparent glaze has countless applications. Woodgrainers and marblers use glazes (and washes) to suggest patina, depth and the complex layering of colour and markings in natural materials. Furniture restorers often use murky tinted glazes to give an instantly 'aged' look, suggestive of centuries of use and wear, to newly painted furniture. Decorators use glazes, and washes, to get subtle colour effects or for distressed finishes that give a soft, rich, spaced out look to interiors. A wash has a particularly vivid spontaneous effect. Whether as a glaze or a wash, transparent colour over white gives glowing pastels; over toning colour it gives a richer version of the same; over contrasting colour it creates effects of astonishing sophistication considering the simplicity of the means. Glazes are a help, too, in keeping one's colour options open – wall colours that have come out wrong can be corrected by applying a suitably coloured glaze on top, distressed or plain. Since thin glazes can be applied over walls in less than half the time it would take to repaint them, this is worth knowing. The right glaze can rescue mistakes.

opposite Making the point that sky blue ceilings need not be sugary confections of cerulean blue dotted with gauzy clouds tinged with sunset gold and pink and the odd cherub, this gloriously stormy, moody ceiling, executed in oil media, moves that decorating cliche forward with impressive panache. The ceiling decoration rounds off a subdued eighteenth-century wall scheme in grand Baroque style.

GLAZES

Depending what goes into a glaze, it can be shiny or matt and more or less transparent, according to the amount of white pigment it contains in proportion to the other ingredients. It should not be confused with that other transparent medium, varnish. Varnish is designed to give a hard, clear, protective coating and though it is sometimes tinted (as with lacquered walls or in furniture decoration) to give a glazed effect, it is not suited to distressing.

Glazes can be bought ready made, requiring tinting, or they can be made up from ingredients available from most artists' suppliers.

Transparent oil glaze

Transparent oil glaze, sometimes sold under the name 'scumble glaze' in the UK [glazing liquid or glaze coat in the US], is a ready mixed glaze base to which colour is then added. This can come in the form of universal stainers [tinting colours],

which are powerful and cheap, but are available in a limited colour range, or artists' oil colours, which offer much subtler and purer colours, but are more expensive. To tint oil glaze, squeeze a blob of colour into a cooking tin or pan and add a little white spirit [mineral spirit] to dissolve it, stirring hard to blend. Next spoon in a cupful or so of the unthinned glaze and stir well, then add the rest of the glaze, stirring continuously.

Proprietary transparent oil glazes [glazing liquids] are convenient and easy for beginners to work with because they stay 'open' and malleable long enough to be distressed with rags, brushes and other equipment. However, it must be said that their very ease and convenience has led to some confusion among amateur painters, who are thereby misled into thinking that proprietary glaze needs only the addition of colour to create a sophisticated wall finish. Used almost neat like this, transparent oil glaze looks like thick jam; wood graining is the sole technique where these products are used full strength.

Oil glaze recipes For special effects on walls, woodwork or furniture, professionals make up a glaze using a relatively small amount of proprietary glaze, much thinned with white spirit [mineral spirit], tinted with oil colour and, more often than not, modified by the addition of a spoonful or so of standard white undercoat. The undercoat softens the glaze colour, giving a slightly blurred rather than hard-edged imprint when it is ragged, dragged. The linseed oil content of a proprietary glaze does contribute to the eventual yellowing and darkening of the tinted colour, which is another good reason for minimizing its use in the modified glaze recipe. Here is a standard professional glaze recipe, which is adequate for many purposes:

1 part proprietary oil glaze [glazing liquid]
3 parts white spirit [mineral spirit]
universal stainers [tinting colours] or artists' oil colours
1 tablespoon undercoat, flat white or eggshell white paint per ½ litre [1 US pint]

It is quite possible to make up your own glaze – artists have done so for centuries. Here is a basic recipe to try:

1 part raw linseed oil
1 part white spirit [mineral spirit]
1 part clear matt varnish (for a softer effect, add one tablespoon or more of white undercoat per ½ litre [1 US pint])

Linseed oil may be purchased 'raw' or 'boiled' and it eventually dries to a hard finish. Boiled linseed oil is a refined and faster-drying version of the raw form. Yet in either form linseed oil can take an impracticably long time to become hard dry, and it may be advisable to add a proprietary product known as 'drier', obtainable from most trade suppliers, which helps the transparent oil glaze to dry to a hard finish more quickly.

Modifying glazes

The above recipes are only guidelines. Beginners find cut-and-dried recipes encouraging, but anyone who works with oil glazes constantly knows that many variables may need to be taken into account. These include the climate, room temperature, type of wall (whether it is an exterior or party wall), depth of the previous finishes, type of base coat and number of layers of base coat. So keep an open mind and critical eye on your transparent oil glaze and be prepared to play around with it, adding and modifying, untill it behaves as it should, taking impressions clearly but not ' jammily'. If dragged markings run together, it is too thin; add a little more transparent oil glaze [glazing liquid]. Often leaving a wet glaze to 'set up' a moment or two longer before distressing will correct a tendency to blur. Be prepared to experiment on boards or on an unseen area inside a cupboard – you can always wipe off the wet glaze with a cloth dipped in solvent.

Non-porous paint ground

Transparent oil glaze [glazing liquid] should be applied over a ground of non-porous paint. Two coats of eggshell (mid-sheen) oil-based paint is the standard professional specification. Today many people cut corners with one coat of eggshell over the undercoat, or they use two coats of vinyl silk emulsion [latex] or acrylic eggshell, which dries much more rapidly.

Applying a glaze

Keep the glaze coat to a thin film for maximum transparency. Take up a small amount of glaze on the bristles of a decorators' paintbrush, brush it on quickly and then smooth out the glaze lightly with the bristle tips of the brush. On a very smooth, eggshell painted surface, glaze can be applied with a bunched up rag – smeared on thinly. If a glaze seems too fluid, leave it a few moments to harden off slightly before distressing.

Keeping the glaze 'open'

Where a transparent oil glaze threatens to dry off too quickly, as it might on a particularly hot day, one solution to prevent this from happening is to add a little clarified raw linseed oil to the glaze mixture – a teaspoon to ½ litre [1 US pint]. Remember that if you have added clarified raw linseed oil to the transparent oil glaze allow longer for overall drying, up to 48 hours.

WASHES Washes of colour diluted in water are trickier to apply and handle than oil-based glazes, just as watercolour is a more difficult medium than oil painting, but they give such luminous colour and airy transparency that some decorators find them irresistible. Walls washed over with clear colours have something of the ethereal freshness of old fresco painting.

Paint consistency A wash can vary in consistency, all the way from emulsion [latex] paint thinned to milkiness, to a mixture that is little more than tinted water, with a dollop of emulsion [latex] for 'body'. Thinned and tinted acrylic scumble can be dragged, rag-rolled, sponged or slapped on every which way for a dappled look. The effect is never going to be as delicately modulated and even as if you were working with an oil glaze, but it gives a streaky homespun effect that you might prefer. Use the ultra-thin colour washes for loose brushing-on only, not distressing, as they dry too quickly to manipulate. Besides, colour applied like this has its own built-in distressing, a brushy quality, especially when the colours are at all strong.

Colour concentration Decorators usually choose to use the purest colours for making washes, favouring gouache colour for its vividness. I find powder colours, either artists' quality or the poster colours sold for children's use, make effective washes too, a bit cruder looking perhaps, but nicely reminiscent of those casually coloured old interiors one sees in France and Italy. Acrylics, also soluble in water, are another possibility but they speed up drying 'open' time.

GROUND A wash is best applied over a flat emulsion [latex] base paint. The flatter the emulsion [latex] base is, in my experience, the more absorbent, and therefore the easier it is to apply an emulsion [latex] wash over it. If you have to apply an emulsion [latex] wash over a mid-sheen surface, adding a drop of liquid detergent will help the wash to 'stick' to the surface. Bear in mind, that a coat of acrylic varnish over the emulsion [latex] base will give you extra 'open time' while you are working, if this is necessary.

THINNING An acrylic scumble suitable for such paint effect techniques as dragging, rag-rolling and sponging should be thinned about one part paint to three or four parts water. Use a thinner version for colourwashing: one part paint to eight or nine parts water. For the 'tinted water' washes, the proportions of colour to water will obviously depend on how vibrant you want the effect to be. A rough guide for a colourwash of this kind is to use one small tube of gouache to ½ litre [1 US pint] water, plus a tablespoon of emulsion [latex] paint. Acrylic 'washes', like colour-wash, dry fast so work quickly to achieve good results.

Tinting washes Tint water-based acrylic scumble washes with gouache colours, acrylic colours, or powder colours. Dissolve the colours in water, then mix before thinning as required. The critical part of mixing your own colours is to mix thoroughly – undissolved specks of pure colour can emerge as huge streaks on a wall.

Applying a wash The most important thing when applying a decorative finish over or with emulsion [latex] paints is to make sure that the surface to which the paint is applied is well cleaned of grease and grime. Water-thinned colours simply won't stick over greasy patches. Use a weak solution of a proprietary paint cleaner, or, if you feel the finish might rub off, wipe over with warm water plus something to cut the grease – ammonia, washing soda, vinegar. Rinse afterwards, and leave to dry out completely before putting on a wash.

The most likely problem in applying a wash, especially in hot weather, is that the wet edge will dry, leaving hard lines of colour that are difficult to disguise. If this happens, adding a spoonful of glycerine – bought from a chemist or druggist – to the wash can help keep the paint 'open' and workable longer. Or spray periodically with a household plant spray filled with clean water.

When you apply two washes on top of each other for richer colour, leave the first wash to dry for at least 24 hours before painting on the second, or the top colour may lift off the one beneath leaving bald patches of base coat showing through, which are not easy to touch up afterwards. A good technique, is to sponge on the second wash, using quick pecky movements so as not to disturb the wash below. If the second wash runs and drips too much, add a little more acrylic scumble to make it thicker. You can drag one wash on top of another, but again brush it on quickly and lightly and try not to go over the same place too much or the wash beneath will soften and begin to lift. Or apply an acrylic varnish between layers.

Don't panic When a glaze or wash doesn't behave quite as you expected, don't panic. Check through various possible explanations – is it too thin, too thick, is the base coat too slippery or greasy, is the weather exceptionally hot or are the walls centrally heated? If it doesn't brush out evenly and looks messy, try sponging or ragging the wet glaze to even it up – use a damp sponge if a glaze has hardened. Really patchy effects can be rescued by sponging a darker or lighter colour on over the top, glazing overall with a creamy colour, dragging with a darker colour, or adding a stencilled border. But before resorting to any of these measures, try hanging a few pictures and putting back some furniture – it is amazing how re-populating the space relegates the wall finish to second place. All decorators agree that some of their happiest effects have been part accidental – some unforeseen reaction that they had the wit to take advantage of.

EQUIPMENT

Apart from basic paints and brushes, you will find it pays to keep a supply of general decorating equipment. The following equipment (*see opposite*) is used for preparation and for many of the paint effect techniques described in the book. The newest finishes – frottage, marmorino, stucco and combing – require some specialist tools listed below. These specialist tools are not illustrated as it is not necessary for the beginner to purchase them.

1 Chamois Leather An alternative to rags for ragging wet glaze. It makes crisper 'prints' than rags but is more of a nuisance to clean. Use white spirit [mineral spirit] for this. Rags can be junked.

2 Mutton Cloth (also called stockinette) For cleaning up; can also be used for ragging and breaking up wet glaze. It will leave some loose fibre but this can be brushed off when the glaze dries.

3 Cotton Rags Used to lift off glaze when ragging and rag rolling, to create distinctive 'prints'.

4 Sandpaper and Wire Wool Available in different grades for rubbing down and finishing. As well as standard abrasive papers, keep some wet-or-dry paper in various grades.

5 Sponges Natural, marine sponges are best for sponging on and off and for dabbing and distressing wet glaze. Synthetic sponges can be used in stencilling and to apply washes.

6 Jam Jar Endlessly useful for storage, keep a box full of spares.

7 Acetate Transparent plastic film can be used instead of card. Its transparency is somewhat illusory since paint soon masks this. But it is immensely tough and usefully bendy for corners, etc. Apt to split while hand-cutting.

8 Stencil Card Oiled manila card is good for making your own stencils as it is easier to cut smoothly without splitting. Not indestructible because water eventually softens it, so make two or more of each pattern on large-scale jobs.

9 Rollers Heads available in a variety of materials including mohair; foam-headed and lambswool heads are shown here. Use to cover a background faster, where absolute smoothness is not critical – such as applying primers, undercoats, emulsion [latex] paints. Some painters use a roller to put glaze on, together with a stippling brush.

10 Cutting Mat Helpful if you are intending to cut a lot of stencils, though I often use layers of newspaper instead.

11 Stanley Knife and Craft Knives For cutting stencils in acetate or card; it has many other uses. Make sure that you never run out of sharp new blades.

12 Trowel Used for plastering and applying materials like proprietary filler [spackle].

13 Scraper Scrapers are multi-purpose tools; depending on size, they may be used for mixing filler [spackle], applying skim coats, stripping wallpaper and loose paint. Choose one with a rigid steel blade. In addition a flexible spatula or artists' palette knife is neat for small filling jobs.

SPECIALIST TOOLS

Plasterer's float Steel tool with rounded corners aids application of stucco finishes.

Plasterer's hawk Smooth board with secure handle beneath, is used to transfer the plaster to wall.

Houseplant water spraymister Used to extend scumble glaze 'open time' and to prepare walls for limewash and colourwash.

Electrically heated 'pen' cutter Makes light work of cutting acetate but use with care as pen can become dangerously hot.

1

3

2

4

5

6

Decorating Equipment
For descriptions of the
equipment see opposite

7

8

9

10

11

12

13

BRUSHES

A brush consists of a handle, bound at the stock (block) to a filling previously 'set' in resin or vulcanized rubber. The filling is usually referred to as the 'bristles', although in fact bristle is only one of the available fillings, which also include hogshair, badger hair, ox hair and synthetic filaments. Indications of quality in a brush are a thick, silky, flexible filling, well bonded to a handle that is balanced and pleasant to hold. You can tell an expensive brush from a cheap one, as the latter has a wide stock [block] running between the bristles. A selection of brushes is illustrated on pages 232–233, and discussed on page 231.

Choosing brushes

Working with well-made equipment, scaled to the job in hand, is pleasurable and also fast. Go to a specialist trade supplier, rather than to a do-it-yourself centre, and ask the experts which brushes they recommend. It pays to buy the best and look after them well – a good brush will last twice as long as a cheap one and does the job more efficiently.

Cleaning and storing brushes

It is worth investing in a proprietary cleaner, too, to keep brushes in shape. These cleaners contain stronger solvents than white spirit [mineral spirit] and they clean the bristles faster. Amateurs invariably skimp the tedious soaking and rinsing ritual, so the use of a brand cleaner will counteract any laziness here. Keep plenty of well-washed glass jars for the purpose – with the lid screwed on tightly to prevent evaporation, the same jar of cleaner can be used over and over again. Brushes used in emulsion [latex] paint must be cleaned immediately after use – either in soap and warm water or in proprietary cleaner. An old-fashioned scrubbing brush, with stiff bristles, is useful for dislodging paint that has worked up the bristles. Lay brushes flat in the sink and scrub away from the handle end under a tap. Never leave a brush standing in solution for days on end – this bends and weakens the bristles. One professional technique for cleaning brushes is to drill a hole through the brush handle, and slot a wire or pencil through, so that you can lay the brush across the top of the jar so that the bristles are suspended in the cleaner without touching the sides of the container, which will bend them. It is worthwhile drilling holes anyway in the brush handle, since hanging brushes from nails is a good way to store them when not in use.

To extract loose hairs from a brand-new paint brush, bang it hard a few times on the edge of a horizontal surface, or spin it between the palms of your hands. The hairs soon work their way into sight, so you can easily pick them out before use. Traditionally, brand-new paint brushes were 'worked in' on primer coats, then undercoats for several days – after all, a loose hair stuck in a priming or undercoat is much less of a problem for decorators than a paint brush hair stuck in the last pristine coat of gloss varnish.

A purpose-made rubber graining comb, extra wide, with flat, spaced teeth, has proved to be the best tool for use with combing paste, giving stronger 'stripes' or ribs. Conventional metal graining combs (see pages 232–233) may also be used for a variety of different decorative painting results.

1–3 Standard Decorators' Brushes Part of any painter's kit. Buy more as special needs arise. A wide, thickly bristled brush (No. 1) is essential for walls – 100 or even 125 mm [4–5 in] wide, depending on how large your hands are. For painting woodwork, use a medium-sized brush (No. 2), between 50–75 mm [2–3 in] wide.

For fiddly 'cutting in' on such surfaces as window frames and door panels, a small brush 25 mm [1 in] or narrower is easier to control. You can use it for painting furniture and other precision work, too. Brushes cut on the diagonal (No. 3) are available for cutting in.

New synthetic brushes, in a range of sizes, have been developed to cut down 'brushmarking' problems with the now popular acrylic scumbles, varnishes and paints – ie gloss [enamel] and eggshell (mid-sheen) acrylic wood paints. These brushes clean up well, in water with detergent, and are long lasting. An old-fashioned paper-hanging brush, extra wide with a not too bushy head of bristles is also worth hunting down to achieve the 'brushy' update on dragged finishes.

4–7 Artists' Brushes A selection of artists' brushes is necessary for decorative work. Soft pointed watercolour brushes are used for fine work in all media. Get the best you can afford in two or three sizes, including one very fine one. Hogshair brushes for oil painting are versatile too. A rounded fitch makes a handy stencil brush for small-scale work, while flat-ended bristle brushes are good for broad lining. Store all these brushes like wooden spoons, handle down in a jam jar.

8 Dusting Brush Useful, versatile and inexpensive. It has soft, medium-length bristles set in a wooden handle. Decorators use it for stippling work on a small scale – furniture, woodwork. You can also use it for softening glazes and washes, although it won't give as fine control as will the badger softener. It should be cleaned carefully – never immerse the stock [block] in cleaner: the solvent will dissolve the resin, causing the bristles to drop out.

9, 10 Badger Softener or Blender This is the finest brush for all softening purposes. Expensive, because it is made of badger hair, but smaller sizes are affordable. It can be used with oil and water media, for softening brushmarks, graining, etc. but should be carefully cleaned after use. Rub bristles as clean as possible on paper or rags, dip into solvent as briefly as possible, then wash in warm water with soap rather than detergent, which dries out the bristles. Rinse, shake and dry flat or suspended.

11 Stippling Brush This hogshair brush comes in various sizes, all with a fixed bridge handle, and is purpose-made for stippling wet glazes, paints and varnish. Because of its size the stippling goes faster and the handle makes it less tiring to use. It is also expensive as brushes go because of the quantity of bristles and should be carefully cleaned and stored so the paint brush bristles don't get bent out of shape.

12, 13, 14 Brushes for Varnishing
Varnishing requires clean brushes, so buy and keep particular ones for that purpose only. You can use a standard decorators' brush, or a glider, a light brush with thin silky bristles which is good for applying thinned varnish and shellac, or an oval varnish brush, which painters use for larger jobs because the generous head of bristle holds more varnish and brushes it out smoothly. Check instructions on varnish tins to determine the correct solvent – white spirit [mineral spirit] for oil-based varnishes, water for acrylics and methylated spirit [denatured alcohol] for shellac. Try to keep a separate paint brush for each type of varnish. Mark them.

15 Camel Hair Mop An ultra-soft brush, like a cosmetic brush, which can be helpful in work using metal powders. I would substitute a cosmetic brush.

16, 17, 18 Fitch A rounded brush with flexible but firm bristles, the fitch comes in sizes ranging from 4.5 mm [⅛ in] to about 30 mm [1¾ in] wide. Traditionally used with oil paints, it is suitable for spattering and stippling.

19–22 Stencilling Brush The traditional stencilling brush (Nos. 20–22) looks like a man's shaving brush – short and fat, with hogshair bristles, blunt cut at the end. It comes in various sizes, between 6–50 mm [¼–2 in] across. With this kind of brush the paint is 'pounced' on, a tiring procedure, and stencillers now often prefer to use a softer, mop-headed brush (No. 19) which allows the paint to be applied in a looser, more swirling fashion that is faster and creates a fine dry image. An artist's fitch is another alternative.

23, 24 Lining Brush Special lining brushes can be bought with long, soft bristles which hold more paint so your line goes further. The swordliner (No. 24) is also a good brush for making fine straight lines freehand. For fine line work I often use a sable artists' watercolour brush. A signwriter's lining fitch has the advantage that you can use it with a straight edge. Lining brushes should be coaxed back into shape after cleaning – fuzzy lines are useless. A trace of soap makes a good setting agent. Store flat.

25–31 Graining Equipment Metal (No. 25) and rubber (No. 26) combs are used for creating the distinctive graining effects, and can also be used for other types of decorative painting. The 'rocker' or heart grainer (No. 27) is used specifically to suggest the whorls of heartwood. An ordinary cork can be whittled to make a knot tool (No. 28). The flogger (No. 29) is primarily a graining brush. Its long, flexible horsehair bristles are flicked against wet glaze to create a woody fibrous texture and also to drag straight grain marking, to which a slight wobble of the handle imparts a naturalistic ripple or bend. This brush can also be used for decorative dragging on woodwork or smaller items. Beginners will find a 'glider' (Nos. 12 and 13) can substitute satisfactorily. Overgrainers (Nos. 30 and 31) are used to put in detail on a dry, previously grained surface.

Brushes

A selection of useful brushes
which are described overleaf.

LIST OF SUPPLIERS

For the readers' convenience the names and addresses are grouped under headings which indicate the range and type of materials they stock. Thus 'Artists' Suppliers' will tend to concentrate on fine arts materials and tools, 'Decorating Suppliers' on more down to earth materials and tools for professional painters and decorators. Some suppliers have a mail-order service. Within each category many shops specialize in particular lines, and these will be listed in each case

ARTISTS' SUPPLIERS

Any good artists' suppliers should carry the following: artists' tube colours in oil, gouache and acrylic; artists' brushes; acrylic gesso; gum arabic; artists' linseed oil; coloured inks; metallic paints; spray varnish; craft knives; stencil card.

Atlantis Ltd
79 Plumber's Row
London E1 1EQ
Tel: 020 7377 8855
Two floors of artists' materials from top-of-the-range to the cheapest student brushes and colours. Open Sundays. Mail order available.

Brodie and Middleton Ltd
68 Drury Lane
London WC2B 5SP
Tel: 020 7836 3289
The stage painter's Mecca, they stock a wide range of cheaper dry pigments, metallic powders, gesso materials, brushes. Mail order available.

Cornelissen and Son Ltd
105 Great Russell Street
London WC1B 3RY
Tel: 020 7636 1045
A very large range of high quality powder pigments, gum arabic crystals, gesso and gilding materials, Vitrail glass painting media, Liquitex modelling paste, acrylic varnish. Mail order available.

A P Fitzpatrick
142 Cambridge Heath Road
London E1 5QJ
Tel: 020 7790 0884
Recent destination for Hackney's artists. Wide range of dried pigments, imported artists' colours, trendy fluorescents. Mail order available.

Green and Stone Ltd
259 Kings Road
London SW3 5EL
Tel: 020 7352 0837
They carry stencil card, pre-cut stencils, specialist brushes, transparent oil glaze [glazing liquid], crackle glaze, gum arabic, casein paints, shellac, craquelure varnishes.

E Ploton (Sundries) Ltd
273 Archway Road
London N6 5AA
Tel: 020 8348 0315
Noted for their competitive pricing, the stock includes acetate sheets, craquelure varnishes, acrylic gesso, metallic powders, gilding materials and transfer gold leaf.
Mail order available.

Stuart R Stevenson
68 Clerkenwell Road
London EC1
Tel: 020 7253 1693
A good range of gilding materials, casein paints [milk paints], specialist brushes, books. Very knowledgeable staff.

Alec Tiranti Ltd
27 Warren Street
London W1P 5DG
Tel: 020 7636 8565
Specialize in sculptors' materials, including burnishing powders (rottenstone, powdered pumice), wire wool in 0000 grade, dry earth colours, bronze powders, coloured bole for gilding, agate burnishers, gilding materials and tools, palette knives.

DECORATING SUPPLIERS

The suppliers listed below stock a good range of state-of-the-art paints, primers, varnishes, plus trade-orientated materials for gilding, marbling and graining. Also specialist brushes, universal stainers, transparent oil glazes, shellac, rottenstone, metallic powders, rabbit skin glue, abrasive papers, basic tools like scrapers, trowels and paint-strippers.

J W Bollom
314–6 Old Brompton Road
London SW5 9JH
Tel: 020 7370 3252
Long established port of call for painters, specialist and otherwise. They keep a huge stock of state-of-the-art paints including distemper and trade eggshell, varnishes, primers etc, plus specialist brushes, transparent oil glaze and universal stainers.

Foxell and James Ltd
57 Farringdon Road
London EC1M 3JB
Tel: 020 7405 0152
Stock a wide variety of paints, primers, varnishes, glazes, plus avant garde heavy-duty floor finishes, and old world materials like whiting, rabbit skin glue, metal powders, liming wax and rottenstone.

Paint Magic Ltd
48 Golborne Road
London W10 5PR
Tel: 020 8960 9960 (for nearest stockist)
UK shops nationwide stock a wide range of own-name paints – emulsions, colourwashes, impasto, marmorino, stucco lustro. Also specialist brushes, varnishes, tile primer, and crackle glaze. Mail order available.

The Paint Service Co Ltd
19 Eccleston Street
London SW1W 9LX
Tel: 020 7730 6408
*Small, but friendly, trade shop with a good
range of decorative painters' materials and
tools. Handy for paints, varnishes, glaze,
shellac, brushes.*

Papers and Paints Ltd
4 Park Walk
London SW10 0AD
Tel: 020 7352 8626
*A comprehensive range of decorative painters'
requirements; paints, brushes, varnishes,
glazes, plus colourmatching service and a
stock of old-fashioned paints like distemper
and limewash.*

Annie Sloan
Knutsford House
Park Street
Oxford OX20 IRW
Tel: 0870 6010082
*Run by author and paint expert. Specializes in
water-based DIY media, emulsions, metallic
and pearl finishes. Also specialist glazes
and varnishes. Mail order only.*

MANUFACTURERS & SUPPLIERS

These are firms which produce materials sold
in many of the above-mentioned stores, but
may also be found in some shops which are
less widely stocked. If a product is not
obtainable locally, these are the people to
phone for nearest stockists or mail order.

J H Ratcliffe and Co (Paints Ltd)
135A Linaker Street
Southport PR8 5DF
Tel: 01704 537 999
*Their transparent oil glaze and emulsion glaze
are a favourite with many painters. Also supply
brushes and graining tools.*

A S Handover Ltd
37h Mildmay Grove
London N1 4RH
Tel: 020 7359 4696

*Importers and manufacturers of every
imaginable specialist and standard brush, at
competitive prices. Also stock hard to find
aids such as 'pinstriping' tapes for effortless
lining. Wholesale, but will deal with private
customers.*

Lewis Ward and Co
128 Fortune Green Road
London NW6 1DN
Tel: 020 7794 3130
*One of the most highly rated brush suppliers
to the trade, with an innovative range,
including small badger softeners, fan brushes
etc. A mine of information.*

Liberon Waxes Ltd
Mountfield Industrial Estate
Learoyd Rd
New Romney
Kent TN28 8XU
Tel: 01797 367 555
*Wood finishing tools and materials (shellac,
sanding sealer, white polish) and an excellent
range of metallic creams, plus ready-coloured
'bole', antiquing waxes and powders.
Mail order available.*

PLACES TO VISIT

Examples of decorative paint finishes can be
seen the world over. My list of 'must see'
places is based on my own experience and is
not exclusively centred around paint effects.

The American Museum in Britain
Claverton Manor
Bath
Avon BA2 7BD
Tel: 01225 460503
*Reconstructed period rooms from Pilgrim
Fathers on, show use of stencilling on floors,
walls and furniture, mixing paints and inventive
finishes. An eye-opener, heart warming.*

Belton House
Grantham
Lincolnshire NG32 2LS
Tel: 01476 566116
*Offers some fine examples of 'Baroque' paint
effects from the seventeenth century. Marbling,
graining and more. An historical context for
much American work of the Colonial period.*

Charleston
Firle
Lewes
East Sussex BN8 6LL
Tel: 01323 811265
*Home of Bloomsbury artists Vanessa Bell and
Duncan Grant, this modest Sussex farmhouse
shows how the pair mixed up distemper
colours, cut stencils, painted murals and
furniture with verve and style. Unmissable.*

Ham House
Ham
Richmond-upon-Thames
Surrey TW10 7RS
Tel: 020 8940 1950
*As above but offers interesting 'oyster' walnut
graining. Recently restored with both taste
and discretion. A National Trust showpiece.*

Sir John Soane Museum
13 Lincoln Inn Fields
London WC2A 3BP
Tel: 020 7430 0175
*A remarkable building by the outstanding
Regency architect. It exemplifies Soane's own
'take' on colours and paint effects in the
classicist spirit of his time. Unique and inspiring.*

Kelmscott Manor
Kelmscott
Lechdale
Gloucestershire GL7 3HJ
Tel: 01367 252486
*The Thameside country retreat of William
Morris, this beautiful stone-built manor has a
haunting romantic 'Englishness'. It is decorated
with inspirational tapestries and wall hangings.*

Queen's House and Painted Halls
National Maritime Museum
Park Row
London SE10 9NF
Tel: 020 8858 4422
*These are two 'must-see' buildings on any
London visit. The Queen's House, a one time
royal palace, is a decorative reconstruction
making much use of old paints like limewash.
The Painted Hall, by Sir John Thornhill, formerly
the Banqueting Hall of Greenwich Naval College
is decorated with murals of heroic scale.*

READING LIST

Painting techniques

A. Bishop and C. Lord *The Art of Decorative Stencilling* Thames and Hudson, London, 1976, revised edition, Viking Penguin, New York, 1985

Jocasta Innes *The Complete Book of Decorating Techniques* Macdonald Orbis, London, 1986
Paintwise: Decorative Effects on Furniture Pyramid Books, London, 1991
Paintability Weidenfeld and Nicolson, London, 1986
Scandinavian Painted Decor Cassell, London, 1990
Trade Secrets Orion Publishing Group, London, 1995

Miranda Innes *The Country Home Decorating Book* Dorling Kindersley, London, 1989, Collins and Brown, London, 1989

The New Complete Book of Decorative Paint Techniques Ebury Press, London, 1999

Ralph Mayer *The Artist's Handbook of Materials and Techniques* 5th edition Faber and Faber, London, 1991

Kevin McCloud *Kevin McCloud's Decorating Book* Dorling Kindersley, London, 1990

I. O'Neil *The Art of the Painted Finish for Furniture and Decoration* William Morrow, New York, 1971

John P. Parry *Parry's Graining and Marbling* 3rd edition, revised by Rhodes, B. and Windsor, J. Sheridan House, New York, 1985 and Blackwell Scientific, Oxford, 1987

W. J. Pearse *Painting and Decorating* 9th edition, revised by Goodier, J.H. and Hurst, A.E. State Mutual Book, New York and Charles Griffin, London, 1980

Annie Sloan *Simple Painted Furniture* Dorling Kindersley, London, 1989

Annie Sloan and Kate Gwynn *The Complete Book of Decorative Paint Techniques* Ebury Press, London, 1992

Stuart Spencer *The Art of Woodgraining* Macdonald Orbis, London, 1989 Marbling Ward Lock, London, 1990

Bill Stewart *Signwork: A Craftsman's Manual* Sheridan House, New York, 1985 and Blackwell Scientific, Oxford, 1987

Janet Waring *Early American Stencils on Walls and Furniture* Dover Publications, New York and Constable, London, 1968

Paint techniques in an historical context

Isabelle Anscombe and Howard Grey *Omega and After: Bloomsbury and the Decorative Arts* Thames and Hudson, London, 1981

Alexandra Artley (editor) *Putting Back the Style: A Dictionary of Authentic Renovation* Evans Brothers, London, 1982

Patricia Bayer *Art Deco Interiors* Thames and Hudson, London, 1990

Jonathan Bourne *Lacquer: An International History and Collectors' Guide* Studio Editions, London, 1990

John Cornforth *The Inspiration of the Past: Country House Taste in the 20th Century* Viking in association with Country Life, London, 1985

Florence de Dampierre *The Best of Painted Furniture* Weidenfeld and Nicolson, London, 1987

D.A. Fales Jr. *American Painted Furniture 1660–1880* Crown Publishers, New York, 1988

Chester Jones *Colefax and Fowler: The Best in Interiors* Barrie and Jenkins, London, 1989

Hugh Lander *The House Restorers' Guide* 2nd edition, David and Charles, Newton Abbott, 1992

Jean Lipman *Techniques in American Folk Decoration: With Practical Instruction by Eve MeLendyke* Peter Smith, 1984

Hiram Manning *Manning on Decoupage* Dover Publications, New York, 1981

Miriam Millman *Trompe L'Oeil Painting: Illusions of Reality* Macmillan, London, 1982

Mario Praz *An Illustrated History of Interior Decoration from Pompeii to Art Nouveau* Thames and Hudson, London, 1964

Peter Thornton *Authentic Decor, the Domestic Interior 1620–1920* Weidenfeld and Nicolson, London 1984

General

Charles Hemming with Mark Aldbrook *The Folding Screen* Lund Humphries, London, 1999

Country House Floors 1660–1850 Temple Newsam Museum Country House Studies Catalogue, 1987

INDEX

Page numbers in *italic* refer to illustrations. Where illustration and caption appear on different pages, the reference is to the caption.

ACKNOWLEDGMENTS

Author's acknowledgments

Updating an existing text is in some ways more of a challenge than starting from scratch, as I think we have all found during *Paint Magic's* fourth overhaul. Without the dedication of my publishing team, notably Carey Smith and Sue Gladstone, the project could never have been realized; I am indebted to their persistence, patience and charm. Not to mention Frances Lincoln herself, who has the vision and determination to keep the show

on the road. I would also like to thank the design and editorial team, Colin Walton and Bella Pringle, who saw how it could be done – performing a brilliantly radical facelift with style and true grit. Thanks also to all those generous 'creatives', both professional and amateur who allowed us to invade their homes to photograph their both progressive and innovative paint effects which take us into the new millenium. Special thanks go to David Carter, Emma Stanhope and Mark Hotham,

Helen Gilmore, Aaron Barker and Jacqueline Hunt and also to my own talented Paint Magic team, Henny Donovan, Kathyrn Quinn, Will McCormac, who all chipped into the projects for this book with their expertize, hard work and imagination.

Finally, thanks to my trade chums, Tony at Foxell James, Stuart at Stuart Stevenson and David Horne at Bedec, who cope with queries on the wing, and share their hard-won paint knowledge so readily.

FLL = Frances Lincoln Limited
d = designed by, p = painted by,
t = top, b = bottom, l = left, r = right, c = centre

PHOTOGRAPHIC ACKNOWLEDGMENTS

2-3 Peter Anderson © FLL d David Carter Interior Design p Benita Houston
6 Ingalill Snitt
9 Tom Stewart © FLL d + p Aaron Barker.
10–11 *The World of Interiors*/Peter Aprahamian d David Carter Interior Design
12 Tom Stewart © FLL d + p Paint Magic Ltd.
13 Tom Stewart © FLL d + p Will McCormac.
14–15 James Mortimer © FLL d + p Graham Carr
17 Peter Anderson © FLL d David Carter Interior Design
18 Max Jordan d + p Paint Magic Ltd.
21 Ray Main/Mainstream d Roger Oates
23 Simon Upton/The Interior Archive d Carol Thomas
24 Peter Anderson © FLL d David Carter Interior Design p Benita Houston
26 Ianthe Ruthven
29 Tim Imrie © FLL p Jocasta Innes
31 Tom Stewart © FLL d + p Aaron Barker.
33 Clive Frost d Miranda Rhys Williams
35 Simon Upton/The Interior Archive d Anthony Collett
36-37 *The World of Interiors*/ Jacques Dirand d + p Gonzalo Gorostiaga
38 Tim Imrie © FLL p Jocasta Innes and Angeles Blasco
41 Tom Stewart © FLL d + p Aaron Barker.
43 Mark Luscombe-Whyte
44 Tim Imrie © FLL d Christopher Nevile p Fiona Sutcliffe and Tania Backhouse
46 Tim Imrie © FLL d Christopher Nevile p Fiona Sutcliffe and Tania Backhouse
49 Tim Imrie © FLL d IPL Interiors p Nicholas Fer
50 Tim Imrie © FLL d IPL Interiors p Nicholas Fer
55 James Mortimer © FLL
58–59 Michael Dunne © FLL p Patricia Boulter and Toby Kalitowski
61 Patrick McLeavey © FLL d + p Paint Magic Ltd.
63 Patrick McLeavey © FLL d + p Paint Magic Ltd.
65 Ianthe Ruthven © FLL
67 Peter Anderson © FLL d + p Paint Magic Ltd.
68 Patrick McLeavey © FLL d + p Paint Magic Ltd.
69 Peter Anderson © FLL d + p Henny Donovan
70 Ingalill Snitt
71 Derry Moore
72 Peter Anderson © FLL d + p Paint Magic Ltd.
74 Elizabeth Whiting and Associates/David George
74–75 Jan Baldwin © *Country Living* The National Magazine Co. Ltd

77 Nadia Mackenzie
78 *The World of Interiors*/James Mortimer p George Oakes
80 Tim Imrie © FLL d IPL Interiors p Nicholas Fer
83 Peter Anderson © FLL d David Carter Interior Design p Benita Houston
85 Peter Anderson © FLL d David Carter Interior Design p Clare Bailey
86 Peter Anderson © FLL d + p Paint Magic Ltd.
89 Richard Glover d + p Allegra Hicks
90–91 Peter Anderson © FLL d David Carter Interior Design p Timna Woollard
93 Tom Stewart © FLL d + p Emma Stanhope and Mark Hotham
95 Ray Main/Mainstream d John Minshaw
96 Andrew Wood/The Interior Archive d + p Arabella Johnsen
100 Ingalill Snitt
103 Peter Anderson © FLL d David Carter Interior Design p Dominic Sharpe
107 Paint Magic Ltd.
108 Michael Dunne © FLL p Nemone Burgess
109 Tim Imrie © FLL p Emma Hardie
110 Tim Imrie © FLL p Emma Hardie
111 tl+bl Tim Imrie © FLL p Emma Hardie r Peter Aprahamian © FLL
112 Bay Hippisley © FLL p Stewart Walton
115 Bay Hippisley © FLL p Graham Carr
117 Tim Imrie © FLL p Cicely Gattagher
121 Bay Hippisley © FLL p Graham Carr
122–123 Tim Imrie © FLL d Christopher Nevile p Fiona Sutcliffe and Richard Sleeman
125 Ingalill Snitt
126 John Hall
127 Thomas Lane d + p Thomas Lane
129 Tom Stewart © FLL p Emma Stanhope and Mark Hotham
131 Peter Anderson © FLL d + p Paint Magic Ltd.
133 John Hall
136 Peter Anderson © FLL d David Carter Interior Design
139 Peter Anderson © FLL d + p Paint Magic Ltd.
142l Fritz von der Schulenburg © The Condé Nast Publications Ltd. p Jim Smart
142–143 Fritz von der Schulenburg/The Interior Archive
146–147 Jan Baldwin d + p Marianna Kennedy and James Howett
149 Hugo Glendinning d + p Gonzalo Gorostiaga
150 *The World of Interiors*/Alex Ramsay
153 Mark Williams d + p Henny Donovan.
159 Simon Upton/The Interior Archive d Anthony Collett
162 Shaker

164 Peter Anderson © FLL d + p Kathyrn Quinn
165 Chalon UK Limited
167 Paint Magic Ltd.
169 John Hall
171 Julia Pazowski/Houses & Interiors
172 Patrick McLeavey © FLL d + p Paint Magic Ltd.
175 Andrew Twort © FLL
177 Bay Hippisley © FLL p Graham Carr and Stewart Walton
178 Tim Imrie © FLL p Jocasta Innes and Angeles Blasco
181 Tim Imrie © FLL p Jocasta Innes and Angeles Blasco
183 Patrick McLeavey © FLL d + p Paint Magic Ltd.
184 Bay Hippisley © FLL p Jocasta Innes and Stewart Walton
186 Tim Imrie © FLL p Cicely Gattagher
189 tl Bay Hippisley © FLL p Stewart Walton cl Tim Imrie © FLL p Cicely Gattagher bl Bay Hippisley © FLL p Graham Carr
190 Andrew Twort © FLL
192 t Tim Imrie © FLL p Sarah Delafield Cook b Bay Hippisley © FLL p John Fowler and Graham Carr
195 Patrick McLeavey © FLL d + p Paint Magic Ltd.
198 Bay Hippisley © FLL p Jocasta Innes
201 William Waldron
202 Andreas von Einsiedel
204 Tim Imrie © FLL p Sarah Delafield Cook
206l Patrick McLeavey © FLL d + p Paint Magic Ltd. r Peter Anderson © FLL d + p Henny Donovan
209 Patrick McLeavey © FLL d + p Paint Magic Ltd.
218–219 Bay Hippisley © FLL d Roger Walton p Stewart Walton
223 Peter Anderson © FLL d David Carter Interior Design p Benita Houston
229 Tim Imrie © FLL
230 Patrick McLeavey © FLL
232–233 Tim Imrie © FLL

ARTWORK
39, 47, 53, 61, 114 Alicia Durdos
98, 99, 105, 140 Jennie Smith